Categorization and Naming in Children

LD&CC **The MIT Press Series in Learning, Development, and Conceptual Change**
Lila Gleitman, Susan Carey, Elissa Newport, and Elizabeth Spelke, editors

Categorization and Naming in Children

Problems of Induction

Ellen M. Markman

A Bradford Book
The MIT Press
Cambridge, Massachusetts
London, England

This book was set in Palatino by Graphic Composition, Inc., and printed and bound by Halliday Lithograph in the United States of America.

Library of Congress Cataloging-in-Publication Data

Markman, Ellen M.
 Categorization and naming in children : problems of induction / Ellen M. Markman.

 p.   cm.—(The MIT Press series in learning, development, and conceptual change)
"A Bradford book."
Includes index.
ISBN 0-262-13239-7
 1. Categorization (Psychology) in children. 2. Induction (Logic) in children. 3. Onomasiology. I. Title. II. Series.
BF723.C27M37   1989
155.4′13—dc19   88-13000
                                                                              CIP

To Shelly
who defies categorization

Contents

Series Foreword

This series in learning, development, and conceptual change will include state-of-the-art reference works, seminal book-length monographs, and texts on the development of concepts and mental structures. It will span learning in all domains of knowledge, from syntax to geometry to the social world, and will be concerned with all phases of development, from infancy through adulthood.

The series intends to engage such fundamental questions as

The nature and limits of learning and maturation: the influence of the environment, of initial structures, and of maturational changes in the nervous system on human development; learnability theory; the problem of induction; domain specific constraints on development.

The nature of conceptual change: conceptual organization and conceptual change in child development, in the acquisition of expertise, and in the history of science.

Lila Gleitman
Susan Carey
Elissa Newport
Elizabeth Spelke

Acknowledgments

I want to express my appreciation to the colleagues who generously read drafts of this book or portions of it. Terry Au, Dare Baldwin, Eve Clark, John Flavell, John Macnamara, Douglas Medin, and Barbara Tversky all provided comments that helped improve the chapters they read. I am grateful for their help. I have had the great pleasure of collaborating with Maureen Callanan, Susan Gelman, Marjorie Horton, Jean Hutchinson, and Edward Smith on some of the studies reported here. All of them have influenced my thinking on these topics. I thank Ed Smith for allowing me to present the results reported in chapter 6. Anne Mark provided expert editorial assistance. I greatly appreciate her help.

I owe a special debt to Susan Carey and Elissa Newport, who provided very detailed, insightful, and constructive comments on two drafts of this book and willingly discussed and debated with me many of the issues that it raises. The book has greatly benefited from their intelligence and insight, and so have I.

I won't even try to express my gratitude to my husband Shelly Markman except to say that he is unique. He is amazing—in a class by himself.

One of the first drafts of this book was written while I was a Fellow at the Center for Advanced Study in the Behavioral Sciences, supported in part by grants from the Spencer Foundation and the National Science Foundation, and I would like to acknowledge their support. I am grateful to the National Science Foundation and to the National Institutes of Health for supporting much of the research reported here (NSF grant BNS 83-00048 and NIH grant HD 20382).

I thank Academic Press for permission to use tables 1 and 2 and figures 1, 2, 3, and 4 from Markman, E. M., and J. E. Hutchinson (1984), Children's sensitivity to constraints on word meaning: Taxonomic vs. thematic relations, *Cognitive Psychology 16*, 1–27 and tables 1 and 2 and figure 2 from Markman, E. M., and G. F. Wachtel (1988), Children's use of mutual exclusivity to constrain the meanings of words, *Cognitive Psychology 20*, 121–157; Cambridge University Press for permission to use figure 1 from Gelman, S. A., and E. M. Markman (1985), Implicit contrast in adjectives vs. nouns: Implications for word-learning in preschoolers, *Journal of Child Language 12*, 125–143; Elsevier Science Publishers for permission to use tables 1 and 2 and figure 1 from Gelman, S. A., and E. M. Markman (1986), Categories and Induction in Young Children, *Cognition 23*, 183–208; table 2 and figure 1 from Markman, E. M., M. S. Horton, and A. G. McLanahan (1980), Classes and Collections: Principles of organization in the learning of hierarchical relations, *Cognition 8*, 227–241 and tables 1, 2, and 3 from Markman, E. M. (1985), Why superordinate category terms can be mass nouns, *Cognition, 19*, 31–53; and The Society for Research in Child Development for permission to use table 1 from Kossan, N. E. (1981), Developmental differences in concept acquisition strategies *Child Development 52*, 290–298 and figure 1 from Horton, M. S., and E. M. Markman (1980), Developmental differences in the acquisition of basic and superordinate categories, *Child Development 51*, 708–719.

Categorization and Naming in Children

Chapter 1

Introduction

My office is overflowing with unsteady stacks of manuscripts because I cannot face the ordeal of trying to file them. The simple filing system that I devised seems to have taken on a vindictive life of its own. If I'd worked at it, I could hardly have created a more cumbersome, aggravating, inelegant scheme. But this certainly isn't what I tried to do. I set out to create a system that would let me readily store each psychology article in its proper place and quickly retrieve it when needed. That didn't seem like too much to expect from a filing system, but mine has fallen pathetically short of that goal.

Examining the problems that I have encountered with my system may help us understand what young children confront in trying to categorize objects in their environment. I started my system as a graduate student studying cognitive development. When my first semester in graduate school began, I was able to remember the individual articles that had been assigned (helped by the syllabus for each course) and had no real need for a filing system. But, given the lengthy reading assignments for these courses, it quickly became impossible for me to remember each individual article, and I was forced to come up with some way of organizing them. The extraordinary difficulty of remembering each unique individual is probably the impetus behind many classification systems.

Once I decided that I needed a way to organize the articles, I considered filing them in alphabetical order by author. Since many authors write several articles, this would save me from having to remember each specific article; moreover, it would give me a quick, reliable way to store a given file and (as long as I knew the author's name) a quick, reliable way to retrieve it.

Despite its advantages, however, this system had two drawbacks. First, if I wanted all the articles on a particular topic, then I would have to be able to recall every author who had written on it and look for each of their files. I preferred a system such that once I found the topical file, it would contain all of the relevant articles, so I wouldn't

have to search through the files of each investigator who had conducted relevant research. The more general concern here is how to
optimize the amount of information each category should contain. A
category may be more useful if, once it is found, it leads to many
relevant entries.

The second, more serious drawback to an alphabetical system was
that I have a terrible memory for names. Now, after studying psychology for many years, I would be capable of using such a system.
As a new student in the field, however, I would have found it especially difficult to keep track of the names of so many psychologists
about whom I'd heard very little. This illustrates a kind of tension
between different criteria for setting up a classification scheme. Even
if a system (such as alphabetical order) provides a simple and efficient
way of storing and retrieving information, if it places too great a
strain on the user's memory, it will not be useful. Moreover, what
might be a reasonable system for someone well versed in an area may
not be feasible for a novice.

Given these problems with an alphabetical system, I decided to
organize my files by topic. I established one file called "Conservation
Studies." It became cluttered with so many assorted studies that finding a specific article required a lengthy search. So I subdivided that
file into files called "Conservation of Number," "Conservation of
Length," "Conservation of Liquid," "Extinction of Conservation,"
"Training of Conservation," and so on. The opposite happened with
my files on attention. I started out with one file called "Dichotic Lis-
tening" and another called "Selective Attention" but later combined
them into a single file called "Attention." This illustrates a pervasive
characteristic of classification systems—their multiple levels of classification. As people learn more about a domain, two complementary
changes occur. First, they notice more distinctions among items in a
given category, leading them to subdivide it to capture the relevant
differences. Second, they detect more commonalities between separate categories, leading them to combine those categories into a more
inclusive one. The existence of multiple levels of classification would
seem to be a natural consequence of trying to organize large amounts
of information. This hierarchical organization is a fundamental property of the way that humans structure their classification systems.
Thus, the changes that I made in these files, to capture the hierarchical structure of the topic areas, are the kinds of changes that should
naturally evolve in a classification system.

Other changes that I made or should have made are more problematic. I had one file entitled "Learning," which contained studies on

probability learning, reversal shift learning, and paired associate learning. At the time "Learning" seemed a reasonable topic. Years later, however, this file would actually hinder me in finding relevant studies. Studies of paired associate learning in children would later seem more relevant to studies of memory development. Studies of probability learning would seem more relevant to problem-solving strategies. What at one time seemed to be a useful system had become obsolete, making it difficult to retrieve relevant studies.

In this instance it is not just that the distinctions I would like to capture now are finer or more general than the ones I noticed before but rather that the whole topical structure needs to be revised. The "Learning" file is not an isolated case. As I learned more about psychology and as the field itself changed, many of the topics I had originally established no longer provided an effective way for storing or finding articles relevant to my current knowledge and perspective on the field. To remedy this situation would require a massive reorganization of the system. This is an enormous amount of work. I assume that other people, like myself, are unwilling to totally scrap an old system and design a new one until they have little other choice. Instead, we tend to create patchwork systems—making duplicate copies of articles that can be filed in different places or sometimes simply sacrificing an article by leaving it filed in such a way that it will fail to be retrieved when a more current topic is searched.

Another kind of change has to do more with the internal structure of the file itself than with its relation to other files. I had one file entitled "Metaphor," which at first included only studies about children's comprehension and production of metaphors. Later I added studies about children's understanding of analogies, which seemed so similar it did not warrant another file. I had one lone study on alliteration in the file as well, but I had reasons for including it there. First, it did not seem worth setting up a new file for a single study on alliteration. Second, I reasoned that since some kinds of alliteration are poetic devices, just like some kinds of metaphor, I could squeeze alliteration into the file. I also had another singleton study in the file, concerning children's comprehension of the words "same" and "different." In this case I reasoned that to understand a metaphor is to find similarities between two disparate things—and this entails studying children's perception of similarity, about which their comprehension of "same" and "different" could be informative. Thus, I stretched the category to accommodate articles that, although they were not quite about metaphor, seemed closer to being about metaphor than to being about anything else I could find in my system. I believe there is a general reluctance to generate an entire new category for a single object, especially when stretching old categories will do fairly well. In Chapter 3 I will argue that this helps account for some of the internal structure of natural categories.

The problems that I encountered with this filing system illustrate the complexity of deciding what classification scheme would be optimal. A large number of factors affect the usefulness of a classification system, including the nature of the material to be classified and the cognitive abilities of the person trying to construct, learn, or use the system. If a person desiring to use a system does not have the knowledge to do so, then the system will not serve its function, no matter how elegant it is.

The example of the filing system also illustrates two forces that I believe play a major role in determining the structure of categories and classification systems. First, there are many pressures on classification systems to evolve and change. Changes in the characteristics of the users of the system, in the functions to which the system will be put, and in what is known about the material will exert pressure on the system for change. Thus, categories should not be viewed as rigid, static, immutable structures but as structures evolving over time. I think this is true for classification in a given culture that will undergo many historical changes, for classification in science, where new discoveries and theoretical advances will necessitate changes, and for classification throughout the lifetime of an individual person whose knowledge, abilities, and perspectives will change from infancy through adulthood.

Hierarchical organization is one kind of natural evolution of a classification system that stems from greater accumulation of knowledge. With greater experience, people notice both more distinctions and more similarities among objects, motivating them to organize categories into hierarchies in which more specific classes are included in more general ones.

There is also pressure for more drastic changes in a classification system. Cultures, sciences, and children can each radically change their theories of the world, rendering a previous classification scheme outmoded. At some point the system may become so unwieldy as to be useless, and a new system will have to be devised. However—and this is the second major force determining the structure of classification systems—I believe that people resist change. It takes an extraordinary amount of effort to develop a totally new organizational scheme. Moreover, the loss of continuity with the old system is probably confusing and disconcerting. In this regard, people are conservative, and they will try to make do with the system they already have rather than develop a new one. Thus, strategies will be stretched to try to accommodate instances that don't quite fit, categories will allow exceptions to general rules, and inelegant systems will result.

In sum, there are, throughout time, two opposing tendencies that need to be reconciled in the evolution of a classification system. On the one hand, there is pressure to change the category system to handle new ways of looking at the world, and new knowledge and abilities on the part of the creators and users of the system. On the other hand, there is reluctance to undertake such massive organizational changes. Given these two opposing tendencies, we would expect to see patchwork systems that have evolved by way of compromise.

Hard as it is, coming up with a way of classifying psychology articles is trivial compared to what children eventually accomplish. Very young children are surrounded by a huge array of objects—all new and unfamiliar. There are hundreds of artifacts created for purposes that the young child could hardly foresee and can barely understand. There are dozens of different kinds of animals, plants, and other natural phenomena to learn about. Each kind of object comes in numerous sizes, shapes, and colors and can be encountered in numerous positions or activities—with the result that there are thousands of ways to group or classify these objects, most of which adults would find peculiar, incomprehensible, or useless. How is it, then, that children quickly arrive at what we do consider to be reasonable categories?

Throughout this book, ideas are offered about how children might accomplish this. To provide some perspective on these ideas, it will be helpful to contrast them with traditional theories of concept acquisition.

Traditional Theories of Concept Acquisition

The seminal development work on categorization and concept acquisition focused on the abilities required for children to organize objects into categories (Bruner, Olver, Greenfield, et al. 1966; Inhelder and Piaget 1964). This view of concept acquisition was based in part on the belief that categories conform to classical definitions. Classical definitions require that categories have an intension and extension that determine one another. The intension of a category is the set of attributes or features that define the category. It is sometimes viewed as the meaning of a category term. The intensional definition of the term "bachelor," to take a well-worn example, is something like "unmarried man of marriageable age." The extension of a category is the set of objects that are members of the category—that is, the set of objects that fulfill the criteria set forth in the intensional definition. In the case of the category "bachelor," the extension consists of the people who are in fact unmarried men of marriageable age. Later I will discuss challenges to this view of categories, but for the moment I will ignore them in order to consider some of the other assumptions the traditional developmental theories have made.

When learning a new concept, children first encounter a small sample of the extension of the concept. For the vast majority of categories, it is impossible to encounter the entire extension of the category even over the course of a lifetime, let alone on first learning the concept. In many cases a child's first exposure consists of a single exemplar. For example, the child might be shown a dog and told it is a dog, or shown a ball and encouraged to watch while it is bounced and rolled. One major assumption of the traditional theories is that from a sample of the extension of a category, children must begin to figure out what the intension is. On this view, then, a child who sees a dog and is told it is a dog needs to analyze the dog into a set of properties (furry, four-legged, brown, barks, and so on) and then evaluate these properties to determine which are necessary and sufficient. As children make progress in determining the intension of a category, this in turn should allow them to more accurately determine its extension. That is, as children come to know the necessary and sufficient criteria, they can use them to evaluate potential members of the category. In sum, on this view, to acquire a concept, a child needs (1) analytic abilities for decomposing the object into its properties; (2) a powerful hypothesis-testing system, for generating possible properties and evaluating them against new exemplars, as well as for revising, rejecting, or maintaining hypotheses in the face of the new evidence; and (3) an ability to use the intensional criteria to evaluate subsequent objects to determine whether they are members of the category.

Given these implicit assumptions about what is required to learn a category, the classical theories of how children acquire categories argue that very young children lack the requisite cognitive abilities. On Piaget's view, children do not have the concrete operations needed to coordinate the extension and intension of categories. On the view of Bruner, Olver, Greenfield, et al. (1966), young children do not have the necessary symbolic abilities. Much research has been conducted to determine more precisely which of these abilities children lack and what the developmental course of classification is like.

Departures from the Traditional Theory

Abilities Needed for Learning Categories
Obviously the question of what cognitive abilities are required for classification and how they develop is an important one, and to some extent it will be addressed in this book as well. Now, however, with the benefit of hindsight, we can see that this may not have been the best formulation of the issues. Although young children have by no means acquired a conceptual system as complete as an adult's, and although they make many mistakes along the way, we should not presuppose that concepts are acquired exclusively by logico-deductive methods. And when we consider not just children's failures at acquiring concepts, but also their extraordinary successes, we are led to ask quite different questions. Even average 3-year-olds, who are years away from the logical and symbolic operations postulated by Piaget and Bruner, have quite thoroughly classified their world. They have formed hundreds of categories of vehicles, clothes, food, toys, furniture, tools, buildings, kitchenware, activities, and so on. They quite readily recognize a novel tricycle, for example, as a tricycle or some kind of vehicle (whether or not they know the term)—that is, they would try to ride it. They would not mistake a tricycle for a tomato just because the two happened to be the same color, or a book for a slice of bread just because the two happened to be the same shape. Even if we took a 3-year-old's vocabulary as a conservative estimate of the concepts he or she had learned, it would seem an enormously impressive accomplishment. Given their level of success in acquiring categories, we need to ask how young children accomplish this, and we need to question the assumption that sophisticated logical abilities are required. In other words, either very young children in fact have the logical abilities that are presupposed by the traditional theories, or they are capable of learning categories by some other means.

I will argue that at least to some extent children acquire categories in ways that circumvent the need for sophisticated hypothesis testing. The most powerful alternative is that young children may come to the task equipped with some assumptions about the nature of categories and about the nature of category terms. These assumptions limit the kinds of hypothesis children consider. In other words, children do not always need to reject hypotheses on the basis of negative evidence. They can implicitly reject them by being biased against them in the first place. Throughout this book I explicitly consider some of the assumptions children make about categories and about category labels and explore the implications of these assumptions.

Another powerful alternative to the hypothesis-testing view, which I present in chapter 3, is that nonanalytic strategies can be used to acquire concepts.

Acquisition of Category Labels
The ideas offered here also differ from traditional accounts in their emphasis on and concern with language. Many of the chapters are about the acquisition of category *terms* as opposed to or in conjunction with the categories themselves. The main approach I have taken to the acquisition of terms—both terms for categories and terms for properties—is to consider the learning of such terms as a problem of induction, analogous to the induction problem involved in learning the categories themselves. When a child hears a word used to label an object, for example, an indefinite number of interpretations are possible for that word. The child could think that the speaker is labeling the object itself as a whole, or one of its parts, or its substance, or its color, texture, size, shape, position in space, and on and on. Given the impossibility of ruling out every logically possible hypothesis, how is it that children succeed in figuring out the correct meanings of terms? Part of the answer is that children are constrained or biased to consider only some kinds of hypotheses. They do not have to eliminate many logical possibilities because they never consider them in the first place. Other, more plausible candidates may be ordered, with some hypotheses taking precedence over others. In this book I consider some of the ways in which children may limit their hypotheses about word meanings—that is, some assumptions they make about new terms. I also consider how these assumptions aid them in acquiring terms, and what problems they may generate as well.

Invention versus Discovery of Categories
The analogy with setting up a filing system, though useful, is not entirely apt. The analogy suggests that each individual is confronted with the task of inventing a classification scheme. This assumption is shared by traditional theories of concept acquisition (Bruner, Goodnow, and Austin 1956; Inhelder and Piaget 1964). It may be more useful, however, to think of children as discovering rather than inventing ways to classify. Traditional theories view the child as inventing ways to classify because they assume that categories are essentially arbitrary. Categories are taken to be arbitrary in the sense that there are an indefinite number of ways to form object categories, and each of these logical possibilities is assumed to be as valid a category as any other. Thus, categorization reflects not the structure of

the world but the order that humans impose on it. To quote Bruner, Goodnow, and Austin (1956, 7): "Do such categories as tomatoes, lions, snobs, atoms and mammalia exist? Insofar as they have been invented and found applicable to instances of nature, they do. They exist as inventions, not as discoveries."

In contrast to this view, Rosch (Rosch and Mervis 1975; Rosch 1973) has argued that, at least for some kinds of categories, it is not right to think of them as defined by arbitrary combinations of features. Rosch takes a Gibsonian view (Gibson 1979) of categories, arguing they have a correlational structure that humans perceive and use in constructing category systems. We do not, for example, start with a list of features such as "has feathers, has fur, has a beak, has teeth, flies, lays eggs, produces milk" and then decide how to combine those features to invent animal categories. We do not have a category defined as "animals with feathers and teeth," for example, even though it is a logical possibility resulting from a simple combination of these features. Instead, on Rosch's view, the world provides us with animals that have feathers, have beaks, lay eggs, and typically fly. We, as individuals and through our culture, discover these correlations and form categories on that basis. Thus, at least to some extent, there is a nonarbitrary quality to many of our categories, and this should aid children in discovering them. In fact, I will argue in chapters 5 and 6 that children may start out expecting categories to have a very rich correlated structure and that this in part guides their acquisition of early categories.

Conceptual Diversity
Traditional theories of concept acquisition did not deal much with differences between kinds of categories. Although distinctions were sometimes noted (for example, between abstract and concrete concepts), little attention was paid to them. Some of the recent advances in our knowledge of human categorization stem from recognizing such distinctions, a partial list of which includes classical concepts versus those defined by family resemblances, collections versus classes, ad hoc categories, natural kinds versus nonnatural kinds, and subordinate, basic, and superordinate categories.

Acknowledging the diversity of categories raises several developmental questions. Are there reasons to think that children use different strategies depending on the structure of the category to be learned, or do they use the same learning strategy for each kind of category? If children use the same strategy to learn all concepts, would that result in any particular ordering of the difficulty of learning the various kinds of concepts? Instead of focusing solely on what logical abilities are needed to learn and represent concepts in general, we must also ask about the particular abilities needed to represent one kind of concept as opposed to another.

This conceptual diversity raises another kind of question that I will be considering—namely, whether the existence of a given kind of concept tells us anything interesting about human cognition. Why is it that concepts would have a given structure? What would the existence of such a structure imply, not just about how hard or easy the concept is to learn, but also about what kind of a mind would generate that particular structure?

Consequences of Categorization

Traditional theories of categorization have in large measure focused on the acquisition of categories. Very little attention has been paid to the consequences of categorization. Yet categories are vehicles for applying information in new circumstances. Categories not only embody knowledge but also are a means of extending it. One reason why this point has been neglected is that traditional theories may have overemphasized the perceptual basis for categorization. If one can readily perceive the necessary and sufficient features needed to classify objects, then it is harder to see what further information, beyond these defining criteria, classification provides. Yet many categories capture nonobvious similarities among their exemplars. Tigers, for example, have similar diets, means of reproduction, and genetic structure, in addition to the more obvious perceptual features they share. Given that categories capture such information, one of the important functions of categorization is to support inductive inferences. Our knowledge about some members of a category is extended to other members. This fact about categorization and induction raises questions about the structure and organization of categories (for example, what kinds of categories can support such inferences?), about assumptions that humans make about categories to allow them to generate such inferences, and about how this relationship between categorization and induction changes developmentally. I discuss these issues in chapter 5 and 6.

General Issues in Categorization

In the remainder of this chapter I touch briefly on several issues—each of which deserves much greater discussion. My purpose is not to resolve these issues but to point them out and highlight their significance for the arguments presented throughout this book. I mention the ubiquity of categorization to provide perspective on the magnitude of the problem we are studying. I mention the relationship between concepts, categories, and word meaning, not to presume to address any of the complex and subtle issues these questions raise, but simply in order to agree on terminology. I consider some of the difficulties involved in deciding what counts as a natural concept and what counts as a feature mainly as a warning to keep these problems in mind. Finally I consider the systematization of categories and what issues this raises for development.

The Ubiquity of Categorization
Categorization is one of the main ways in which children attempt to make sense of their environment. Bruner, Goodnow, and Austin pointed out in the introduction to their seminal book (Bruner, Goodnow, and Austin 1956) that if we responded to each object that we come across as if it were a unique individual, we would be overwhelmed by the complexity of our environment. Categorization, then, is a means of simplifying the environment, of reducing the load on memory, and of helping us to store and retrieve information efficiently. As many investigators have pointed out, categorization is a fundamental cognitive process, involved in one way or another in almost any intellectual endeavor. In identifying objects, in perceiving two things as similar, in recalling information, in solving problems, in learning new information, in acquiring and using language—in all of these cognitive processes and more, categorization plays a major role. Forming categories is also one of the major ways in which we learn from experience. Through induction, we note similarities among objects and are thus able to make important generalizations about the categories.

By far the most striking advantage of categorization is that it provides information that goes beyond the knowledge we have about a specific object. If we know, for example, that a given object is a cat, we can be fairly certain about whether it has fur, how it moves about, how it stalks its prey, how it reproduces, and even what internal organs it has. We know all of this information even about a new cat we have never seen before. It would be hard to overestimate this advantage. The time and energy that would be required to learn this amount of information for each individual cat that we encounter, let alone for all the rest of the hundreds of object categories that we know about, would be staggering.

Thus, the importance of categorization is very clear: most of human cognition depends on it. We cannot fully understand perception, memory, problem solving, learning, language, or induction without understanding categorization. But the converse possibility is daunting: perhaps we cannot fully understand categorization without understanding all of human cognition. A more accurate, and less pessimistic, way of stating the issue may be that we never are able to fully isolate a person's ability to classify from some cognitive context, however minimal. This point is acknowledged to some extent in the literature. To take one example, our ideas about how children form categories are influenced by our knowledge of the limitations on children's memory. If children could recall every instance of a concept that they had seen and what information they had been provided about its category membership, our theories of how they learn would be quite different. In the case of memory, then, theories of categorization consider, to some extent, how categorization may interact with memory limitations. More generally, however, information gained about categorization is always information about categorization in a given context. Quite often the conclusions drawn from categorization research are stated more boldly and generally than the evidence warrants. This may be especially true for developmental studies, where minor differences in task demands or difficulty can obscure or reveal abilities young children have.

Concepts, Categories, and Meaning
As Katz (1972) has argued, the answer to the question "What is meaning?" requires, not a simple definition, but a theory. Similarly, an analysis of what counts as a human concept or category cannot be presented in a short paragraph. Nonetheless, I would like to briefly set out the relationship among concepts, categories, and meaning, to clarify subsequent discussion and avoid confusion.

One of the main functions of human concepts is to *categorize* the world into objects, events, properties, and so on (a category being a set of objects, events, properties, etc.). The *meaning* of a word refers to the *concept* that the word expresses. Some but not all concepts are encoded into single words. Many human concepts are not represented by single words in a language. In English, for example, we do not have a single word to refer to concepts such as "tall, generous children" or "buildings overlooking a major freeway." Thus, word meanings constitute only a subset of the possible human concepts. Many concepts could have been represented by single words but just happen not to be. These are referred to as "accidental gaps" in the lexicon. There does not seem to be any principled reason for excluding such concepts from the lexicon, and we could imagine that if one or another of them became useful or interesting enough to a given culture, a word would be coined to represent it. English, for example, has "bachelor" and "spinster," referring to an unmarried man and an unmarried woman, but does not (to my knowledge) have a single word that refers to an unmarried brother or an unmarried sister. Nothing principled, however, would prevent us from coining such terms if they were needed. In other cases, however, there are principled reasons for excluding certain kinds of meanings from being represented by single words—for example, because the concept itself is not a natural human concept.

Natural Concepts
On the issue of what can constitute a concept or category, there is some tension between logic and psychology. If we view a category simply as a class of objects, then, on logical grounds alone, any odd assortment of objects can be in the same set. To take an example from Savin 1973, consider the concept "either a bachelor or a no-deposit-no-return Coke bottle." Savin argues that this is an example of an unnatural concept, though it is a perfectly respectable set. This point raises the question of what makes a concept natural or not. A first, intuitive response is to say that bachelors and no-deposit-no-return Coke bottles have nothing in common. They share too few properties; they are just not similar enough to be united in a single concept. There is probably a great deal of truth to this argument, and many analyses of human concepts that psychologists make rely on the notion of assessing how many features objects share. The problem is that unless we can specify what counts as a feature, the argument fails. If features can be anything, then even bachelors and no-deposit-no-return Coke bottles can share an infinite number of features. Both are not dogs, for example, both are found in the twentieth century; both are less that 15 feet tall; both are less than 16 feet tall; both are less than 17 feet tall;. . . . A further problem is that many categories that are widely agreed upon as natural concepts (for instance, "tree," "dog") seem to defy any simple analysis into perceptual features (Herrnstein 1982; Rosch and Mervis 1975). An even more pessimistic view is that either there are no such things as features and thus a featural account of concepts will fail or that psychologists and linguists are too far away from discovering features to make such an analysis feasible (Armstrong, Gleitman, and Gleitman 1983).

Another intuitive argument about why concepts such as "either a bachelor or a no-deposit-no-return Coke bottle" seem unnatural is that they don't make any sense. There is no apparent reason why these diverse objects would be united into a single concept. Some recent arguments in psychology are relevant in this regard. Several investigators have proposed that concepts embody lay theories about

objects, arguing that people represent concepts in terms of explanations or simple theories about objects (Carey 1985; Miller and Johnson-Laird 1976; Murphy and Medin 1985). Moreover, conceptual
change throughout development might be best explained by thinking
of it as theory change (Carey 1985). A related issue is considered here
in the discussion of natural kind categories in chapters 6 and 7. For
other discussions and attempts to grapple with this difficult problem
of conceptual naturalness, see Goodman 1955, Quine 1960, Murphy
and Medin 1985; Osherson 1978, Herrnstein 1982.

Even if the concept itself is a perfectly natural human concept,
however, there still may be principled reasons for not representing it
as a single lexical item in a human language. Although "the dog and
its bone" and "the spider and its web" are comprehensible, sensible
phrases, each composed of two elements that are strongly associated
with one another, I believe that there are principled reasons for not
representing such categories with single words. These arguments are
presented in chapter 2.

The Systematization of Categories
The systematic organization of categories may be one of the major
intellectual achievements of human conceptualization (Markman and
Callanan 1983). Human categories tend to be organized into systems
where the categories are related to each other in various ways rather
than each concept being represented in isolation. One striking example is that many categories are organized into taxonomies of
nested class-inclusion relations. That is, many categories form hierarchies that consist of more and more general levels of categorization
(for example, "delicious apple, apple, fruit, food"; "poodle, dog,
mammal, animal"). Taxonomic systems are a pervasive and extremely important kind of organization of categories.

A taxonomy is particularly useful in extending information because, by grouping objects into more and more general categories (for
example, "Siamese cat, cat, feline, mammal, animal"), it creates a rich
set of deductive possibilities. You should be able to state with a fair
degree of certainty whether a Siamese cat breathes oxygen or carbon
dioxide and whether it produces chlorophyll or not. Even though you
may have never thought about these questions before with respect to
a Siamese cat, and even if you have never seen such a cat yourself,
you can still readily deduce the answer to these questions. Because a
cat is an animal, all of the properties of animals, such as that they
breathe oxygen, can be deduced to be true of cats. You should also
be fairly certain that a Siamese cat does not lay eggs but instead bears
its young live, that it has a heart and lungs, and that it is warm-

blooded. By virtue of being mammals, cats should have these properties. Because it is feline, a Siamese cat can be known to have certain more specific catlike physical features and behavior. And its size and ferocity can be deduced from its being a common cat rather than a wild cat. Thus, an object that is categorized at a given level of the hierarchy will inherit all of the properties that are known to characterize each of the more general categories in which it is included. An extraordinary amount of knowledge is passed on in this way, saving us from having to learn it anew for each object.

Developmental Issues

One important developmental question is to ask what needs to develop—or, conversely, to ask what abilities we can safely assume that even babies have. We know that babies can recognize some individual objects as individuals. Babies do not see their family members as just being other people but identify them as particular individuals. The same is true for some inanimate objects—children know own cribs, blankets and favorite stuffed toys as individuals. Moreover, by 18 months to 2 years of age, children are capable of learning proper names for individuals—that is, for animate objects and stuffed animals (Katz, Baker, and Macnamara 1974; Macnamara 1982; Gelman and Taylor 1984).

Very young children are also capable of forming object categories at least at some intermediate level of categorization, roughly what Rosch et al. (1976) have called the *basic level*. "Bottle," "ball," and "dog" are just a few examples of the kinds of objects that can be categorized by children as young as 2 and probably younger.

Young children also acquire information about their environment that enables them to recognize certain kinds of thematic relations—causal, spatial and temporal. Babies know, for example, that they sleep in cribs, drink from bottles, get wrapped in blankets.

Thus, from very early childhood or even infancy the basic abilities needed to classify objects, to recognize objects as individuals, and to comprehend relations between objects already exist. The interesting developmental question, then, is how children figure out which of the many ways to categorize objects are the culturally specified ones and which of these categories are referred to by specific word meanings.

One classificatory ability that appears to be less available to young children is the ability to work out hierarchical categories—at both the superordinate and subordinate levels. There may be many reasons for this, which I will explore throughout the chapters to follow. The issue is complicated, however, by the complexity of what it means to "have a concept." On the one hand, many investigators have argued that young children do not have superordinate categories. On the other hand, children must already know some of the reasons for categorizing objects at higher levels. Young children may not group couches, high chairs, and stools together on a classification task; yet they would know that these objects are for sitting on. The problem is that the fact that children know this should not lead us into thinking that they therefore must "have" the category and that little is left to develop. Implicit in many psychological discussions of categorization is that some categories are so available, stable, habitual, and familiar that they achieve a special status. The most common and useful have often been lexicalized into single words in the language (Brown 1958). Other categories are unstable, unfamiliar, and less available, yet in some sense we know them or construct them as well. We know, for example, that we can stand on a table or a ladder to reach a high place, yet we don't think of ladders and tables as the same kind of thing. We know that apples and fire engines are both red, yet we don't think of them as the same kind of thing. Thus, a child may know that we sit on chairs and on stools and on couches yet not think of them as the same kind of thing. This argument is made most clearly by Barsalou (1983), who distinguishes between ad hoc categories and those that can claim greater consensus. In chapter 4 I consider in more detail the possibility that children may only implicitly represent or construct superordinate categories, as adults implicitly represent and construct ad hoc categories (Horton 1982).

Children are faced with two general problems, then, in trying to learn the conventional object categories of their culture. The first problem concerns the acquisition of single categories. Because there are an unlimited number of possible ways of forming categories, how is it that children come up with the conventional categories encoded by their particular culture? Second, children must organize and structure the knowledge they acquire. They must be able to relate categories to each other in terms of class-inclusion hierarchies, and the categories that they form and the organization that they impose on these categories must eventually come to match that of the adults who live in their culture.

For convenience, I will discuss these two problems separately, although in actuality they are closely related. The question of how children acquire single categories leads us to examine the structure of natural categories and to consider what makes a category psychologically natural or useful. It leads to questions about how children obtain information about categories and what principles of organization they use to generate new categories. As we will see, these questions are complicated by the diversity of categories.

The second developmental question is how children learn and represent the relationships among the categories themselves. Because of their importance I will focus mainly on how children learn and deal with hierarchical relationships among categories. This will lead to examining the evidence for whether children do in fact represent categories hierarchically or not and to consider why this relationship seems so difficult for children to understand.

To the extent that it is possible, this book is organized around these two questions: the acquisition of single categories, and the organization of categories with respect to each other. However, there are many mutual influences between the nature of categories and the classification system, and many overlapping issues that blur this distinction. To take just one example, consider the single categories "rocking chair" and "easy chair." In these cases it may be somewhat misleading to speak of learning the single category apart from the hierarchical relations. Even the names of these single categories presuppose the existence of a more general category "chair" that is being divided into contrasting kinds of chairs. Thus, with respect to the single category "rocking chair," the relation between it and other categories, such as "chair" and "easy chair," will influence how it is learned. It is somewhat artificial to talk of learning a single category in this case as if the hierarchical relations did not matter. It will become more apparent that these issues are tightly intertwined. Nevertheless, there are enough differences between these two developmental problems that it is helpful to try to consider them separately.

Chapters 2 through 6 consider the acquisition of single categories. Chapter 2 presents the problem of the acquisition of category labels as a problem of induction and argues that children are able to acquire category labels so quickly because they are biased to assume that labels refer to objects of the same type. Given that children treat labels as referring to object categories, we need to consider which of the many ways to categorize objects children focus on. Chapters 3 through 6 discuss these issues. Chapter 3 concerns the internal structure of categories, chapter 4 concerns basic, superordinate, and subordinate categorization, and chapters 5 and 6 concern natural kinds and other richly structured categories. Chapters 7 through 9 consider the problem of the systematization of categories—how categories are related to each other. Chapter 7 focuses on hierarchical classification, and chapters 8 and 9 propose that to systematize categories, children begin by assuming that category terms are mutually exclusive.

Chapter 2
Acquisition of Category Terms

To begin thinking about what children must accomplish in learning how to categorize objects in their world let us consider what is involved in learning labels for object categories.

Quine's Problem of Induction

A simple, straightforward way in which young children learn new category labels is through ostensive definition. That is, an adult or other teacher points to an object and labels it. It is important to consider how much can be learned by way of ostensive definition, because very young children who are learning their first language may have little else to rely on. We cannot explain or describe to the young child what "rabbit" means, because the child does not yet understand the language needed for the explanation. At first, then, adults are limited to pointing to an object (such as a rabbit) and labeling it ("rabbit"). What is required for the child to conclude, in this situation, that the word "rabbit" is the label for a rabbit? First, the child must be able to interpret the pointing gesture correctly. The child's gaze must follow the direction of the pointing finger (see Churcher and Scaife 1982, Murphy and Messer 1977, Scaife and Bruner 1975 for discussion of how children make use of eye gaze and pointing). Then the child must assume that the word is somehow related to what he or she views. How is it that the child settles on an interpretation? At first glance this would seem to be quite a simple problem, and in fact children correctly make hundreds of such inferences when acquiring new vocabulary. But this apparent simplicity belies an incredibly difficult inferential problem. To illustrate the problem, I will summarize the example used by Quine (1960) to make his well-known argument about translation.

Quine asks us to imagine that a linguist visits an unknown country and attempts to learn the native language. A rabbit passes by and a native of the country says, "Gavagai." How is the linguist to figure out what "Gavagai" means? Like us, the linguist hypothesizes that

it refers to "rabbit"; but that hypothesis of course requires confirmation. After all, "Gavagai" could refer to "white" or "furry" or
"medium-sized" or the like, as well as to "rabbit." To decide whether
the "rabbit" hypothesis is correct, the linguist might set up certain
test situations in order to be able to point to various objects and ask
whether or not "Gavagai" applies. The native would then assent or
not, thereby allowing the linguist to test the hypothesis. (This procedure requires that the native can understand that the linguist is
asking about the meaning of the term and that the linguist can determine what gestures or words refer to "yes" and "no," but I will ignore
these problems.)

To test the hypotheses for the potential meaning of "Gavagai," the
linguist will point to carefully selected objects and ask whether each
is a Gavagai. If the native denies that "Gavagai" applies to other
white furry objects, then those hypotheses can be rejected. Quine
points out, however, that through this procedure alone we can never
settle on the meaning of "Gavagai," because there will always be
some other hypothesis that is consistent with the data. That is, if all
we are allowed to do is to compare the objects that can correctly be
called "Gavagai" to those than cannot be, we will not have enough
information to rule out all but one meaning for the term. For example, "Gavagai" could refer to some abstract concept "rabbithood"
or even to "undetached rabbit parts." As Quine puts it, "Point to a
rabbit and you have pointed to a stage of a rabbit, to an integral part
of a rabbit, to the rabbit fusion, and to where rabbithood is mani-
fested" (p.52).

Young children beginning to acquire their native language face the
same problem as Quine's linguist. Someone points in some direction
and utters a word. On what grounds is the child to conclude that a
new unfamiliar word—say, "rabbit"—refers to rabbits? What is to
prevent the child from concluding that "Rabbit" is a proper name for
that particular rabbit, or that "rabbit" means "furry" or "white" or
any number of other characteristics that rabbits have? Finally, what
prevents the child from concluding that "rabbit" means something
like "the rabbit and its carrot" or "the rabbit next to the tree" or
"mother petting the rabbit"? These last examples of thematic relations pose a particular problem because children are so interested in
such relations and often find them more salient than categorical relations. Although children are biased toward organizing objects thematically, single words, in particular nouns, rarely encode thematic
relations. English does not have a single noun for thematically related
objects such as a boy and his bike, a spider and its web, or a baby
and its bottle. Before we consider a possible solution to this problem,

let us look in more detail at the differences between these kinds of thematic relations and categorical or taxonomic relations between objects.

Taxonomic versus Thematic Organization

A *taxonomic* organization groups objects of the same type together. There are many different ways that objects might be considered to be of the same type, and much of this book will be devoted to this issue. For the moment I will simply mention some of the possibilities. Such taxonomic organization could be based on the existence of certain features—be they perceptual, functional, or something more abstract—that are shared by the exemplars of a category and that distinguish them from exemplars of other categories. These features might constitute necessary and sufficient criteria for category membership or they might be only probabilistically related to the category (see chapter 3) for a more complete discussion of this issue). In either case, to decide whether an object is a member of a given category, it suffices to consider its relevant properties, appearance, function, or behavior.

However, many external relations between objects are not captured by this internal analysis of an object's properties. Objects can be found in various spatial relations to each other ("next to" or "on top of"); they can be related to each other through a large variety of causal relations (a can opener opens cans; a light switch turns on a light; a bat is used to hit a ball); and more generally they can be related to the extent that they are involved in the same event (dogs chew bones; people read books; spiders build webs; a child owns a doll). These various types of external relations between objects are referred to as *thematic* relations, to reflect the idea that the objects participate together in a theme or event. We continually rely on our knowledge of such thematic relations between objects in order to interpret ongoing events, to comprehend what is happening, to make simple decisions, to solve complex problems, to predict the consequences of actions, and so on. In other words, thematic relations encompass an enormous amount of knowledge. This point is worth emphasizing for two reasons: first, because the literature often gives the impression that thematic relations are something only younger children attend to, which is clearly false; and second, because, despite their ubiquity and importance, thematic relations are not the (sole) basis for (adult) categories. This second point contains hedges that need to be explained. The claim I am making is that even though, for example, dogs and bones are highly associated in a clear thematic relation, we do not think of them as the same kind of thing. We could of course come up with some criterion by which "dog" and "bone" would be considered the same kind of thing—say, by virtue of being physical objects, or being dull-colored, or not being very heavy—but it would not be by virtue of the fact that dogs eat bones. In other words, the existence of thematic relations between two objects does not render them things of the same type. The fact that spiders build webs does not make spiders and webs similar. The fact that children play with blocks does not make children and blocks the same kind of thing. The fact that shoes are worn on feet does not make shoes and feet the same kind of thing. There are many categories, however, that are both taxonomically and thematically organized. "Dishes" can be defined by their perceptual and functional features and are clearly also thematically related (as when stacked in a cabinet or laid out in conventional spatial relations when a table is set). "Articles of clothing" can be defined by perceptual and functional features and are also thematically related when hung together in a closet or when worn in a particular configuration. So although thematic relations often exist between members of a taxonomic category, they are not the sole basis for the formation of the categories. Even very powerful thematic relations—for instance, between shoes and feet or between a spider and its web—are not sufficient to make us consider those objects the same kind of thing. Of course, functional features do sometimes contain hidden relational information. "Shoes," for example, are "coverings for feet," so external relations between objects are being mentioned. But the main point here is that the objects involved in that relation—namely, shoes and feet—are *not* being united into a single category. Further, relational information can be the basis for taxonomic organization as well (socks and mittens might be taxonomically related because both are used to cover appendages), but the category would unite objects that play the same role in the relation rather than ones that play different roles (socks and mittens could be categorized for that reason, but not socks and feet). Although thematic relations are not the basis for adult categories, it has been argued, in fact, that such thematic groupings are the basis for children's categorization.

This chapter will sketch the initial arguments that children's categories are thematically based and outline reasons for rejecting that argument. A more detailed review of this literature appears in chapter 7, where classification tasks are considered as evidence for hierarchical organization. Although the conclusion that children's concepts are thematically based will be rejected, there is little question that children find thematic relations very compelling and, in some circumstances, more compelling than taxonomic relations.

Children's Preference for Thematic Groupings

One widely used procedure for studying how children form categories—on what basis they form them, what principles of organization they use, and so on—is to ask them to classify objects by sorting them into groups. Typically children are presented with objects from several different categories (for example, vehicles, animals, clothing, and people) and are instructed to put together the objects that are alike or that go together. Other variants of the procedure are also frequently used, one being an oddity task in which children are presented with three objects, two from the same category and one from a separate category, and are asked to find the two that go together. In the most unstructured variant, children are simply presented with various objects and given relative freedom to sort them as they like. In this way the child's own organizational preferences can be discovered.

Children older than 6 or 7 sort objects on the basis of taxonomic categories, placing all and only the vehicles together, all and only the clothing together, and so on. Younger children sort on some other basis. Sometimes, especially when geometric figures are used, young children create spatial configurations with the objects, arranging them into designs or patterns. When more meaningful objects are used, children represent causal and temporal relations among the objects as well as spatial relations. These thematic relations emphasize events rather than taxonomic similarity. For example, children might sort a man and a car together because the man is driving the car. Or they might place a boy, a coat, and a dog together because the boy will wear his coat when he takes the dog for a walk. This attention to relations between objects rather than to how objects are alike is a common finding replicated in many studies. In fact, in addition to being found in studies using classification and oddity procedures, this thematic bias shows up in studies of memory and word association (see Markman 1981).

Again, I want to emphasize that it is not surprising that children notice these thematic relations. They are obviously very important for making sense of the world even for adults. During all sorts of normal activities, we observe people interacting with each other or using tools, machines, or other artifacts to accomplish some goal. We view natural occurrences such as storms, and we admire scenery.

Much of our perception is interpretive, making sense of what we encounter, trying to figure out what is happening and how. Thus, these eventlike meaningful structures are a universally important and natural way of organizing information (Mandler et al. 1980). This is in marked contrast to the cross-cultural and developmental differences found in studies of taxonomic classification. In sum, interest in thematic relations is not limited to young children. Nor should attention to thematic relations be viewed as an immature, useless, or nonproductive bias. Noticing the way in which objects interact, attending to causal, spatial, and temporal relations between objects, is essential for understanding the world (Mandler 1983). It is a heightening of interest in categorical relations, and not a loss of interest in thematic relations, that takes place with development.

From these studies of classification, we can conclude that children are more interested in the thematic relations among objects, or that thematic relations are simpler or more readily constructed than taxonomic relations. However, some investigators have placed a more radical interpretation on these results. Inhelder and Piaget (1964), Vygotsky (1962), and Bruner, Olver, Greenfield, et al. (1966) have interpreted this result to mean that children lack taxonomic categories and categorize solely on the basis of thematic organization. It is difficult to make sense of this interpretation of the results, however (Markman and Callanan 1983).

If children were capable of organizing objects only into the categories that correspond to the stories they create in classification tasks, the consequences would be dramatic. Suppose one were to try to teach such children the concept of "animal." Their concept of "animal" might include a cow and grass (because the cow is eating the grass), a dog and a leash (because the dog is on the leash), a cat and a bowl of milk (because the cat is drinking the milk). Thus, the child's concept would consist of cow, grass, dog, leash, cat, and milk. Casual observation of 5-year-old children should convince anyone that this is not true. The 5-year-olds who participated in these classification studies certainly do not believe that grass, a leash, and milk are animals even when accompanied by a cow, a dog, and a cat. Although children's concept of "animal" is not fully formed (for instance, they may not believe that insects are animals), their notion of "animal" would not allow "leash" and "milk" as exemplars. It would be impossible to communicate with children whose concepts had this structure (Fodor 1972). Moreover, children can certainly correctly answer simple questions such as "Do animals eat?" though they would deny that a leash eats. And if explicitly asked, they would deny that these objects are animals.

To summarize, although children's concepts may be incomplete and differ from the adult form in many ways, this extreme form of thematic grouping is not characteristic of their categories, at least not those categories for which they have labels.

Moreover, we know that under simplified conditions children are able to understand categorical organization (for reviews, see Carey 1985; Gelman and Baillargeon 1983; Markman and Callanan 1983; Horton 1982), even though they prefer thematic relations. Aspects of the classification task may obscure early knowledge of categories that children have. For example, one difficulty children have with the sorting task is that they may take the spatial nature of the task too literally. Markman, Cox, and Machida (1981) have argued that children may interpret the spatial arrangement of the objects to be an important part of the task and that this may bias them to construct meaningful scenes or storylike groupings. Just as adults may organize objects thematically if asked to place objects in a theater (that is, on a stage with curtains), children may be misled by the spatial nature of the task to construct meaningful scenes. We attempted to reduce the salience of the spatial arrangement of objects by asking children to sort objects into transparent plastic bags rather than into spatially segregated groups on a table. Children displayed more taxonomic sorting when they sorted objects into bags than when they sorted the same objects on the table. Thus, the spatial demands of the task confuse children and mask some of their knowledge of categories.

Another problem children may have with the standard sorting task is that they have to cope with a very large number of objects. Children are typically faced with a scrambled array of 16 different objects, four each from four different categories. To successfully classify the objects, children must scan this bewildering array, find some of the categories salient enough to emerge from this confusion, and keep them in mind while trying to impose some order on the remainder of the objects.

Children's preferences for thematic sorts may conceal any categorical knowledge that they have. Smiley and Brown (1979) tested whether 4- and 6-year-old children can understand taxonomic relations even though they prefer thematic ones. They presented children with a target picture and two choice pictures. One of the choices was thematically related to the target, and the other was taxonomically related to it. For example, children were shown a spider (target), a spider web (thematic choice), and a grasshopper (taxonomic choice). The experiment pointed to the spider and asked for "the one that goes best with this one." As usual, these young children tended to pick the spider web, rather than the grasshopper, thereby indicating a thematic relation. Nevertheless, when they were asked about the grasshopper, all of the children except the very youngest could explain the taxonomic relation. Thus, children have a rudimentary ability to organize objects taxonomically, but it is often obscured by their attention to thematic relations.

Although we cannot conclude from the classification studies that children's concepts are organized thematically, children do find it more difficult in this task to focus on categorical relations, and they do in fact seem captivated by thematic relations. Repeatedly, in many different kinds of studies, children prefer to organize objects into eventlike structures. They find the causal, temporal, and spatial relations between objects of interest, and their attention is drawn to these relations. Why is it, then, that in learning category labels children do not assume they refer to thematic relations?

The Taxonomic and Whole Object Assumptions

Thus, to return to Quine's problem of induction, we are faced with a kind of paradox. Children seem to readily learn terms that refer to object categories. Their vocabulary is filled with words such as "ball" and "dog," simple concrete nouns referring to object categories. Yet children often notice and remember thematic relations between objects more readily than an object's category. How is it that children readily learn labels for categories of objects if they are attending to relations between objects instead? To take a concrete example, imagine a mother pointing to a baby and saying, "Baby." Based on the classification studies, we should assume that the child will be attending to the baby sucking on the bottle, or to the baby being diapered. Why, then, doesn't the child infer that "baby" means something like "baby and its bottle" or "baby and its diaper"?

Jean Hutchinson and I (Markman and Hutchinson 1984) have proposed that the solution to this paradox is that children, even extremely young children, expect certain constraints on the possible meanings of words. Regarding Quine's problem of induction, children rule out many possible meanings of a new term, in particular many thematic meanings. That is, they do not consider thematic relations as possible meanings for words despite the fact that they consider them good ways of organizing the objects themselves. Children may well prefer to structure the environment in a way that conflicts with the way that language is organized. But children may have implicit hypotheses about the possible meanings for words that help them acquire words for categories. Even very young children may be aware of the constraints on word meaning so that when they believe that they are learning a new *word*, they shift their attention from thematic to categorical organization.

Although Markman and Hutchinson (1984) refer to this constraint as the "taxonomic constraint," Carey (1988) has correctly noted that in fact two constraints are being hypothesized. One is that children assume that terms refer to taxonomic categories, and the second is that children are biased to interpret novel labels as referring to whole objects, rather than properties, actions, events, and so on. In other words, the taxonomic assumption applies to categories of color, substance, shape, and so on, as well as to objects. Thus, to be more precise, children may be biased to treat novel labels as referring to whole objects (the whole object assumption) and to treat them as referring to objects of the same type (the taxonomic assumption). When children do consider terms as referring to substances, colors, or other properties, the taxonomic assumption should still be met.

Experimental Evidence for the Taxonomic and Whole Object Assumptions
The studies of Markman and Hutchinson tested both the taxonomic assumption and the whole object assumption: children should interpret novel labels as labels for objects of the same type rather than objects that are thematically related.

To test this hypothesis, we conducted a series of studies, each of which compared the way children would organize objects when they were not given an object label with the way they would organize them when they were given a novel label. Study 1 investigated whether hearing a novel word will cause 2- to 3-year-old children to shift their attention from thematic to categorical relations. Basic level categories (such as "dog" and "chair"; see chapter 4) were used with these young children rather than general superordinate level categories (such as "animal" and "furniture").[1] There were two conditions in study 1. In both conditions children were first shown a target picture; they were then shown two other pictures and asked to select one of them as being the same as the target.

In the no word condition children were introduced to a hand puppet and were told to put the picture they chose in the puppet's

1. Rosch et al. (1976) showed that 3-year-old children are capable of using category membership to sort objects at the basic level of categorization, even though they fail to sort objects taxonomically at the superordinate level. In this study children were presented with two objects related at the basic level, along with an unrelated distractor, and were asked to find the two that were alike. Three-year-olds almost always selected the two category members over the unrelated distractor. Because this study failed to include any competing thematic relations, however, it did not establish the relative salience of thematic and categorical relations. In a preliminary study we demonstrated

mouth. On each trial the puppet pointed to the target card and told the child, "Look carefully now. See this?" The two choice pictures were then placed on the table and the child was told to "Find another one that is the same as this."

One of the choice pictures was a member of the same basic level category as the target; for example, the target might be a poodle and the taxonomic choice a German shepherd (both dogs). We attempted to make the two category exemplars fairly dissimilar yet still readily identifiable to these young children. The other choice card was a strong thematic associate to the target, in this case dog food. In all there were ten such triads, which are listed in table 2.1.

The novel word condition was identical to the no word condition, with one exception. Children in this condition were told that the puppet could talk in puppet talk. They were instructed to listen carefully to find the right picture. The puppet gave the target picture an unfamiliar name and used the same name in the instructions for picking a choice picture. For example, the puppet might say, "See this? It is a sud. Find another sud that is the same as this sud."

When children in the no word condition had to select between another category member and a thematically related object, they often chose the thematic relation. They selected other category members a mean of only 59% of the time, which was not different from chance. In contrast, when the target picture was labeled with an unfamiliar word, children were significantly more likely to select categorically. They now chose the other category member a mean of 83% of the time, which is greater than chance. This effect held up over every item. As predicted, when children think they are learning a new word, they look for categorical relationships between objects and suppress the tendency to look for thematic relations. These results supported the hypothesis at least for very young children and basic level categories.

Study 2 tested the hypothesis that hearing a new word will induce older preschoolers to look for taxonomic relations rather than thematic relations at the superordinate level of categorization. Four- and 5-year-old children participated in this study. The procedure used in the no word condition of study 2 was very similar to that used in the

---

that when a competing thematic relation is present (say, a baby and a bottle), 2- and 3-year-olds often select it over the basic level category (say, two babies). When an unrelated distractor was used, children selected the categorical associate 94% of the time, as in Rosch et al.'s (1976) study. When a thematically related distractor was used, however, children selected the categorical associate only 56% of the time. This finding allowed us to address the main question about the role of a word in inducing categorical organization.

Table 2.1
Triads used in study 1 of Markman and Hutchinson 1984

Standard object	Taxonomic choice	Thematic choice
Police car	Car	Policeman
Tennis shoe	High-heeled shoe	Foot
Dog	Dog	Dog food
Straight-backed chair	Easy chair	Man in sitting position
Crib	Crib	Baby
Birthday cake	Chocolate cake	Birthday present
Blue jay	Duck	Nest
Outside door	Swinging door	Key
Male football player	Man	Football
Male child in swimsuit	Female child in overalls	Swimming pool

no word condition of study 1 except that now superordinate level categories were used. Associated with each target picture were two choice pictures, one related in a thematic way to the target (for example, as milk is to cow) and the other a member of the same superordinate category as the target (related, for example, as pig is to cow). An attempt was made to use a variety of thematic relations rather than just one, so as not to limit the generality of the results. A list of the materials used is shown in table 2.2.

On each trial in the no word condition the experimenter, using a hand puppet, said, "I'm going to show you a (new) picture. Then you'll have to find another one that is the same kind of thing." The experimenter then placed the target picture face up on the table directly in front of the the child and said, "See this?" She placed the two choice pictures to the left and right of the target and then said, "Can you find another one that is the same kind of thing as this one? Find another one that is the same kind of thing as this one."

The procedure for the novel word condition of study 2 was identical to the procedure for the no word condition, except that the target picture was now labeled with a novel word. Children were told that the puppet could talk in puppet talk and that they were to listen carefully to what he said. The instructions now included an unfamiliar label for the target: "I'm going to show you a kind of dax. Then you'll have to find another kind of dax. See this? It's a kind of dax. Can you find another kind of dax?"

As is typical for children this age, they did not often make categorical choices when no word was present. When children in the no word condition had to select between another member of the same superordinate category and a thematically related object, they chose

Table 2.2
Triads used in studies 2 and 3 of Markman and Hutchinson 1984

Standard object	Taxonomic choice	Thematic choice
Cow	Pig	Milk
Ring	Necklace	Hand
Door	Window	Key
Crib	Adult bed	Baby
Bee	Ant	Flower
Hanger	Hook	Dress
Cup	Glass	Kettle
Car	Bicycle	Car tire
Sprinkler[a]	Watering can	Grass
Paintbrush[a]	Crayons	Easel
Train[b]	Bus	Tracks
Dog[b]	Cat	Bone

[a]This set was used only in study 2.
[b]This set was used only in study 3.

the categorical relation a mean of only 49% of the time. This was not different from chance. As predicted, the presence of a new word caused children to seek taxonomic relations. When the target picture was labeled with an unfamiliar word, children now chose the other category member a mean of 69% of the time.

In sum, children were more likely to look for another object from the same superordinate level category when an object was labeled with an unfamiliar word than when it was not labeled.

Study 3 was a replication of study 2, except that we changed the wording of the instructions somewhat and the children were slightly younger.

The procedure used in the no word condition of study 3 was very similar to that used in the no word condition of study 2. On each trial the experimenter said, "I'm going to show you something. Then I want you to think carefully, and find another one. See this? Can you find another one?"

The materials and procedure for the novel word condition were identical to those of the no word condition, except that a novel word was used to describe the target picture. Children were told that the puppet could talk in puppet talk and that they were to listen carefully to what he said. The instructions included an unfamiliar label for the target: "I'm going to show you a dax. Then I want you to think carefully, and find another dax. See this dax? Can you say dax? Can you find another dax?"

As usual, when children in the no word condition had to choose between another member of the same superordinate category and a thematically related object, they often chose the thematic relation. They selected the other category member a mean of only 25% of the time. This was less often than would be expected by chance. When the target picture was labeled with an unfamiliar word, children were much more likely than children hearing no label to select categorically. They now chose the other category member a mean of 65% of the time, which was greater than chance.

In sum, when young children are asked to classify things, they often classify them thematically. But hearing a new word induces children to look for categorical relationships instead of thematic relationships.

From these studies we wanted to conclude that children focus on categorical relations because of the sheer presence of the word, and not because of any particular knowledge about the meaning of the word. Thus, we wanted to make sure that the effect could not be due to children translating the novel word into a familiar word. One indirect source of evidence for this comes from children's justifications for their selections. Older children's justifications corroborated their choices. Children who heard a novel word tended to give more justifications that referred to the categorical relations between the objects, whereas children who did not hear a label for the objects referred more to thematic relations. Even when children chose thematically in the novel word condition, they seemed reluctant to justify the thematic choice with a thematic explanation. For example, when children select a dog and a dog bone as being the same, they ordinarily justify this by saying that the dog eats the bone. However, those children who had heard the dog labeled with an unfamiliar term, yet nevertheless selected the dog bone, would now justify their choice by saying that the dog and the bone were both white, for example, or would refuse to explain their selection. There was no such reluctance to justify thematic choices thematically when no label was given. More direct evidence that translation cannot account for the effect is needed, however, and is provided by study 4.

In study 4 pictures of artificial objects were used instead of pictures of real objects. Children were not likely to translate unfamiliar names for these objects into known words, because they did not know real word names for them. If the presence of an unfamiliar word still caused children to shift from thematic to taxonomic responding when the materials were also unfamiliar, then this would rule out translation as an explanation for the effect.

Four- and 5-year-old children participated in study 4. The design and procedure were essentially the same as those of the earlier studies. The main difference was that the experimenter first taught children the taxonomic and thematic relations for the artificial objects before asking them to select the picture that was like the target.

In the no word condition children were shown eight sets of pictures. Each set included a target picture and two choice pictures, one thematically related and one taxonomically related to the target. Before children saw the target picture and the two choices, they were shown two training pictures that illustrated how the target picture related to each of the choice pictures. One picture showed the target object and the taxonomic choice, side by side. For these pairs children were told a common funation that the two objects shared. An example taxonomic training picture is shown in figure 2.1 For this example the experimenter said, "This swims in the water" (pointing to the left-hand object), "This swims in the water" (pointing to the right-hand object).

A second training picture showed the target and the thematic choice in an interactive relationship. The experimenter told the chil-

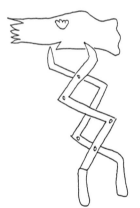

Figure 2.1
A taxonomically related pair of objects from Markman and Hutchinson 1984

 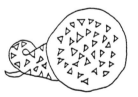

Figure 2.2
A thematically related pair of objects from Markman and Hutchinson 1984

dren how the two objects interacted. The thematic training picture for the set just given is shown in figure 2.2. For this example the experimenter said, "This catches this" (pointing to the objects she was referring to as she said the sentence). Children were asked to repeat the spoken information, to make sure that they were paying attention. The first training picture was left on the table as the second training picture was introduced, so that children could see the connection between the target in the first picture and the target in the second picture.

A second example taxonomic training picture is shown in figure 2.3. For this example the experimenter said, "This pokes holes in things" (pointing to the left-hand object), "This pokes holes in things" (pointing to the right-hand object). The thematic training picture for the same set is shown in figure 2.4. For this picture the spoken information was "You keep this in here."

After children saw the two training pictures in a set, the pictures

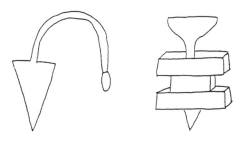

Figure 2.3
A taxonomically related pair of objects from Markman and Hutchinson 1984

Figure 2.4
A thematically related pair of objects from Markman and Hutchinson 1984

were removed from the table. The procedure for the rest of the trial was identical to the earlier procedures. The experimenter said, "I'm going to show you something. Then I want you to think carefully, and find another one." The experimenter then placed the target picture face up on the table directly in front of the child and said, "See this?" She placed the two choice pictures to the left and right of the target and then said, "Can you find another one?" Note that the choices were pictures of the individual objects, as in the previous studies, rather than pictures of two objects together.

The materials and procedure for the novel word condition were identical to those of the no word condition, except that a novel word was used to label the target picture. After children saw the training pictures, the experimenter said, "I'm going to show you a dax. Then I want you to think carefully, and find another dax. See this dax? Can you say dax? Can you find another dax?" A different unfamiliar word was used for each set.

The results for the choices were parallel to those of the previous studies. As usual, when children in the no word condition had to select between another member of the same superordinate category and a thematically related object, they often chose the thematic relation. They selected the other category member a mean of only 37% of the time, which was less then chance. When the target picture was labeled with an unfamiliar word, children were more likely to select categorically. They now chose the other category member a mean of 63% of the time, which was greater than chance. This effect held up over every item.

Thus, children could not have been translating in this study because they did not know what these unfamiliar objects were and had no familiar labels for them. Nevertheless, the results from this study replicated the results from the studies that used familiar objects. Again, the presence of an unfamiliar meaningless word causes children to shift from selecting objects that are thematically related to selecting objects that are taxonomically related. This suggests that children have placed an abstract constraint on what words can mean that is not mediated by the meaning of known terms.

Related Findings
Results from related studies also supported the hypothesis. Markman and Hutchinson (1984) tested 3-year-olds only at the basic level of categorization. Waxman and Gelman (1986) have found that a label will induce 3-year-olds to classify taxonomically at the superordinate level as well, at least for superordinate categories for which the children do have a label. Moreover, they found that a novel label (actu-

ally a Japanese term) helped children organize objects taxonomically in a free classification task, instead of the oddity procedure that we had used. Hutchinson (1984) has also provided evidence for the generality of the effect. She raised the concern that the oddity task forces children to select another object to go with the target. Although children who hear a label select taxonomically under these conditions, they may not be so likely to generalize when they are not forced to. So Hutchinson (1984) used a procedure that was designed to more closely resemble naturalistic conditions. Children were taught a novel word for the target object, as before, but were not forced to select exactly one alternative as going with that object. Children were free to select none, one, or two additional objects, one of which was related taxonomically to the target and one of which was related thematically. Hutchinson (1984) used basic level categories for 3-year-olds and superordinate level categories for 4- and 5-year-olds. With the exception of the 3-year-old boys, Hutchinson replicated the results of Markman and Hutchinson (1984) with this procedure. That is, 3-year-old girls and 4- and 5-year-old children will spontaneously extend a term to label taxonomically related objects, even when they are free not to. Thus, both Hutchinson (1984) and Waxman and Gelman (1986) have replicated the effect using different procedures.

Waxman and Gelman went on to compare different ways of focusing children's attention on categorical relations: providing an English superordinate label, and presenting typical instances with instructions to think about them as a group. Four-year-olds benefited from both of these manipulations. Three-year-olds, however, were helped by the use of labels but not by seeing typical instances. Moreover, 3-year-olds did just as well when Japanese labels were provided for these familiar superordinate categories as when the known English labels were provided.

By 4 or 5 years of age, hearing a label will cause children to look for categorical relations even for superordinate level categories for which children do not have a ready label (Markman and Hutchinson 1984). For example, with no word present, children often selected a car and a car tire as being the same kind of thing. When the car was called "a dax," however, and children were asked to find another dax, they more often selected a bicycle because car and bicycle are both in the same superordinate category, vehicles.

Implications of These Findings
By constraining the meaning of a term to categorical relations, children are able to rule out many other potential meanings for any given term. For example, suppose an adult points to a cup and says, "Cup."

With no constraints on possible meanings, a child would have to consider that the table might also be a "cup" because the cup was on the table, or that coffee is also called "cup" because the cup was filled with coffee, or that mother might be a "cup" because mother was lifting the cup. All of these relational meanings would be eliminated from consideration by the constraint that nouns refer to object categories. By limiting the number and kinds of hypotheses that children need to consider, this constraint simplifies the problem of learning category terms.

These findings raise the question of how children come to constrain their hypotheses about what a word can mean. What leads children to assume that a word is likely to refer to objects that are similar in some way rather than to objects that participate in the same event or context? There are at least two possibilities. One is that sensitivity to the constraint appears in prelinguistic infants—thus, by the time children begin learning language, they would assume that words refer to categories of similar objects. Having such implicit knowledge would provide children with an entry into the formidable problem of learning language. Children would at least be able to readily acquire count nouns, and once they had a reasonable vocabulary of category terms, they could then begin to comprehend other linguistic forms. In fact, a large proportion of children's first words are count nouns (Clark 1983; Nelson 1973; Huttenlocher 1974).

Another possibility is that the constraint is induced from early language experience. Having learned many count nouns, almost all of which refer to objects that are taxonomically related, children may come to expect this to be true of subsequent terms they learn. If so, then this induction must take place fairly rapidly at an early point in language acquisition, since we found that even 2-year-olds believe that count nouns are more likely to refer to objects that belong to the same category than to objects that are thematically related.

There is also the question of the specificity of this constraint. It is not clear whether or not very young children limit the constraint to count nouns as opposed to all words or all stressed terms, for example. Especially if this constraint appears very early, children may at first overextend it, indiscriminately believing that any word they hear must refer to a taxonomic category. Only somewhat later might they become sensitive to form class and expect count nouns to be more likely than other classes of words to refer to categorical relations.

Children's sensitivity to this constraint raises the possibility that language may help children acquire new categories. In contrast, it is often argued that words must map onto concepts that have already been worked out nonlinguistically (Clark 1973; Huttenlocher 1974; Macnamara 1972; Nelson 1974; Wittgenstein 1953, 1958). On this view, language plays little role in concept learning. But this view may underestimate the importance of language. Young children may create concepts to fit new words, guided by abstract constraints on word meaning. This alternative view is a mild form of linguistic determinism (Whorf 1956), in that language is believed to shape thought. It is quite different, however, from Whorf's conception that each language imposes a particular world view on its speakers and that cognition is determined and limited by the specific language one speaks. First, all languages are likely to share similar constraints on possible meanings for count nouns. Thus, the hypothesis is that, regardless of native language, children look for categories of similar objects when they hear new nouns. Second, although nouns help focus children's attention on categorical relations I am not arguing that children would be incapable of forming categories without exposure to language.

The small amount of research that bears on this milder form of linguistic determinism suggests that children can use abstract knowledge of the semantic correlates of form class to help them discover the concept to which a word refers. Brown (1957) found that 3- to 5-year-old children interpreted an unfamiliar count noun ("a dax") as referring to a new concrete object, whereas they interpreted an unfamiliar mass noun ("some dax") as referring to a novel undifferentiated mass. In a study by Katz, Baker, and Macnamara (1974), children as young as 1½ years old interpreted an unfamiliar proper noun ("Dax") as referring to an individual. At the same time these young children understood an unfamiliar count noun ("a dax") as referring to a category of similar objects.

Why is language organized this way? Why don't words refer typically to objects that are thematically related? As noted earlier, thematic relations between objects certainly are important for adults as well as for children. In naturally occurring situations objects are not found organized by category but rather are embedded in spatial, temporal, and causal contexts. Such relational structures as events and themes are a common way of organizing information to make sense of what we encounter (see Mandler 1979; Markman 1981).

Given that these thematic, eventlike organizations are a natural way of construing the world, why should languages force a taxonomic or categorical structure rather than capturing this thematic bias? Why don't we have single words for a boy and his bike, a baby and its bottle, a spider and its web? One reason may lie in the advantages of hierarchical organization and in the fact that if nouns referred exclusively to relations such as a baby and its bottle or a boy and his bike, there would be no easy way to express hierarchical tax-onomic relations. Because a taxonomy groups objects into categories nested within broader categories, it allows us to make deductive in-ferences that go beyond the firsthand knowledge we have about a specific object. If we know, for example, that a particular object is an animal, we can be fairly certain that it takes in food, moves about, reproduces, and has internal organs. In contrast, knowing that some-thing is a "dax," where "dax" could be a boy or his bike, tells us very little else about it.

Another—perhaps the major—reason why nouns refer primarily to taxonomic categories rather than to thematically related objects is that if they did not, the enormous expressive power of language would be lost. The expressive power of language derives from its ability to convey new relations through combinations of words. There are a potentially infinite number of thematic relations that we might want to express. These relations can easily be described through combinations of words (sentences and phrases). If single words were used to express them, however, there would be an ex-traordinary proliferation of words, probably more than humans could learn. We could need separate words for a baby and its bottle, a baby and its crib, a baby and its mother, a baby and its diaper, and so on. Thus, the combinatorial power of language would be wasted.

In sum, the taxonomic and whole object assumptions go a long way in enabling children to figure out what object labels refer to. They rule out the large set of hypotheses that would have to be eval-uated if children considered the terms as possibly referring to the-matic relations as well. Nevertheless, given the many ways in which objects can be categorized, children are still faced with a formidable task. In other words, we need to consider the problem of conceptual diversity: what are the possible ways to categorize objects and which of these ways are children most prone to consider? The next few chapters address these issues.

Chapter 3
The Internal Structure of Categories

I begin this chapter on the internal structure of categories by contrasting the classical view of categories with the family resemblance view. In doing so, I summarize some of the advantages of the classical view that must be sacrificed whenever categories conform to a family resemblance structure. I also review evidence bearing on whether or not adult categories are organized according to family resemblances. To the extent that the family resemblance view is correct, it has implications for how children represent categories and for how they learn them. It predicts that central exemplars will be learned before peripheral ones and that central exemplars provide children with a better source of information from which to learn a given category. The family resemblance view also raises questions about the strategies children use to learn categories. Given the disadvantages of a family resemblance view of concepts, we need to consider why human concepts would have such an organization. I conclude the chapter by considering three different kinds of explanations for the existence of family resemblances.

The Classical View of Categories

Until recently most theories of conceptual organization have assumed the classical view of concepts that was discussed in chapter 1 (see also Smith and Medin 1981). The main assumptions of this view are that for any given category, one can specify criteria that define the category, and that all objects that are members of the category satisfy the criteria. For example, "bachelor" is defined as "unmarried man"—that is, "unmarried" and "man" are necessary and sufficient features for being a bachelor. The definition of the category or the criteria for membership are referred to as the "intension" of the category, whereas the objects that are members of the category are referred to as the "extension" of the category. According to the classical view, there is a straightforward reciprocal relation between the intension and the extension. That is, all objects that have the necessary and sufficient criteria are members of the category, and all members of the category must have the necessary and sufficient features. For example, anyone who is unmarried and a man is a bachelor and every bachelor is unmarried and a man.

Advantages of the Classical View

There are many advantages to this simple, powerful theory of categorization.

Intuitive Appeal.   Intuitively the classical view is very appealing. It captures what most of us would assume about the way our categories are structured. On first thought, anyway, if someone asks us to define "mother," or "square," or "vehicle," we react as though this is a fairly simple task. After all, we know what the words mean and assume, therefore, that we can come up with a kind of classical definition. We take it for granted that our definition for the category will cover all objects we know to be members of the category. So "mother" is a female parent, "square" is an equilateral quadrangle with 90° angles, and so on.

Simplicity and Elegance.   The classical view is also simple and elegant. It presents a kind of ideal that definitions should strive for. It would be rather disturbing if the criteria that defined a given category did not apply to all of the members of the category. Under these circumstances, what would it mean to be a member of the category? Having necessary and sufficient features for membership offers a simple and sure way of deciding whether something is a member of a category.

Combining Concepts.   Most of the time we use concepts in combination with other concepts—as for example when we combine words into phrases and sentences. Therefore, a theory of concepts should be able to explain how concepts are combined. On the classical view, new complex concepts can be defined by combining the necessary and sufficient criteria from each of the simpler concepts. "Pet fish," for example, would be defined as something that is both a pet and a fish and therefore would fulfill the criteria necessary for both (something like "domesticated animal kept for pleasure" and "cold-blooded, water-breathing vertebrate"). Of course, even on the classical view, many concepts do not combine in this straightforward way. "Big," for example, may mean something different when applied to "mouse" and "elephant." "Good" means something different when combined with "person" and "knife." "Red" means something different when applied to "fire engine" and "hair." (This issue is discussed from a different perspective in chapter 6.) Nonetheless, in general the classical view provides a simple way of figuring out how concepts combine to form new concepts. On the family resemblance view, there are no necessary and sufficient features that define categories; hence, there is no simple way to state how features should combine when categories are combined (Armstrong, Gleitman, and Gleitman 1983; Osherson and Smith 1981). For example, consider one possible implication of a family resemblance structure: that members of a category differ in the extent to which they exemplify the category, with some exemplars being prototypical or best exemplars of the category. For the category "pet," dogs and cats are good exemplars, whereas tarantulas and snakes are less good. For the category "fish," trout and salmon might be good exemplars. However, a good example of a "pet fish" (for instance, a guppy) is neither a good example of a pet nor a good example of a fish. Thus, the typicality of the single categories does not predict the typicality of the combined category. Although categories defined by family resemblances do not combine in as simple a way as finding the conjunction of necessary and sufficient features, as would be expected for classically defined categories, there are more complex ways of combining prototypes that do well at predicting the typicality of the composite concept. Smith and Osherson (1984) and Smith et al. (in press) describe a model that determines how to weight features that define each concept in a composite and then combines the weighted features to predict the typicality of the composite concept.

Developmental Implications.   The classical view provides a reasonable developmental theory of how categories are acquired (see Carey 1982 for an interesting discussion of this and other consequences of the classical view). If category terms are composed of necessary and sufficient features, then the child must learn what features define the category. In fact, many developmental theories of the acquisition of categories and of word meanings implicitly assume the classical view (Bruner, Olver, Greenfield, et al. 1966; Inhelder and Piaget 1964; Vygotsky 1962; Clark 1973).

Support for Certain Logical Distinctions.   Certain arguments in philosophy and logic depend on the classical view. Notions of analytic truth assume that we can deduce with logical certainty something that follows from the definition of a term. For example, if we know that John is a bachelor, then we can conclude that John is a man. We do not have to check this empirically; we know that John must be a man because, by definition, bachelors are men.

Thus, we do not want to abandon the classical view of concepts lightly. Intuitively it seems right, it is simple and elegant, it provides a clear way of combining simple concepts into more complex ones, it allows for a straightforward way of learning categories, and it forms the basis for certain kinds of logic. Nevertheless, it is now widely believed that the classical view may fail to characterize many of our categories.

Family Resemblances

In opposition to the classical view, Wittgenstein (Pitcher 1966) argued that many of our natural categories are organized by family resemblances. To make his point, Wittgenstein challenged us to discover necessary and sufficient features for the common category "games."

> Consider for example the proceedings that we call 'games.' I mean board-games, card-games, ball-games, Olympic games, and so on. What is common to them all?—Don't say: 'There *must* be something common, or they would not be called "games"—but *look and see* whether there is anything common to all.—For if you look at them you will not see something that is common to *all*, but similarities, relationships, and a whole series of them at that. To repeat: don't think, but look!—Look for example at board-games, with their multifarious relationships. Now pass to card-games; here you find many correspondences with the first group, but many common features drop out, and others appear. When we pass next to ball-games, much that is common is retained, but much is lost—Are they all 'amusing'? Compare chess with noughts and crosses. Or is there always wining and losing, or competition between players? Think of patience. In ball-games there is winning and losing; but when a child throws his ball at the wall and catches it again, this feature has disappeared. Look at the parts played by skill and luck; and at the difference between skill in chess and skill in tennis. Think now of games like ring-a-ring-a-roses; here is the element of amusement, but how many other characteristic features have disappeared! And we can go through the many, many other groups of games in the same way; can see how similarities crop up and disappear.
>
> And the result of this examination is: we see a complicated network of similarities overlapping and crisscrossing: sometimes overall similarities, sometimes similarities of detail.
>
> I can think of no better expression to characterize these similarities than 'family resemblances'; for the various resemblances

between the members of a family: build, features, color of eyes, gait, temperament, etc. etc. overlap and criss-cross in the same way. (pp. 188–189)

"Games" is not an isolated example. Many other categories seem to defy any simple definition. Inspired by the work of Rosch and her colleagues, there are now many psychological studies supporting the view that categories are organized around family resemblances among the members rather than around necessary and sufficient features (Rosch and Mervis 1975; Smith and Medin 1981; Mervis and Rosch 1981). This view states that categories are structured in a way similar to the resemblances that family members have to each other. Resemblances between members of the same family can be striking, with each member resembling every other member, yet there may be no single feature or set of features that every member of the family possesses. There are a number of different dimensions along which family members can resemble each other, including bone structure, coloring, mannerisms, and facial features. These features crisscross and overlap in different combinations rather than any one or two of them being defining. On analogy with the family, then, the family resemblance view states that there is pool of features that define a given category, none of which is necessary or sufficient. To be a member of the category, an object must have enough of the features. There are various ways of defining "enough" (Smith and Medin 1981)—for example, setting a lower bound on the number of features needed, or weighting the features according to how well they predict category membership and then summing the weights.

Given the disadvantages of a family resemblance structure compared to classically defined categories, we need to consider why categories should be defined by family resemblances. I will return to this issue after presenting some of the evidence about whether family resemblances can serve as a model of how natural categories are structured.

Evidence That Concepts Have a Family Resemblance Structure
I will briefly summarize the kinds of evidence that support a family resemblance view (for more complete discussion, see Smith and Medin 1981 and Mervis and Rosch 1981). One procedure that has been used to determine how a category is defined is to ask subjects to report features of category members and then observe the type of feature structure that occurs within the category. In this procedure, subjects are given various category members, one at a time, and asked to list as many properties of each object as they can. For ex-

ample, for the category "vehicle," subjects are asked to list as many properties as they can for "car," "bus," "truck," "boat," "train," "airplane," "sled," and so on. The resulting lists of properties are then examined to see whether any of the properties listed across category members are necessary and sufficient. That is, are any properties listed for every instance of the category, and do any properties, alone, guarantee membership? The answer is that necessary and sufficient properties do not often emerge from these lists of properties of the instances. A family resemblance structure is much more likely to characterize the category than a classical definition.

One potential problem with this source of evidence, however, is that there may be implicit demands associated with this task that prevent subjects from listing the necessary and sufficient features that they may, nevertheless, know. Subjects certainly do not list everything that they know about the objects they are asked to respond to. For example, subjects are much less likely to list "has feathers" for "robin" than they are for "bird." Tversky and Hemenway (1984) argue, following Grice's (1975) cooperative principles of communication, that subjects attempt to list features that would be informative given the implicit contrast sets that they are using. When subjects are asked to list features for "robin" and "sparrow," then, they would not list the property "has feathers" because it fails to distinguish between these two kinds of birds. Murphy and Medin (1985) argue that attribute listings are constrained by lay theories that the categories are involved in. They point out that most people will acknowledge that "flammable" applies to wood, money, and certain plastics, yet it would most likely appear only on subjects' listings for wood. Thus, subjects' attribute listings are not a completely reliable source of information about how categories are defined.

Another procedure that has been interpreted as revealing category structure is to show subjects an instance of a category and ask them to judge how typical or how "good" an instance it is (Rips, Shoben, and Smith 1973; Rosch 1973; Tversky 1977). The rationale is that if the category is defined by a family resemblance structure, then some instances will have more of the features (or more of the important features) than others. Moreover, some of these will also have fewer features that define other categories. Thus, these "good instances" will be highly representative of their own category, yet quite dissimilar from other categories. In contrast, some instances of the category may have just enough features to qualify and may also have features that define other categories as well. This would predict a range in terms of how representative various instances are of a given category, from prototypical instances that exemplify the category to peripheral instances that can just barely be included. To take one example, a robin is a prototypical bird. It flies, and it has the right size and overall shape for a bird. An ostrich, on the other hand, is not a very good bird. Its size and shape are not right and it does not fly. A bat is at the boundary: it is not a bird, yet it has many of the bird features. If categories were defined by necessary and sufficient features, then all exemplars of the category would have the required features, and we would not expect this variation in typicality of exemplars. The results of many studies indicate that people can readily judge the "goodness" of an exemplar. That is, people find the question of how good an instance is to be reasonable and sensible, and, moreover, there is reasonable agreement among people as concerning the ordering of exemplars. Moreover, the typicality rating for an exemplar can be predicted by its family resemblance score, that is, by how many of the relevant features it has. Many psychological implications of this structure have been demonstrated, such as that people are faster at judging that a typical instance is a category member than that an atypical instance is.

Problems with the Family Resemblance View
Armstrong, Gleitman, and Gleitman (1983) have raised some questions about the interpretation of these findings. We have been assuming that if the classical view held, then there would be no reason for categories to exhibit internal structure; that is, all members of a given category should be equally good instances because all will have fulfilled the same necessary and sufficient criteria. However, Armstrong, Gleitman, and Gleitman have demonstrated that even classically defined concepts can have an internal structure. To do this, they asked subjects about categories that do in fact have clear defining criteria—for example, "odd number." (All odd numbers are integers that cannot be divided by 2, and every integer that cannot be divided by 2 is an odd number.) They asked subjects to judge how good an instance of the category "odd number" various numbers were. They discovered that, as with the categories Rosch and others have used, subjects found it sensible to make these judgments and that they in fact agreed about their ratings. People feel that 7 is a good example of an odd number, whereas 23, for example, is less good. Moreover, as with the object categories, people are faster to judge that a typical exemplar is a member of a category than that an atypical exemplar is. For example, they more quickly say that 7 is an odd number than that 23 is. Thus, people's agreement concerning the "goodness" of exemplars is not enough evidence to rule out a classical view in favor of the family resemblance view. The existence of a

graded structure cannot be taken to indicate a lack of defining criteria or the presence of a family resemblance rather than a classically defined category. Even classically defined concepts have graded membership.

Another potential problem in interpreting these results comes from work by Barsalou and Sewell (1984). As in previous studies, subjects were asked to rate how typical or good various examples of a category were. In this case, however, they were to make these judgments from several different perspectives, for example, from the point of view of a businessman, housewife, or redneck. Barsalou and Sewell found that the typicality ratings varied with the perspective. For example, for the category "hobbies," fishing was thought to be a highly typical exemplar from the perspective of a redneck but not from the perspective of a housewife. Barsalou (1987) concludes from these and other findings that there is no stable graded structure of categories. Another way to view these findings, however, may be to claim that subjects are actually rating different categories, rather than the same category from different perspectives. They may have considered, for example, a category such as "hobbies a redneck would enjoy" versus a category such as "hobbies a housewife would enjoy." These more specific categories would differ in their internal structure both from each other and from the more inclusive category "hobbies." Thus, Barsalou's (1987) work might be better interpreted as demonstrating people's ability to construct and evaluate the exemplars of more specific categories, rather than as demonstrating the instability of graded structure. The graded structure of the more specific categories may well be very stable.

Another concern is that once the correct features that define a given category are known, then, on the family resemblance view, there must be some way of summing the features a given object possesses to determine whether it is a member of the category in question. As mentioned earlier, there are a number of different ways of defining this criterial number of features. According to Medin (1983), what all these definitions have in common is that this summing of the evidence accepts members and excludes nonmembers of a category. This translates into a formal criterion that the categories be "linearly separable." Linearly separable categories can be distinguished by a weighted, additive combination of their features. Medin and his colleagues (Medin 1983; Murphy and Medin 1985) argue that if linear separability is a general feature of human categories, then people should be sensitive to whether or not categories are linearly separable and find the linearly separable ones easier to learn. Medin and Schwanenflugel (1981) tested this hypothesis by studying how easily subjects could learn artificial categories that were either linearly separable or not. They could find no benefit in linear separability.

The work of Armstrong, Gleitman, and Gleitman (1983), Barsalou and Sewell (1984), and Medin (1983) forces us to be more cautious about deciding that categories are organized into family resemblance structures. We cannot assume that the fact that a category has a graded structure clearly rules out a classical definition for that category. Thus, additional criteria must be invoked to argue against the classical view. Subjects' persistent failure to come up with defining features for certain categories has been used as one such criterion. Again, some of the experimental evidence for this failure must be interpreted cautiously, since the attribute-listing tasks may have many implicit demands that prevent subjects from listing what would be necessary and sufficient features. On the other hand, the difficulty of providing classical definitions for many natural categories extends to philosophers, psychologists, linguists, and lexicographers as well.

Implications of Family Resemblances for Development
Under the assumption that categories are organized by family resemblance structure, what are the implications for how children might learn them? Mervis and Pani (1980) suggest that instances that better exemplify the category should be easier to learn than more peripheral instances. They further suggest that the category itself may be acquired more effectively if it is first taught with prototypical instances rather than peripheral ones. For example, we might expect children to learn the category "bird" more effectively if they are first shown a robin, a sparrow, and a blue jay than if they are shown a penguin, an ostrich, and an egret. Mervis and Pani (1980) argue that the good examples should provide the most accurate basis for generalization to new instances because they are maximally similar to members of their own category and minimally similar to members of other categories. There is evidence that children tend to learn typical instances of a category before atypical ones (Anglin 1977), but this could be largely because parents tend to teach the typical ones first. To test whether children learn a category better when presented with good instances rather than peripheral instances, Mervis and Pani (1980) taught children labels for new object categories. There were two different training conditions. Some children were taught the categories based on exposure to good exemplars, and others were taught the categories based on exposure to poor exemplars. Following training, they were presented with objects they had not seen before, some of which were members of the category and others of which were mem-

bers of other categories. As predicted, children who had been exposed to the good exemplars were better able to learn the category than those who had been exposed to the poor exemplars.

In a second study Mervis and Pani (1980) hypothesized that even when exposed to a range of exemplars, children will tend to learn the good exemplars of a category more readily than the poor exemplars. In this study they also compared how well children learned the category when exposed to the full range of exemplars and how well they learned it when exposed to just the good exemplars. In fact, children were better able to learn the new categories when they were exposed only to the good exemplars than when they were exposed to all of the exemplars. And when they were taught the category by being exposed to all of the exemplars, children learned the good exemplars more readily than the poor ones, as predicted. In sum, the good exemplars of a category, because they are representative of the category and dissimilar to other categories, are more readily learned and appear to provide a better basis for generalization to other category members compared to peripheral instances. However, it is possible that with more extensive training, learning based on the peripheral instances would improve and would ultimately provide a better basis for generalization to other nonprototypical instances than would training on prototypical instances alone (Homa and Vosburgh 1976).

Another implication of family resemblance structure for how children acquire categories comes from the kinds of strategies one might use to learn a category (Kemler-Nelson 1984; Kossan 1981). Before examining the evidence for this with children, I will first consider an analysis by Brooks (1978) on how adult strategies for acquiring concepts vary with the nature of the concept to be learned. Brooks argues that some of our knowledge is likely to be exemplar based rather than based on more abstract defining rules. That is, we may have learned a list of exemplars of a given category rather than a more abstract set of criteria. On this model, to decide whether a new object is a member of the category, we would compare it to the exemplars. If it is similar enough to one or more of the exemplars then we would count it as a member of the category (see Smith and Medin 1981 for a detailed discussion of exemplar-based models). To demonstrate the feasibility of this model, Brooks taught adults new categories for which the defining rules were deliberately designed to be exceptionally difficult to learn; in other words, they were designed so that the information-processing abilities of adults would be strained in trying to acquire them. These ill-defined categories were letter strings that were generated by a grammar that would be very hard to discover in the time allotted. Subjects were exposed to these letter strings in one of two ways. Subjects in the first group were told that each letter string came from one of two categories and that they were to learn the correct category for each one. On each trial they were shown a letter string, asked which category it was from, and told whether they were correct or not. Subjects in the second group were not told that there were two categories of objects and were not given any training or feedback about which category any given letter string belonged to. Instead, they were instructed to learn an arbitrary paired associate to each letter string. As each string was presented, they were told a name that they were to learn for it. The name had no relation to the string, nor was it related to the category. After this training, the two groups of subjects were tested on their ability to divide new letter strings into the two categories. The subjects who had been trained to categorize the letter strings trial after trial were unable to do this. This result is not surprising. The categorization rule was expected to be very difficult for the subjects to figure out, and it was. Subjects were unable to discover the basis of categorization and, as a consequence, they did not know how to classify the new strings. When the subjects who had learned the paired associates to the items were told they now had to classify the letter strings into two categories, they protested that they had no idea how to do so. Nevertheless, and this is the surprising result, they were better able to categorize the new letter strings than the subjects who had known all along that this was what they would have to do.

Brooks interprets these results as supporting an exemplar-based model of categorization. The subjects who had tried to figure out the rule presumably would formulate a hypothesis on each trial, check it against the instance, and then try to revise the hypothesis. They would not attend to or remember very much about the specific instances because they were concentrating on figuring out the rule. As a consequence, when they failed to figure out the rule, they had, in addition, lost specific information about the instances. The other subjects were forced to learn a name for each instance and therefore recalled the specific instances quite well. Although they did not have a rule to classify by, they could use what Brooks referred to as "analogical reasoning." Each new instance might remind them of one or more of the other instances and therefore would be classified along with it.

Brooks considers when this kind of analogical reasoning might be more efficient than trying to figure out the defining rule. Basically, he suggests that if the rule is too difficult to be figured out in the time allotted, then the learner may actually be better off attending to specific instances and not attending to the rule. The learner would then have learned the specific exemplars and could reason about the category by comparing new instances to the familiar ones.

Brooks's findings with adults may be applicable to young children trying to learn a category defined by a family resemblance structure. Because there is no simply stated classical definition for categories defined by family resemblances, it is likely that young children will find it difficult to figure out the defining rule for such categories. If so, then, like Brooks's adults, these children may actually be better able to learn the category when they try to memorize instances than when they deliberately try to learn the category. Older children, however, may not find the family resemblance rule so difficult and may learn the category better when they are in fact trying to learn it.

This developmental hypothesis was tested by Kossan (1981). She taught second and fifth graders one of two kinds of categories of novel animals. Table 3.1 presents the structure of the categories used. The novel animals were characterized by five dimensions: they could be dotted, striped, or plain; they could have two, three, or six legs; short, medium, or long legs; a short, medium, or long neck; and a straight tail, a curly tail, or no tail at all. One kind of category was defined by a simple rule that provided necessary and sufficient criteria for membership. For example a novel creature would be a member of the category if it had a long neck and a straight tail. It was expected that children of both ages would find this to be a fairly simple rule to figure out and therefore, that children would be better able to learn the new category when they were instructed to do so and would find learning paired associates for the instances to be disruptive to learning.

The other kind of category was defined in terms of a family resemblance structure. No single feature was necessary, although some were sufficient. For example, some but not all members of the category could be identified because they had dots, others by their straight tail. This kind of rule was expected to be difficult for the younger children to discover. Thus, Kossan predicted that the second graders would learn the category better when they were in the paired associate condition than when they were in the concept acquisition condition. The fifth graders, however, should have less trouble learning the rule and should thus be better able to learn the category in the concept acquisition condition.

The two training conditions for this experiment were modeled after the ones used by Brooks (1978). Children in the concept acquisition condition were told that there were two kinds of animals, "zonks" and "nonzonks," and that their job was to learn which was which. On each trial the children were shown an animal picture, asked

Table 3.1
Feature structure of categories in experiment 1 from Kossan 1981

Dimensions	Rule-defined concept		Sufficient feature concept	
	Category A	Category B	Category A	Category B
Body design	Dots/strips	Dots/strips	Dots/plain	Stripes/plain
Number of legs	Six legs/two legs	Six legs/two legs	Six legs/three legs	Two legs/three legs
Length of legs	Short legs/long legs	Short legs/long legs	Long legs/medium legs	Short legs/medium legs
Length of neck	Long neck	Long neck or straight tail but not both	Short neck/medium neck	Long neck/medium neck
Type of tail	Straight tail		Straight tail/no tail	Curly tail/no tail

Note: Each exemplar of the sufficient feature concepts contained three or four of the sufficient features for its own category.

which kind of animal it was, and told whether they were right or wrong. Children in the paired associate condition were told that they had to learn a masculine first name—for instance, "Tom"—for each animal. On each trial they were shown an animal picture, asked to say its name, and told what the correct answer was.

Immediately before they were tested on how well they had learned the categories, children in both conditions were shown each training exemplar one more time and told whether it was a zonk or a non-zonk. Thus, children in the paired associate condition participated in only one trial in which information about the category membership of the exemplars was provided. After this final presentation of the training exemplars, children were shown the training exemplars plus additional transfer items and asked to judge whether or not each was a zonk.

The results of this experiment were just as predicted. For the simple, classically defined category, children of both ages were better able to learn the category when they were instructed to do so. The rule that defined the category was simple enough for them to discover, so it was to their advantage to try to figure out the rule rather than just memorize instances. For the categories defined by a family resemblance rule, the results were different. The older children were able to learn this kind of category under both kinds of instructional conditions. The second graders, however, were better able to learn the category when they memorized names for the animals than when they learned the category. That is, children who on each trial had to decide whether the animal was, say, "Tom" or "Robert" were later better able to decide whether an animal was a zonk than those children who trial after trial learned which animals were zonks. Extending Brooks's argument here, apparently the ill-defined category was difficult for children to figure out. By memorizing the specific instances, children would at least be able to reason analogically; that is, they could base their category judgments on how much a new exemplar reminded them of an old one. In fact, Kossan (1981) reports that the children who were in the paired associate condition often mentioned that they decided about a new exemplar based on its similarity to the old ones. One second grader said, "I thought about the old ones, you know, that looked like Tom."

Kossan conducted a second experiment to obtain more evidence about whether children in a paired associate training condition later use an exemplar-based strategy to categorize objects. In this experiment only one kind of category was taught under the two different training conditions. It was an ill-defined category designed to be more difficult than the first. In this case no features were necessary or sufficient. Thus, it was expected that even fifth graders would be better able to learn the category in the paired associate condition. One other important change was made. Some of the features of given exemplars were distinctive features. That is, they characterized that particular training animal and no other. Other features were common features that applied to some but not all of the animals. These distinctive features allowed Kossan to test whether children were using an exemplar-based strategy or not. During the test phase children were shown objects that would be classified in one way based on their common features but in another way based on their distinctive features. If children were trying to extract general rules, they should have judged new exemplars based only on the common features and not on the distinctive features that applied to only one animal. If, however, children were using an exemplar-based system, then, if a new animal had the same distinctive feature as an old exemplar they should have used that as a basis of classification.

The results were that children of both ages were better able to learn the categories in the paired associate condition. Even the fifth graders, who for trial after trial had judged whether or not an animal was a zonk, were not very successful at later classifying objects into zonks and nonzonks. Children who had learned names for each animal, without any extended practice at categorizing the animals, were nevertheless better able to classify in the end. Based on the pattern of responses to distinctive and common features, Kossan was not able to determine that the second graders were using an exemplar-based strategy. The second graders who learned the paired associates correctly classified more objects based on both common features and distinctive features than children in the concept acquisition condition. The results were more clear-cut for the fifth graders. For those instances in which were was a conflict, children in the concept acquisition condition almost always classified on the basis of the common features, whereas children in the paired associate condition usually classified on the basis of the distinctive feature.

Kossan's (1981) and Brooks's (1978) studies demonstrate that the most effective strategy for learning a new concept varies with both the kind of concept to be learned and the cognitive abilities of the learner. Sometimes, of course, a deliberate attempt to formulate hypotheses about the concept will be the best strategy. However, in other cases, when a child's information-processing abilities are strained, it may actually be to the child's disadvantage to deliberately set out to formulate the rule that defines the category. For young children trying to learn categories defined by family resemblances, an exemplar-based strategy may be most effective.

Although it is not completely clear how to generalize these findings to a naturalistic setting, children probably begin learning some category terms using an exemplar-based strategy. First, children are often taught categories one exemplar at a time, as when a parent sees a single new object and labels it for the child. For example, seeing a dog pass by, the parent says, "Dog." The child must begin forming the category on the basis of only one exemplar. Although with just one instance, children could begin hypothesizing about what features define the new category, they might be more likely to remember just that the particular object was called "dog." In fact, children may have a great deal of experience with one particular dog before encountering even one other instance. Intensive exposure to a limited number of instances should promote an exemplar-based strategy for acquiring concepts (Brooks 1978). Once a greater number of instances has been encountered, if the concept is simple enough, the children might abstract out the defining features. But if the concept is ill defined, children may continue to represent it as a list of exemplars. Thus, it is reasonable to expect that young children might begin to learn family resemblance categories using an exemplar-based strategy.

Family Resemblance Structures and Complexive Groupings
The family resemblance structure of natural categories is in some ways similar to the principles of organization young children use to group objects in classification tasks. Based on this similarity, one might be tempted to conclude that children would find it easier to learn a category defined by family resemblances than a classically defined category, because the family resemblance structure is consistent with their own principles of organization. Although there are some important ways in which the parallel between family resemblance structures and complexive sorting is revealing, there are some ways in which it is misleading. Before discussing what we can legitimately conclude from this similarity, I briefly review some of the findings from studies of classification.

The classification task is commonly used to determine the principles of organization children apply to form categories. Children are presented with an array of assorted objects and asked to put together the ones that are alike. At first children may form thematic groupings in which they place objects together to tell a kind of story or represent an event rather than because they are similar. But Inhelder and Piaget (1964), Bruner, Olver, Greenfield, et al. (1966), and Vygotsky (1962) have all reported that even once children get the idea that they should look for commonalities among the objects, they still fail to

categorize as an adult might. Vygotsky and Bruner call these immature kinds of classification "complexive" sorting.

To take a concrete example of a commonly used classification problem: The subject is presented with an array of geometric forms that
vary in shape (circles, squares, triangles, and trapezoids), color
(green, blue, red, and yellow), and size (small, medium, and large).
The forms are mixed together on a table and laid out in a haphazard
order. The subject is then told to put together the ones that are alike.
Adults typically sort in a way that is consistent with a classically defined concept. They might sort on the basis of shape, for example,
making one category for each shape. According to Inhelder and Piaget (1964), it is as though the adults were quite explicitly defining
the category, using necessary and sufficient criteria, and then being
sure to include all and only those objects that meet the criteria.
Adults might not sort on the basis of shape—they might select color
or size instead—but for whichever dimension they were to select,
they would define the concept in accord with a classical definition.

Children under the age of about 7 classify in a different way. A
number of different kinds of complexive groupings have been described (Bruner, Olver, Greenfield, et al. 1966; Vygotsky 1962), but all
of them differ from classically defined concepts. In each case objects
are put in the same group not because they fulfill the necessary and
sufficient defining features but because they are similar to some other
members of the category in one way or another. Some objects may
share the same shape, others the same color, and others the same
size. One rather advanced kind of complexive sorting is known as
"key-ringing" (Bruner, Olver, Greenfield, et al. 1966). In this case the
child selects a focal object and includes other objects in the grouping
if they are similar in some way to the initial object. In our concrete
example a child might first select a big red triangle, then a big green
circle (because it is big), a small blue triangle (because it is a triangle),
a small red trapezoid (because it is red), and so on. Thus, in these
kinds of complexive groupings objects are alike in some way or other,
but there are no necessary and sufficient features to define the class.
These groupings, then, are defined by family resemblances.

What can we conclude from this similarity between the family resemblance structure of natural categories and the family resemblance
structure of the classifications children construct? Do children prefer
family resemblance structures and therefore find them easier to
learn? On the contrary, although little research has been done on this
particular question, we can be fairly confident both on logical and on
empirical grounds that—if the number of dimensions or criteria were
held constant—children as well as adults would find classically de-

fined concepts easier to learn than concepts defined by family resemblance structure. First, it seems logical that children should find classical concepts simpler, as they did in Kossan's first experiment. Classical concepts have a simple, straightforward, elegant definition, and once the criteria for a category are known, it is simple to identify new members. Why should it help children to take the same criteria but make the definition more complex, more probabilistic, and less certain? It is unlikely that a child would be aided in learning a category such as "furniture" because the rule takes the form that some but not all pieces of furniture have legs, some but not all have seats, some but not all are made of wood, and so forth. It would certainly be much easier if all pieces of furniture were made of wood and had legs and seats.

There are some empirical findings that suggest that classically defined concepts are easier for children to learn. Many studies have compared children's ability to learn artificial concepts that are defined by a simple conjunctive rule with their ability to learn such concepts that are defined by a disjunctive rule (Bourne 1966). A conjunctive rule states the necessary and sufficient criteria for being an example of the concept; for example, "big circle" is defined as being big and a circle. A disjunctive rule states that one or another of the properties is sufficient for an object to count as an exemplar; for example, "big or circle" defines a concept that includes a big triangle because it is big and a small circle because it is a circle. This disjunctive concept is an example of a family resemblance structure, albeit a meager one. Numerous studies have demonstrated that children find the classical conjunctive concepts far easier to learn than such disjunctive versions of a family resemblance concept. In general, I would expect that a category with a family resemblance structure that approximates a classical structure will be easier to learn than one that greatly departs from the classical view.

If family resemblance structures are not easier to learn, then why are children so likely to sort according to a family resemblance rule rather than a classically defined rule? One answer concerns the task demands. Children are not asked to *learn* categories in a sorting task; they are forced to *create* their own categories. Someone presents them with a complex, confusing array of 16 or so objects, and they must make sense of it. Although it is easier to learn a simple, elegant rule, it is very difficult to come up, unassisted, with a simple rule that will describe all the objects belonging to one category and differentiate them from objects belonging to another category.

It may be too much to expect children to be able to cope with this complexity and devise a streamlined, classically structured system.

Children might begin, not by carefully and systematically scanning the whole array, but by grabbing a couple of interesting objects and placing them together. Thus, children will begin sorting without having a clear plan for how to optimize the grouping for all objects. Once young children have formed some groups of objects, they are unlikely to keep revising the grouping until they find a perfect solution. Rather, in playing this game, children stick with what they have and make the best of it.

Despite their poor performance on classification tasks, children could well prefer simple, elegant classification systems. I do not know of a formal study on this point, but informally I have asked children to judge which kind of classification scheme they think is better, and I have found that they prefer the simple, classical type of organization. In one case in particular, a little boy proceeded to make a complexive mess of a deck of 16 cards. After he had finished, I told him that I was going to sort the cards a different way, and I began to sort them by suit. He became very interested, exclaimed that my idea was much better than his, and asked if he could finish sorting for me. He then proceeded to sort perfectly by suit. Not only do children probably prefer this kind of organization, they should find it simpler to learn and deal with as well. It is important to emphasize the difference between what it is easy to create on one's own with limited foresight and resources, and what it is easy to learn and work with. As I discovered with my own filing system, simple and elegant systems cam be extremely difficult to create.

The argument just put forward about why classical definitions might be preferred to family resemblance sorting depends on several important assumptions being met. First, it assumes that the kind and number of criteria being compared in a classical and a family resemblance structure would be equated. Second, it depends on the availability of a simple, elegant solution that can somehow be conveyed to children. Third, it depends on children or adults searching for rules to define categories. When these assumptions are not met, then in fact family resemblance structures might well be preferred to classical definitions—not only by children but also by adults. That is, if one compares a rich family resemblance structure with many characteristic features to a classical definition involving only a single dimension, then the family resemblance structure might be easier to notice and learn. If the category to be learned defies any simple classical definition that could pick out the relevant exemplar and also exclude nonexemplars, then family resemblances might work better. Finally, finding a classical definition might often require an analytic hypothesis-testing strategy that is not characteristic of people's ordinary approach to classification. Children in particular are much more likely to attend to objects per se and not features and combinations of features in first acquiring categories. Under these kinds of circumstances, family resemblance structures may be preferred to classical definitions. A series of studies by Medin, Wattenmaker, and Hampson, in which adults were asked to sort objects into two categories, helps address this issue (Medin, Wattenmaker, and Hampson 1987). The categories were constructed in such a way that subjects could elect to sort the objects by family resemblances or by a classical definition. In this study, however, the number of dimensions that were useful in deciding how to categorize the objects was deliberately not equated in the two ways of sorting. The materials were designed in such a way that the family resemblance sorts would result in better classification schemes in the following sense: partitioning the objects into categories on the basis of family resemblances would result in more within-category matches and fewer between-category matches than would partitioning the objects on the basis of a classical definition. To accomplish this, the family resemblances were defined over a number of different dimensions, whereas the classical sorts were defined by a single dimension. Because the number of dimensions was not equated, this task was an example of a situation in which a family resemblance structure could be preferred to a classical definition.

Even in this situation, however, there was no evidence that adults preferred sorting on the basis of family resemblances. To the contrary, despite many attempts to modify the materials and task demands, Medin, Wattenmaker, and Hampson found almost no sorting on the basis of family resemblances. Subjects clearly preferred to sort on the basis of a single feature instead. The one exception to this finding was that when subjects were provided with information that gave them some way of understanding how the properties that defined the family resemblance structure were related, they then began to sort on the basis of family resemblances. Medin, Wattenmaker, and Hampson conclude that people do not have a general preference for family resemblance structures per se. Instead they organize object categories around implicit theories. These lay theories predict not just what properties are relevant for identifying members of a category but also how these properties are related to each other. In the absence of any knowledge that could provide a structure for making sense of the overlapping features that define a family resemblance structure, people will prefer classifying on the basis of a single dimension.

In sum, even when a family resemblance structure involving several dimensions was pitted against a unidimensional basis of sorting, subjects avoided the family resemblances as a basis for categorization and relied on the more impoverished classical definition instead. The findings of Medin, Wattenmaker, and Hampson may be limited in their generality, however. The sorting tasks used required that subjects subdivide what was roughly a basic level category into two subordinate level categories. (The distinction between basic and subordinate level categories will be explained more fully in chapter 4.) That is, subjects were presented with a set of objects that looked more or less alike and were asked to subdivide this category into two categories. (Imagine being presented with a group of chairs, for example, all of which are clearly chairs, and being asked to divide them into two groups.) Given this task subjects may look for some distinguishing feature that forms the basis for contrasting similar things. In the case of chairs, for example, they might look for rockers or arms or cushions to subdivide the category "chairs." The task of trying to distinguish between subcategories of similar things may be quite different from the task of trying to figure out how objects are alike in the first place. Family resemblance sorting might be more prevalent when subjects find the basis for the similarity of objects to be more obscure and when they perceive their task as being that of finding some basis for treating things as similar, rather than as being that of finding some basis for treating similar things as distinct.

The studies of Medin, Wattenmaker, and Hampson therefore suggest that the prevalence of family resemblance structures in natural categories does not indicate that people prefer family resemblance structures to classical definitions, although the question remains open about what would happen at a different level of categorization.

There is, however, evidence that children prefer categories defined by family resemblance structures over classically defined categories, again in situations where the number of dimensions is deliberately not equated. Following Kemler (1983) and Smith (1979), Kemler-Nelson (1984) has argued that young children are more limited in their analytic abilities and will determine category membership on the basis of overall similarity rather than by analysis into component features. In order to classify an object on the basis of necessary and sufficient features, one must be able to analyze it into its component features. Lacking such analytic abilities, a child would respond on the basis of overall similarity, rather than on the basis of any criterial features. This holistic processing strategy would result in using family resemblances rather than classical definitions as the basis of classification. As expected on this argument, Kemler-Nelson (1984) found developmental differences in which kind of category was easier for children to learn. Five-year-olds found categories defined by family resemblances easier to learn, whereas 10-year-olds found classically defined categories easier. Moreover, when adults were induced to take a nonanalytic attitude towards the tasks, they too found the family resemblance structures easier to learn. Thus, family resemblance structures can be a consequence of a nonanalytic, holistic strategy in learning categories.

I will conclude this chapter by reconsidering the issue of why categories might be organized into family resemblance structures.

Why Should Natural Categories Have a Family Resemblance Structure?
To the extent that natural categories are organized into family resemblances, why might this be so? Why should the advantages of the classical view be sacrificed? Three different kinds of explanations have been mentioned, each of which makes quite different assumptions about what categorization involves and about what the family resemblance structures reflect. At present there is not enough evidence to rule out any of these explanations entirely. It is very possible that family resemblance structures may be multiply determined. First, they could result from stretching classically defined categories to encompass exemplars that do not quite fit in the category in question but fit better there than anywhere else. Second, they could be consequences of implicit theories that form the basis for categorization. Third, they could result from nonanalytic strategies for acquiring categories.

Family Resemblances Result from Stretching Categories to Allow Exceptions.   Family resemblance structures could arise even if people in general preferred classically defined categories. That is, the prevalence of family resemblance structures does not necessarily mean they are preferred. Humans, individually or through their culture or language, create classification schemes as well as learn them, and are forced to create them to encompass a world that may not fit a simple, elegant classification scheme.

Some concrete examples will help to illustrate this point. One of the most fundamental distinctions people make in biological categories is the distinction between plants and animals. Among the many features that differentiate them are that plants but not animals can produce chlorophyll and that animals but not plants have means of locomotion. There exists, however, a one-celled organism that has one or more flagella and is therefore capable of locomotion, like an animal, but produces chlorophyll, like a plant. The existence of such an organism forces us to modify our ideas about plants and animals.

We could decide that the distinction has no merit, abandon the current taxonomy in biology, and start over from scratch. We could maintain the distinction but decide that chlorophyll and method of locomotion are irrelevant rather than defining features. We could decide that there are three categories of living things: plants, animals, and these odd organisms. Biologists have resolved this problem by deciding instead to stretch the category of animals to accommodate these organisms. The are considered to be one-celled animals that are exceptional in that they produce chlorophyll.

As another example, consider the category "bird." Assume that the category began as people noticed the similarity between robins, blue jays, ravens, and so on. These birds are perceptually similar in many ways: they have very similar body parts such as beaks and wings, and they share a great many other features such as having feathers, laying eggs, and being able to fly. Now imagine that we come across a penguin for the first time. Should it be considered a bird or not? If not, then we need to decide what other category it fits in better. No other animal category seems better than "bird," so we must decide either to include the penguin as a bird or to allow it its own category. Although the penguin does not fly and does not have the typical bird shape, it is similar to other birds in many ways. Its body parts, the fact that it has feathers, the fact that it lays eggs, and so on, make "bird" an informative and useful category. Thus, there would be good reason to include the penguin in the category "bird" even though it does not fly. We would try to salvage the classical definition to some extent by noting that penguins are exceptions and that in general we can assume that birds fly. By including the penguin as a bird, we sacrifice some of the simplicity of a classical definition that states that all birds fly. Yet stretching the category to cover this unexpected instance is preferable to the other alternatives we have.

Family Resemblances Are a Consequence of Lay Theories.   One quite radical departure from the classical view of concepts had been made by Carey (1985) and by Murphy and Medin (1985). On this view, categorization is guided and determined by implicit theories that people hold. This view denies that there is some theory-neutral sense in which people look for features or similarity per se as the basis of categorization. Instead, people rely on lay theories or knowledge to determine how to categorize objects. Which features are considered salient, or relevant, and how they relate to each other does not depend on some neutral similarity metric but instead is theory relative. Medin, Wattenmaker, and Hampson (1987) apply this view to explaining family resemblances by arguing that family resemblance structures exist when they make sense in terms of a given theory or knowledge structure. They argue, for example, that properties of the category "bird," including feathers, wings, and building nests in trees, can be interpreted as adaptations to flying. Thus, family resemblance structures can be superficial manifestations of a deeper explanatory principle that makes sense of what the features of the category should be and how they should be related to each other.

Family Resemblances Result from Nonanalytic Processing.   The classical view assumes that people, in attempting to categorize the world, are looking for criteria. This may not always or perhaps even often be true. Instead, people, especially children, may adopt a nonanalytic approach to acquiring categories—thinking about exemplars in a holistic way. Using overall similarity to known exemplars as the basis of categorization will result in categories structured into family resemblances (Kemler-Nelson 1984).

Wattenmaker, Nakamura, and Medin (1988) point out that this kind of holistic strategy can be very adaptive. They make the very interesting observation that using overall similarity to make decisions about category membership would prevent children from prematurely settling on dimensions that might turn out to be wrong. In the absence of knowledge about what dimensions are relevant for classifying (according to what the culture has decided or according to what will be most useful), children could select any of a number of dimensions to sort on, many of which would be fruitless. Another disadvantage of prematurely deciding on a dimension along which to classify objects is the one brought out by Brooks (1979) and by Kossan (1981). In attempting to analyze objects and sort on the basis of a single feature or some combination of features, one discards information about other dimensions. In attempting a premature analysis, one can lose information that is relevant. In other words, nonanalytic strategies—exemplar-based, holistic processing—allow children to retain useful information, prevent them from discarding relevant information, and prevent them from prematurely settling on erroneous dimensions.

There is another related benefit concerning the induction problem raised in chapter 2. Recall that part of the problem is to understand how children can so quickly settle on object labels as the referents for terms, given that a label could, in principle, refer either to an object or to its color, size, shape, and so on. But to think of hypotheses such as color, size, and shape requires analyzing the object into those dimensions in the first place. Thus, these competing hypotheses may not be so readily available to the young child. Another way of stating this is that a limitation on young children's information-processing abilities may actually provide part of the solution to the induction problem. This is reminiscent of an argument put forward by Newport (1984) to explain how it is that children are so competent at acquiring language. In an ingenious discussion of the acquisition of syntax, Newport raises the possibility that some cognitive limitations of children may actually work to their advantage in learning language. Here too, in the domain of acquiring categories and category labels, a limitation may work to children's advantage. Their limited analytic abilities may effectively narrow down the hypothesis space that they need to consider. The hypothesis space that children generate would not expand to encompass all of the possible features and Boolean combinations of features. By not generating the hypotheses in the first place, children do not have to subsequently rule them out. Thus, children's focus on objects per se rather than on sets of properties or features, the use of exemplar-based learning strategies, and holistic processing of exemplars fit well with the taxonomic and whole object assumptions hypothesized in chapter 2.

Chapter 4

Basic, Superordinate, and Subordinate Level Categories

According to the argument put forth in chapter 2, when children hear an object label, they first assume that it refers to the object taken as an exemplar of a category of objects, as opposed to referring to its properties or its extrinsic relation to other objects. In chapter 3 we saw that exemplar-based holistic strategies that children may be prone to use fit well with the whole object and taxonomic assumptions. However, this still leaves open the question of which of the possible object categories children consider. Suppose, for example, that someone points to a Honda Civic in a child's presence and says, "See the car." On the basis of the taxonomic constraint, the child should assume that "car" refers to the Honda Civic as a whole—not to its color or size, not to "a man driving the car," and so on. Yet "car" could refer to Honda Civics (but not other Hondas), to Hondas (but not other cars), to Japanese cars, to cars, to four-wheeled vehicles, or to vehicles. On what basis does the child determine which of these categories is the referent of "car"? Two closely related and overlapping lines of investigation are relevant to answering this question. One concerns children's acquisition of category terms, and the other concerns children's acquisition of categories. The distinction between the acquisition of category terms and the acquisition of categories is often blurred in this type of work, and in fact little is known about how the acquisition of the lexicon might differ from the acquisition of categories per se. In this chapter, then, evidence regarding differences between the acquisition and use of basic, superordinate, and subordinate category terms will be summarized along with evidence regarding differences between the categories themselves.

In a classic paper entitled "How Shall a Thing Be Called?" Roger Brown (1958) noted that there is tremendous regularity in the way adults label objects, at least when they are labeling them for children. In teaching young children the labels for objects, adults could select any number of terms that differ in how specifically they categorize the object. For example, we could call the same object "a dog," "a boxer," "a quadruped," "a canine," "a mammal," or "an animal." Although there are many possible labels to choose from, there is a striking tendency to select the label "dog" above all the others. Brown proposed that the first labels that are given categorize objects in a maximally useful way.

Eleanor Rosch and her colleagues have more fully described the principles that determine the most useful level of categorization (Rosch et al. 1976). They have distinguished three levels of categorization: the basic, superordinate, and subordinate levels. An example of a basic level category is "chair." According to Rosch et al. (1976), all chairs are fairly similar to each other, yet they are quite different from other kinds of furniture, such as beds and dressers and tables.

At the superordinate level the category is more general than the basic level and includes objects that are relatively diverse. At this level it is more difficult to perceive the similarities among objects in the same category. Furniture, for example, includes objects as diverse as chairs, tables, dressers, and beds.

At the subordinate level the category is more specific than the basic level category and includes objects that are quite similar. An example of a subordinate level category is "rocking chair." Rocking chairs are more similar to each other than chairs are in general. But, according to Rosch et al. (1976), there is a cost to this gain in similarity. The subordinate categories do not contrast as well with each other and are therefore more confusable. Thus, although rocking chairs are similar to each other, they can also be confused with arm chairs, kitchen chairs, and so on.

In short, basic level categories provide a good compromise between two different goals of categorization: (1) maximizing similarity between category members and (2) minimizing similarity with members of other categories.

Distinguishing Basic Level Categories from Other Levels of Categorization

There is now a great deal of evidence attesting to the special status of basic level categories (for a review, see Mervis and Rosch 1981). First, as already implied by Brown's examples, the basic level seems to be the most natural level at which to label objects. If people are shown objects and simply asked to label them, most often they will give the basic level labels. People tend to label an object "a car" instead of "a convertible" or "a vehicle," "a bed" instead of "a king-size bed" or "a piece of furniture," "a dog" instead of "a poodle" or "an animal." Second, the basic level is the highest level at which experimental subjects have been found to form concrete images of objects. Third, subjects are faster at verifying that a picture belongs to the basic level than at assigning it to the other levels. They are faster at saying, for example, that a rocking chair is a chair than at saying that it is a rocking chair or a piece of furniture (Rosch et al. 1976).

Having Parts in Common
According to Rosch et al. (1976), what sets the basic level apart from superordinate and subordinate levels of categorization is that the objects at the basic level share many features with each other while sharing few features with other contrasting categories. Tversky and Hemenway (1984) have argued that what sets the basic level apart is that objects at this level have many parts in common, rather than sharing any kind of feature. That is, the basic level is the most general level at which objects share parts. To take one example, consider the categories "clothing," "pants," and "Levi's." The superordinate level, "clothing," consists of shirts, pants, and socks, among others. These categories do not have many parts in common. In contrast, at the basic level, "pants," the various kinds of pants, such as Levi's, dress pants, and double-knit pants, all have a waist and two legs, and many have buttons, zippers, and cuffs. At the subordinate level there is not much gain in parts shared, and in fact many of the distinctions between categories at the subordinate level consist of modifications of basic parts, witness "straight-legged" pants versus "bell-bottoms."

Tversky and Hemenway (1984) cite several different sources of support for their analysis. In general, they find that, as predicted, subjects tend to list far more parts at the basic level than at the superordinate level. Moreover, subjects do not tend to list many additional parts at the subordinate level. Instead, nonpart features tend to differentiate subordinate categories from each other.

This analysis raises an interesting developmental question. We know that children tend to acquire basic level categories prior to superordinate and subordinate level categories. Is the ease of perceiving this categorical level dependent on the shared features being parts? Some evidence bearing on this comes from a classification study by Tversky (1983). In this study 4- and 5-year-old children were presented with 15 objects that fell into five categories (animals, clothes, furniture, tools, and vehicles). There were two main conditions to this study. In one condition the objects that were presented as members of the categories were judged to be relatively good, typical examples of the category but did not share many parts. In the other condition the objects that were presented as members of the categories were judged to share many parts and were somewhat less typical examples of the category. For example, for the category "animals" one group of children saw a cat, a fish, and a snake—three examples that do not have many parts in common—whereas another group saw a bear, a cow, and a deer—three examples that do share many parts. Children were first shown the objects from one condition (that is, the objects that share parts or the objects that do not) and then objects from the other condition. The results were that children were better able to group together objects from the same category when those objects shared parts.

This finding suggests that parts play a significant role in children's analysis of categories. What we really would like to know, however, is this: if we were to find or create categories that shared many non-part features, would they serve just as well as categories even at the basic level? To my knowledge, this study has not been done, nor is it an easy one to design. The reason for the difficulty is that having parts in common is correlated with (confounded with) many other characteristics. As Tversky and Hemenway (1984) note, if two objects have many parts in common, they will also tend to have a very similar overall configuration or shape. Perhaps this overall shape is what dominates children's attention, rather than the parts per se. Further, having parts in common means that the objects are likely to have the same function, since the parts will be used for the same purposes. Thus, again there is a problem of deciding whether the part or the function is dominating children's cognition.

This last issue illustrates an important characteristic of basic level categories: they tend to be overdetermined. That is, the objects in these categories tend to have the same overall shape, many features in common, many parts in common, and many functions in common. Perhaps this level is basic because so many defining criteria tend to converge here rather than because any one of them is essential.

Cue Validity

This conclusion is reinforced by attempts to more formally discriminate the basic level from other hierarchical levels. Rosch et al. (1976) argue that two complementary criteria partially determine how useful a category will be. The first criterion is that it should be relatively easy to detect the basis of categorization. That is, we should readily be able to perceive the similarity among objects that are members of the same category. The second criterion is that it should be relatively easy to distinguish a category member from other potentially confusable categories. That is, categories should contrast well with each other. Thus, basic level categories are maximally useful because they reflect a reasonable compromise between these two criteria of categorization. According to Medin (1983), however, there has been no concrete proposal that specifies precisely how this compromise is achieved. Rosch et al. (1976) and Rosch and Mervis (1975) argue that the basic level category should maximize the cue validity of the category. Cue validity is the extent to which the properties can predict membership in that category over other categories; in other words, it is the probability that something is a member of the category, given that it possesses a given feature. The feature "flying," for example, makes it more likely that something is a bird compared to animals that are not birds. Medin (1983) and Murphy and Medin (1985) argue, however, that this measure incorrectly assigns the highest cue validity scores to the most general categories. Something that flies, for example, is likely to be a bird—but it is at least as likely to be an animal. As Medin (1983) notes, this is not to say that cue validity is not important in categorization; but it cannot be the sole basis for determining a concept's utility.

Maximizing Within-Category Similarity and Between-Category Contrast
Cue validity does not achieve the compromise between within-category similarity and between-category contrast that Rosch et al.'s (1976) analysis calls for. It is not possible to simultaneously maximize within-class similarity and between-class contrast (Tversky 1977). One can, however, attempt to maximize some function of within- versus between-category similarity. In his evaluation of attempts to accomplish this, Medin (1983) points out two types of problems with this criterion. The first is that some of the logical consequences of the attempts to maximize within-category similarity and minimize between-category similarity are counterintuitive. The second is that these models make some rather strong assumptions about the way information is combined, namely, that component features are independent and additive. There is reason to question these assumptions (Smith and Medin 1981).

Rosch and Mervis (1975) emphasized that categories are not defined by arbitrary combinations of attributes but instead reflect a correlational structure of attributes that exists in the world. Creatures that have feathers, for example, have beaks and claws rather than mouths and paws or hands. Animals with hair or fur, on the other hand, are not likely to have beaks, claws, or wings. They claimed that basic level objects are the most inclusive categories that reflect the correlational structure of the environment. There is evidence that naturally occurring categories tend to have correlated attributes, and in experiments in learning artificial categories subjects have been shown to rely on correlated attributes in forming categories (for a review, see Medin 1983). Murphy and Medin (1985) now argue that it is not correlational information per se that people rely on, but that correlations provide a basis for primitive theories or explanations, which in turn are the conceptual glue that makes some categories more coherent than others. In chapter 5 I will return to examine the question of correlated attributes from a somewhat different perspective.

Developmental Implications

Based on their analysis of hierarchical levels, Rosch et al. (1976) hypothesize that basic level terms should generally be the first category terms that children acquire. This is not a trivial prediction; other reasonable theories in fact make different predictions on this point. For example, if we assumed that the more similar the objects in a category were to each other, the easier the category would be to learn, then we would predict that subordinate categories would be easiest to learn. That is, a child should find it easier to learn a category such as "Volkswagen" than a category such as "car," because Volkswagens are more similar to each other than cars are. Another theory of how children acquire terms, the "semantic features hypothesis" (Clark 1973), states that the fewer features that a child has to notice, the simpler the term will be to learn. Because superordinate terms refer to more general categories, these terms have fewer defining features than the more specific basic level terms. Since vehicles have fewer features in common than cars do, this hypothesis would predict that "vehicle" would be acquired before "car."

Thus, there are other reasonable analyses that would predict that subordinate or superordinate terms should be acquired first, but the analysis of Rosch et al. (1976) predicts that children should acquire basic level categories first. It is, of course, unreasonable to expect that all basic level terms would be acquired before any superordinate terms. One could expect, though, that the first words learned by children might be mainly basic level terms. Moreover, within any given hierarchy a child might acquire at least some basic level terms before learning the subordinate or superordinate terms for that hierarchy.

Vocabulary Acquisition and Sorting Studies

There is a fair amount of evidence supporting the developmental progression I have just sketched, some of which comes from studies of young children's vocabulary. Rosch et al. (1976) examined the vocabulary of one child who had participated in Roger Brown's extensive longitudinal study of language acquisition. They found that the great majority of her first acquired words were basic level terms. A review of studies of vocabulary development also suggests that of the first

50 or so words that children learn, many are basic level terms (Clark 1973). Finally, in a study by Rosch et al. (1976) in which 3-year-old children were asked to name pictures of objects, it was found that they used almost exclusively basic level labels.

Other evidence in support of this hypothesis comes from studies of categorization in which children are shown objects and asked to place the ones that are alike together. Typically these studies require children to sort at the superordinate level of categorization, putting together all of the furniture, clothing, animals, and so on. Children aged 5 or younger have trouble sorting these superordinate categories (Bruner, Olver, Greenfield, et al., 1966; Inhelder and Piaget 1964; Vygotsky 1962). Rosch et al. (1976) compared 3- and 4-year-old children's abilities to classify objects at the superordinate level versus the basic level using an oddity procedure. In this procedure children were shown three objects, two of which were from the same category and one of which was a random distractor. At the basic level, objects from the same category included two cats or two cars. At the superordinate level, objects from the same category included a cat and a butterfly (both animals) and a car and an airplane (both vehicles). At the basic level of categorization, both 3- and 4-year-olds were virtually always able to select the two category members. They did so 99% and 100% of the time, respectively. In contrast, 3-year-olds did much more poorly on the superordinate categories, finding the two category members only 55% of the time, though 4-year-olds performed quite well, choosing correctly 96% of the time. In another study Rosch et al. (1976) used a more difficult sorting procedure in which four exemplars from four categories were mixed together and children were asked to "Put together the ones that go together." Now even 5- and 6-year-olds had trouble sorting at the superordinate level, but both ages again sorted virtually perfectly at the basic level.

Although this evidence about vocabulary growth and early categorization indicates that children do generally learn basic level terms before subordinate or superordinate terms, it cannot be taken alone as strong evidence in favor of the primacy of basic level categories. One problem with the vocabulary data is that children may overgeneralize the meanings of some terms (Clark 1973) and so may use a basic level category term ("dog") to refer to a more general category ("four-legged mammals"). In fact, it would be interesting to use the nature and extent of such overgeneralizations as evidence for what might be the most natural level of categorization, when it does not coincide with what Rosch et al. (1976) would have termed the "basic level." There are many problems in interpreting overgeneralizations and they would, of course, need to be addressed (Huttenlocher

1974). Assuming they were, then suppose that children might prefer to form a category consisting of porcupines and hedgehogs, for example, rather than either alone or some higher or lower level category. If so, they should then overgeneralize "porcupine" to include hedgehogs. A more general way of stating this point is that Rosch et al. (1976) have imposed a trichotomy on what is often likely to be a much more elaborated hierarchy of categories. There may not always be a single basic level that fulfills all of the criteria proposed.

Another problem in interpreting the vocabulary acquisition data is that adults tend to use basic level terms when speaking to children (Anglin 1977; Callanan 1985; Shipley, Kuhn, and Madden 1983). In fact, Callanan found that even when teaching their children new superordinate category terms, parents label objects at the basic level as well as the superordinate level. For example, when teaching their children the term "machine" parents labeled objects as "blender" or "sewing machine" before teaching "machine." This was true even when the basic level categories were unfamiliar to the children. Parents appear sensitive to the fact that basic level categories may be easier for their children to grasp. (Parents may also be sensitive to the mutual exclusivity constraint discussed in chapter 9.) On the other hand, the difference in the frequency with which the two types of terms are mentioned could at least partially account for the vocabulary data. Children might acquire basic level terms first because adults teach them first and not because basic level categories are simpler to acquire. Thus, we need some way of controlling for what children are taught before we can determine whether basic level categories are simpler for children.

Experimental studies that deconfound frequency of exposure to a category term with its level of generality can avoid this problem. Horton and Markman (1980) summarize some indirect evidence from concept formation studies (for example, Bourne, Ekstrand, and Dominowski 1971; Bruner, Goodnow, and Austin 1956) that bears on the relative difficulty of superordinate versus basic level categories. As mentioned in chapter 3, disjunctive categories are relatively difficult to learn (Conant and Trabasso 1964; Haygood and Bourne 1965; Hunt and Hovland 1960). Superordinate categories are like disjunctive categories in that few criterial features are shared by all members. The experimentally created disjunctive concepts usually require only that an object have one feature or another to be a member of the category. The family resemblance structure of natural superordinate categories is richer than these simple disjunctive categories in that there is a larger pool of features to select from and an object must have a number of them to qualify as a member of the category. Nevertheless, the similarities between disjunctive and superordinate concepts suggest that superordinate categories should be more difficult to learn than basic level categories. Thus, these studies of concept learning provide some indirect evidence that some of the principles that characterize superordinate categories render such concepts more difficult to learn.

Learning of Artificial Categories

More evidence for the primacy of basic level objects comes from a training study by Horton and Markman (1980). We argued that a person should find it relatively simple to learn basic level categories from viewing some of the exemplars, because those exemplars will be perceptually similar. In contrast, at the superordinate level the categories are more inclusive, with greater perceptual dissimilarity among members. A child who views exemplars of a superordinate category might be unable to perceive the similarity among members and thus be unable to infer the basis for category membership from this perceptual information. For superordinate categories, then, some additional means of identifying the relevant criteria may be needed to acquire the concepts. One potentially important way of specifying the criteria would be to use language to point them out. For example, one could help a child understand why koalas, possums, and kangaroos are all marsupials by pointing out that marsupials have a pouch for carrying their young.

If linguistic specification of the criteria is important for acquiring superordinate categories, then that suggests one further reason why superordinate categories are acquired later than basic level terms. Young children may be unable to use linguistic description for purposes of classification as well as older children. To use such information to classify exemplars, a child must keep the descriptions in mind and systematically evaluate objects against the set of features described. In other contexts such comparisons have been found to be difficult for children (Anglin 1977; Asher 1978; Gholson, Levine, and Phillips 1972). If young children do not have such efficient processing abilities, they may rely mainly on the similarity that they can detect through purely exemplar-based information.

To summarize the predictions (from Horton and Markman 1980): Children should be able to learn new basic level categories simply by being presented with examples of the categories. Describing the relevant features should not help. In contrast, describing the features should help children learn superordinate categories, where the commonalities are more difficult to discover. Finally, younger children should be less able than older children to use the linguistic information to its full advantage despite its value for the learning of superordinate categories.

In this study children were taught artificial animal categories, two of which were designed to be at the superordinate level of categorization and two at the basic level. The categories were modeled after natural biological categories (for instance, ungulate at the superordinate level and salamander at the basic level). For each artificial category the overall body shapes of the natural animals were retained but novel features were added. For example, the ungulate category member "horse" possessed horns, a feathered tail, and a special type of feet yet was still recognizable as a horse because its overall body and head shapes were retained. Members of each basic level category varied in their size, body orientation, and skin markings, so that they did not look identical. Examples of the categories used are presented in figure 4.1.

Children were taught these categories in one of two ways. In the linguistic training condition linguistic descriptions were used that mentioned the criterial features. For example, the child was told, "Here is a danker with horns on the top of its head and a tail made of feathers." In the exemplar training condition children were told to attend very closely to the exemplars but were not told what features to look for.

Preschoolers, kindergartners, and first graders were told that they would be seeing animals from another planet. They were then introduced to a puppet zookeeper and told they could help him by learning about these animals so that they could find the ones that were supposed to live in the zoo.

The results of this study were just as predicted. First, basic level categories were easier for these young children to learn. Telling children what features defined the categories helped only for learning the superordinate level categories. It did not help children learn either of the basic level categories. Moreover, the preschoolers did not benefit from the linguistic descriptions. Only the kindergartners and first graders were better able to learn the superordinate categories when told what features were relevant.

Using linguistic information about criterial features is one means for learning superordinate categories, and young children's failure to benefit from such information is one factor accounting for their difficulty with categories at this level. However, there are certainly alternative ways in which superordinate categories can be learned. First, there are nonlinguistic ways of drawing attention to criteria. Functional criteria, for example, can be discovered by viewing objects in

BASIC LEVEL: SALAMANDERS

EXEMPLARS

DISTRACTORS

SUPERORDINATE LEVEL: UNGULATES

EXEMPLARS

DISTRACTORS

Figure 4.1:
Examples of exemplars and distractors of the basic level category "salamanders" and the superordinate level category "ungulates" from Horton and Markman (1980).

use. Second, it may not always be necessary to abstract out relevant features. For superordinate concepts in particular, one may, at least initially, work with a list of exemplars. One may learn, for example, that chairs, tables, lamps, and so on, are kinds of furniture without attempting to abstract out the defining properties of furniture. This is an exemplar-based model like that proposed by Brooks (1978) and Kossan (1981), discussed in chapter 3. Such a learning process would account for the acquisition data: it would predict that basic level concepts should be acquired first since superordinate concepts are defined in terms of basic level concepts. New exemplars could be admitted based on their similarity to one or more of the basic level categories subsumed under the superordinate category, rather than on their possession of defining features.

Although this research compared only basic and superordinate categories, the analysis may apply to the acquisition of subordinate categories as well. At the subordinate level the contrast between categories is more difficult to perceive, so information about the defining features may be helpful. In fact, category labels at the subordinate level often consist of an attribute term that specifies the relevant criterion, for example, *rocking* chair and *arm*chair. Thus, at the subordinate level we would expect children to benefit from explicit information about the relevant contrast.

More experimental evidence for the relative simplicity of basic level terms for children comes from work by Mervis and Crisafi (1982). Children in this study were taught artificial categories designed to be at different hierarchical levels. Children were again found to be better able to learn the basic level category than the superordinate or the subordinate category. The main purpose of this study, however, was to compare the relative difficulty of learning subordinate and superordinate level categories. Mervis and Crisafi predicted that subordinate category terms should be acquired last. Thus, the predicted order of difficulty from simplest to most difficult is basic, superordinate, and subordinate.

Mervis and Crisafi (1982) argue that the degree of differentiation of the categories should predict their order of acquisition. Differentiation is a measure based on the relationship between within-category similarity and between-category similarity. (To estimate degree of differentiation, they averaged adult ratings of object similarity which is subject to the previously mentioned criticisms of Medin (1983)). A category is highly differentiated when the members of that category are highly similar to each other but not very similar to members of other categories at the same level. According to Mervis and Crisafi (1982), superordinate categories are more differentiated than subordinate level categories. Presumably the gain in similarity of members at the subordinate level (within-category similarity) cannot compensate for the still high similarity at the basic level (between-category similarity). In the same vein, the loss of similarity at the superordinate level (within-category similarity) would be compensated for by the low similarity between different superordinate level categories (between-category similarity).

In contrast to Mervis and Crisafi's (1982) argument, one might expect instead that whether the subordinate or superordinate categories are more differentiated would vary from category to category and might depend on how elaborated the hierarchy is, that is, on how many levels there are. For some categories, Mervis and Crisafi's analysis seems correct. The contrast between a kitchen table and a dining room table seems very slight to me, so I would expect these categories to have low differentiation scores. Similarly, the contrast between Levi's and double-knit pants seems slight and might be more difficult for children to detect. In fact, Mervis and Crisafi (1982) offer evidence from adult ratings that such subordinate categories have lower differentiation scores than the superordinate categories of furniture and clothing. But not all subordinate categories differ by such minor features. The difference between a daschund and a sheep dog seems quite striking, so these categories might well be highly differentiated. Similarly, the difference between a robin and a flamingo seems fairly striking, as does the difference between a Volkswagen bug and a luxury sedan or a station wagon. Thus, although degree of differentiation may predict order of acquisition as Mervis and Crisafi argue, it is not clear that superordinate categories will always be more differentiated than subordinate categories.

In their training study Mervis and Crisafi (1982) taught 2-, 4-, and 5-year-old children categories of abstract figures that were defined by their shape. The basic level categories had very similar overall shapes. The subordinate level categories were very much like the basic level categories except that the figures differed in where a minor detail was placed. For example, a basic level category consisted of two triangular objects, each of which had three extra small points and one dark bar protruding from it. This basic level category consisted of two subordinate categories that differed in the placement of one of the points and the bar. The superordinate level categories were defined as angular versus curved figures. Mervis and Crisafi constructed these categories in such a way that the subordinate category was less differentiated than the superordinate category (as confirmed by the ratings of adult subjects). In accord with the predictions, children found the subordinate category more difficult to learn than the superordinate one.

It would be interesting to follow up this study by manipulating differentiation score independently of hierarchical level. That is, from this study we do not know whether the differentiation of the category or its absolute position in the hierarchy accounts for how readily it is learned. We need to compare children's learning of the kind of hierarchy that Mervis and Crisafi taught to their learning of a hierarchy in which the subordinate categories are more differentiated than the superordinate ones. Differentiation is likely to be very important and could matter more than the absolute hierarchical position of the categories. Moreover, as I just argued, in naturally occurring hierarchies the superordinate categories may not always be more differentiated than the subordinate ones.

Difficulty of Superordinate Categories

Functional Criteria
Murphy and Smith (1982) have a somewhat different interpretation of the distinction among superordinate, basic, and subordinate categories. They argue that it may be the superordinate rather than the basic level that is distinctive. At the basic and subordinate levels category members are quite similar to each other, and justification for considering them the same is readily apparent. Superordinate categories differ in this regard. It is much more difficult to find commonalities at the superordinate level, and functional criteria take on much more importance.

Relational Information
Another way in which superordinate terms may differ is that they may contain some relational information (Murphy and Wisniewski 1985). As I will argue in chapter 8, children sometimes interpret superordinate category terms as collections rather than classes. Collections (for instance, "pile," "family," "forest") refer to objects that are related to each other in some way, for example, by spatial proximity. A child who interprets the superordinate category term "toy" as a collection will agree that a group of toys that includes a doll are called "toys" but will deny that the doll alone is a toy (Callanan and Markman 1982). Thus, for the child the category term refers to the group of related objects instead of to any single object that fulfills the criteria for category membership. Murphy and Wisniewski (1985) suggest that there may be a vestige of such relational meanings in adults' representations of superordinate categories. Although adults may not define the categories as collections, relational information may often be invoked as part of the representation of the category. If so, they argue, then providing some relational context should help adults access superordinate categories but should not be needed for basic level categories. In support of their hypothesis, they found that embedding objects in scenes helped subjects to identify objects at the superordinate but not the basic level.

Ad Hoc Categories
Barsalou has investigated two related types of categories that he has termed "ad hoc" (Barsalou 1983) and "goal-derived" (Barsalou 1985) that may help explain why children find superordinate categories so difficult. Goal-derived categories are categories that people use to achieve goals, such as "things to take on a vacation." The exemplars, which in this case include a suitcase, a novel, suntan lotion, and

plane tickets, are grouped together not because they are similar to each other but rather because they achieve some goal or function. Ad hoc categories are unfamiliar goal-derived categories that are created on the spot to achieve a goal. Ad hoc and goal-derived categories cross-classify objects that would more conventionally be thought of as part of different categories.

Ad hoc categories exhibit the same kind of internal structure that is characteristic of common categories. Barsalou (1983) asked subjects to rate exemplars of ad hoc categories and common categories for their typicality. Ad hoc categories were found to be like common categories in that both possess typicality gradients and unclear cases. Subjects used the same range of values for rating the goodness of exemplars for both ad hoc and common categories. Moreover, there was equally good consistency in subjects' judgments about how representative an exemplar was, whether it was from an ad hoc or a common category.

Although ad hoc categories possess an internal structure that is similar to that of common categories, there are important differences in the way the two kinds of categories are represented; and it is these differences that may parallel the developmental differences in the representation of categories. The main difference is in how explicitly the category is represented. Common superordinate categories are likely to be explicitly represented or associated with their exemplars, at least for adults. For example, as adults, we probably quite readily think of a chair as a kind of furniture. In contrast, a given object can be cross-classified into an indefinite number of other categories. To take an example from Barsalou, "chair" can be cross-classified into ad hoc categories such as "things to hold a door open with" and "things that can be sold." It is unlikely that all of these indefinite number of classifications are explicitly represented in memory. Rather, Barsalou (1983) argues that most ad hoc categories are probably implicitly represented. The associations or categories are inferrable from information about the objects in question. Given that ad hoc categories are only implicitly represented, they should be less accessible in memory than common categories.

From this analysis, Barsalou (1983) predicted that ad hoc categories would not be as effective mnemonic devices as common categories are. To test this hypothesis, subjects were asked to learn a list of words. One group of subjects learned a list that was organized into blocks of words belonging to the same common superordinate category. A second group of subjects learned a list that was organized into blocks of words belonging to the same ad hoc category. In both of these conditions the subjects were told, for each block of words, what the categories were. A third group of subjects learned a list of unrelated words. Subjects were then asked to recall the words they had learned. Subjects who had studied common categories recalled more categories than subjects who had studied ad hoc categories, and they recalled more exemplars per category than subjects who had learned ad hoc categories. In fact, the subjects who learned lists organized by ad hoc categories did not seem to benefit from the categorical organization at all. They recalled no more than the control subjects who had learned unrelated words.

To foreshadow an argument by Horton (1982) to be discussed soon, note that this finding is reminiscent of a common developmental difference in how effective common categories are as a mnemonic device. Older children are more likely to benefit from the category structure than are younger children.

Barsalou (1983) argues that because ad hoc categories are not well established in memory, they may come to mind only when triggered by a relevant context. For example, you may think of a chair as something to stand on to reach the ceiling only when you are trying to change a light bulb in an out-of-reach fixture. To test this, subjects (in this case college students) received lists of items that belonged to ad hoc or common categories and were asked to think of a category label for each. Half the subjects heard a brief story that primed the relevant category. As might be expected, these adult subjects had no trouble coming up with the labels for the common categories and did not require a context to trigger the relevant category. Moreover, they agreed on the labels they gave. In contrast, it was difficult for subjects to find a label for the ad hoc categories without the context. Subjects who heard the stories that provided a relevant context readily discerned the relevant categories and agreed about which categories they were. But without the context subjects found it hard to come up with a category that encompassed the diverse items and disagreed on the labels they did generate.

Again, this finding has an analogue in the developmental literature. The classification task is similar to this labeling task in that subjects have to decide what unites various objects. Young children find it difficult to categorize objects at the superordinate level and create idiosyncratic sorts. By contrast, older children sort with good agreement, on the basis of the common taxonomic category.

One of the reasons why young children have difficulty with the superordinate level of categorization, then, may be that these categories function as ad hoc categories for them. Older children and adults have had enough experience with superordinate categories that they become explicitly represented. But for young children the categories are as yet implicit and must be inferred by the child as needed. This is the hypothesis tested by Horton (1982). A young child might well be unfamiliar with the category "kitchen utensils," for example. Nevertheless, the child might know the individual exemplars of the category—that is, be able to recognize an eggbeater, a spatula, a knife, and so on. The child would find it difficult to group these objects together as being the same kind of thing and would have trouble detecting the similarity among them. Yet this same child would agree, if asked, that each object is used in the kitchen.

Horton's (1982) argument is that an important reason why children fail on tests of their knowledge of superordinate categories is that quite often this knowledge is only implicit. That is, from children's failure on sorting tasks we should not necessarily conclude that their ability to learn and represent categories is qualitatively different from that of adults, any more than we would draw the same conclusion from adults' failure when ad hoc categories are involved. We know that adults have the ability to represent and use superordinate categories, and perhaps the same is true of children.

This argument predicts that the same child should display two different ways of dealing with superordinate categories, depending on whether the categories are explicitly or implicitly represented for the child. Following Barsalou, it further predicts that with contextual priming of the implicit categories, children should be better able to solve categorization tests as the adults did with ad hoc categories.

Horton (1982) tested these predictions with two different tests of children's knowledge of categories. These tasks were selected to represent the two ends of a continuum ranging from tasks that require very explicit knowledge of categories and systematic, deliberate strategies for their solution, to tasks that are automatic and nonstrategic and perhaps require only implicit knowledge of categories. The first is the object classification procedure, which is relatively difficult for children. The second is a measure of release from proactive inhibition, which will be described later.

Although, it was important in this study for the categories themselves to be unfamiliar to the children, the individual exemplars of the categories needed to be familiar. For a category to be used in this study, the exemplars had to be familiar even to young children and, when asked, children had to agree on the superordinate classification. For example, in order to use the category "food," children had to know each individual exemplar (say, "apple") and had to agree that it was something people eat. Before children could participate in the classification study, Horton needed to determine which categories were explicit and which were implicit for each child. A few weeks before their participation in the study the children, ranging in age from 3½ to 7 years old, were pretested for their knowledge of the categories. A category was considered to be explicitly represented for a child if he or she could explicitly provide the relevant defining criteria or give the correct label for the category. It was considered a candidate for an implicitly represented category if the child demonstrated little explicit knowledge about the category—that is, if he or she was unable to explain how the objects were alike.

In the experiment proper, children were shown four objects from each of three or four categories and told to put the ones that were alike together. Children sorted twice: once they sorted categories that were explicit for them, and once they sorted categories that were hypothesized to be implicit for them.

Two instructional conditions were compared. In the standard, nonprimed condition children were simply given the standard instruction to put the objects that were alike together. In the primed condition children were told that they were going to hear a secret that could help them, and then they were given a label and description of the categories. For example, they would be told that "some of these things are food—things that people eat."

To summarize, there were two main predictions: (1) children should be better able to classify categories that they have explicitly represented than those that are only implicitly represented, and (2) priming should help children classify the implicit but not the explicit categories.

The first prediction was clearly supported. At both ages children were better able to sort categories that were explicitly represented than those that were only implicitly represented. Thus, even 3- and 4-year-olds have some capacity to represent categories at the superordinate level of categorization.

The results for the second prediction were more complex. The findings for the older children agreed with the prediction. They sorted explicit categories just as well whether or not they were primed. In contrast, when given a description of an implicit category, they became better able to use the category as a basis of classification.

The younger children did not show this pattern. The priming helped them to sort the explicit but not the implicit categories. In fact, their sorting of implicit categories was actually hurt by telling them what the categories were.

These two findings from the younger children need to be accounted for. Horton (1982) suggests that this pattern of results may be caused by a limitation in young children's processing capacity. We know from the pretest data that even the 3- and 4-year-olds understood the descriptions of the categories when they were presented for each object, one at a time. But it may be that the children were unable to remember the description of four relatively unfamiliar categories and then apply them systematically to the objects in the array. Horton mentions that this is consistent with evidence from several different kinds of studies, including studies of concept acquisition (Horton and Markman 1980), classification (Anglin 1977), referential communication (Asher 1978), and discrimination learning (Gholson, Levine, and Phillips 1972). Young children find it difficult to use linguistic information in tasks that require systematic evaluation of the information against a series of objects. Thus, instead of helping them discover the implicit categories, the additional information simply gave them one more thing to keep track of, further disrupting their performance.

Horton's (1982) suggestion could also help explain why the younger children benefited from the priming when sorting explicit categories. Although the categories were explicitly represented, the children may still have found the sorting task somewhat confusing given an array of 12 or 16 objects from different categories that needed to be sensibly organized. The priming may have not only helped children access the relevant category but also helped them figure out the best strategy for solving the classification task.

The classification task was selected because it was thought to require rather explicit knowledge of the categories for its solution. A memory procedure that measures buildup and release of proactive inhibition was selected as the second task because such a task involves no deliberate strategies and thus provides a good contrast to the demands of the classification procedure.

To study proactive inhibition, subjects are given short lists of words to remember over a series of trials. If the words come from the same category, trial after trial, then subjects start to recall fewer words. This is the buildup of proactive inhibition. The argument is that having already recalled words from the same category over several trials interferes with recall of new words from the same category. If on a subsequent trial the category is changed, then there presumably is a release from the proactive inhibition, and in fact there is a marked increase in the number of words recalled. This procedure can be used as a measure of category knowledge (Huttenlocher and Lui 1979) in that the buildup and release of proactive inhibition presumably depends on some recognition of the categories.

In Horton's (1982) study 4-year-old children were asked to remember lists of words over several trials. Half of the children learned words from explicit categories and half learned words from implicit categories. (As in the first study, children were pretested to determine for each child which categories were explicitly known and which were implicitly known.) In each case half the children participated in an experimental group and half in a control group. In the experimental group the children learned words from the same category over several trials and then on certain shift trials the category was switched. In the control group the category was changed on every trial.

The results for the explicit categories were as predicted. Children showed a clear buildup of inhibition over trials and a release from inhibition when the categories were changed. That is, children's sensitivity to the explicit categories had the expected effects on their memory. The results for the implicit categories were somewhat more equivocal. Although the pattern of recall looked as though there might have been a slight buildup of proactive inhibition and a slight release from it, these results were not significant. Only for the explicit categories did the pattern of results differ significantly between the experimental and control groups.

In summary, using two very different tasks, one requiring deliberate strategies for its solution and one in which the effects are automatic and nonstrategic, Horton (1982) found a similar pattern of results. It is possible to find superordinate categories that even 3- and 4-year-old children have explicitly represented. Their performance on those categories looks somewhat more like the performance of older children and adults. But for the categories that they have only implicitly represented, their performance looks more like the typical findings for young children. This argues against a view of conceptual development that attributes young children's failure on tests of classification to an inability to learn superordinate level categories or to understand principles of categorization. Horton's (1982) results suggest that, on analogy with Barsalou's adults dealing with ad hoc categories, children fail on tests of classification at the superordinate level not only because of structural differences between superordinate and basic level terms but also because they are usually forced to deal with categories that, for them, are as yet only implicitly represented.

Violation of Mutual Exclusivity
A final reason why superordinate terms may be more difficult to learn is that they violate the principle of mutual exclusivity. I will argue later (chapters 8 and 9) that one constraint on word meanings, in addition to the taxonomic constraint discussed in chapter 2, is that children assume that category terms are mutually exclusive. That is,

each object should have only one category label. In fact, at the basic level of categorization, categories and category terms do largely conform to this principle. "Cat," "dog," and "rabbit" and "chair," "table," and "couch" are nonoverlapping, mutually exclusive categories. Given that children acquire basic level terms first, then superordinate terms and subordinate terms will violate mutual exclusivity. A child who knows that a given object is a dog will be troubled or confused by claims that it is a poodle or an animal.

Summary and Conclusions

To return to our original question, how is it that when children hear a category label, they determine which of the many possible categories the label refers to? The answer is that a number of factors may bias children toward assuming that the term refers to some intermediate level of categorization. It is not that children consider a variety of alternatives and settle on the basic level, but rather that the basic level, or something approximating the basic level, is the level of categorization that first comes to mind for children, as long as they do not yet have a label for the object. Many factors have been proposed to account for the relative simplicity or relative salience of the basic level category compared to others, and conversely for the relative difficulty of the superordinate level of categorization. Superordinate categories may be more difficult for children because they have few perceptual features in common and are instead defined in terms of common function; they may behave for children as ad hoc categories do for adults—being less explicitly represented and requiring a context to be retrieved or generated; and they violate the principle of mutual exclusivity.

Basic level categories may be simpler because category exemplars are relatively similar, while contrasting well with other categories at the same level, because they often have a common overall shape, and because they have many parts in common. In addition, they are defined by correlated attributes.

As I argued earlier, the basic level may be relatively simple and relatively salient because it is the level at which these various criteria tend to converge rather than because any one of them is definitive. Individual tests of these criteria have often failed to show them as being sufficient for determining the way in which people categorize. The one criterion that stands out from the rest as potentially the most important is that basic level categories mirror the correlational structure of the world. Correlated features have been demonstrated to be an important cue that serves as the basis of categorization (see Medin

1983). In the next chapter we will see that the correlational structure is important for the implications and consequences of categorization, and not just for the acquisition of categories. Moreover, we will see that children not only use correlated features to acquire categories, but in fact may start out assuming that categories have a correlated structure that goes well beyond what can be determined by visual inspection of exemplars. That is, children may assume that category members have properties in common that are not apparent from their perceptual features.

Chapter 5
Natural Kinds

In this chapter about natural kind terms I pursue the suggestion that children might expect categories, or at least categories of a special status, to have a correlated structure.

Recent arguments in philosophy about natural kind terms provide another challenge to traditional theories of concepts (Kripke 1971, 1972; Putnam 1970). According to these analyses, natural kind terms do not have meaning in the traditional sense.

The term "natural kind" has various uses in philosophy and psychology, but to begin with some clear cases, natural kinds are categories that are found in nature, such as various categories of plants and animals. For example, the categories "mammal," "gold," and "water" are all natural kinds.

One of the most distinctive characteristics of natural kinds is the remarkable richness of their correlated structure. According to Mill (1843),

> Some classes have little or nothing in common to characterize them by, except precisely what is connoted by the name. (p. 135)

Consider the category of white things.

> White things are not distinguished by any common properties except whiteness or if they are—it is only by such as are in some way dependent upon or connected with whiteness. . . . But hundreds of generations have not exhausted the common properties of animal or plants. . . . If anyone were to propose for the investigation the common properties of all things which are of the same color, the same shape, or the same specific gravity, the absurdity would be palpable. . . . Of these two classifications, the one answers to a much more radical distinction in the things themselves than the other does. One classification is made by *nature*, the other by us. (p. 136)

Thus, some categories allow us to infer a great deal about their members. A related point has been made about basic level categories, which also have a correlated structure (Rosch et al. 1976); for example, if we know that something is a bird, we know that it has feathers and wings, that it is quite likely to have a beak and to fly, and so on. Mill's claim is that some categories have such an extraordinarily rich correlated structure that even after extensive study of the category, we have not exhausted all there is to learn about it. We have sciences devoted to discovering and understanding different animal species such as mammals. Although a category such as "mammal" may have originally been delimited by a few superficial features, such as having fur or hair, members of the category have unforeseen properties in common. We have continued to discover properties that are characteristic of mammals, so much so that separate scientific disciplines are needed to account for the accumulation of knowledge. The properties of mammals figure in scientific laws or generalizations from various sciences, including physiology, anatomy, genetics, and ethology. The fact that several scientific disciplines continue to discover new facts about this category is testimony to how richly structured it is.

Now, to take Mill's contrasting example, consider a category defined as "white things." If it seemed important or useful, we could certainly define such a category; yet we could not have a science devoted to determining what these diverse objects that happen to be white have in common. This category has a minimal correlated structure. It includes a white cloud but excludes a grey one. It includes a white car but excludes cars of any other color. It includes white paper but excludes yellow paper, and so on. Being white does not tell us very much about an object beyond the fact that it is white. Whiteness does not correlate with or predict much else.

The Causal Theory of Reference

The new theory of reference for natural kinds poses several problems for traditional theories of meaning. According to the traditional view (see chapters 1 and 3), each category term has both an intension (the set of necessary and sufficient properties that define the concept) and an extension (the set of objects to which the term applies). The intension specifies the criteria that determine which objects will make up the extension. That is, in order for an object to be in the extension of the term, it must satisfy the relevant criteria. To take a concrete example, consider the concept "square." The intension of the term "square" is an equilateral quadrangle with four right angles. In order for an object to be a square, it must fulfill these criteria; that is, it must have four sides, four right angles, and so on. The extension of the word "square" is the set of objects that meet these criteria. That is, the extension of the word "square" is composed of the objects that are squares.

One view of category terms that contrasts with this traditional view has already been discussed in chapter 3, under family resemblances. On this view, there may be no features that are necessary and sufficient; instead, the intension of the term consists of a set of features some number of which must apply to an object for it to qualify as an instance of the category. As long as an object has enough of the relevant features, it will qualify; it is not required to fulfill all of them.

What these two views have in common, however, is that they are both criterial accounts of category terms; that is, both claim that the meaning of a category term derives in some way or another from a set of criteria associated with that category. In this regard, the causal theory of reference contrasts with both the classical view and the family resemblance view of categories. In a major departure from the typical way of looking at category terms, Kripke (1971, 1972) and Putnam (1977) suggest that category terms be treated on analogy with proper names. This is a radical view, because on their treatment, at least, proper names do not have criterial meaning in the ordinary sense. (For a good summary of the issues, see Schwartz 1977.) As an example, consider the proper name "Shakespeare." We know a fair amount about Shakespeare—for example, that he was the author of *Hamlet, Romeo and Juliet,* and so on. Imagine a list of such facts about Shakespeare that we would use to identify him or describe him to someone who does not yet know who he is. It is possible, however, that we are mistaken about these facts. It could turn out that Shakespeare never really wrote those plays and that our beliefs about him were therefore erroneous. Nevertheless, the name "Shakespeare" would still apply to the same person. We wouldn't decide that we were wrong and that that person isn't really Shakespeare. We would conclude instead that Shakespeare did not write those plays. Thus, the facts or descriptions that we might use to identify Shakespeare do not function as *criteria.* They are not necessary and sufficient features of what it takes to be Shakespeare. They are beliefs about Shakespeare that are helpful in *identifying* him, but they do not constitute criteria in the traditional sense.

Kripke argues that instead of being based on criteria, the "meaning" of a proper name derives from the causal history of its use, going back to its first introduction, on analogy with a baptismal ceremony. Moreover, he claims, proper names refer to the same individual, even in counterfactual situations. When we ask, "If Johnson had not declined to run again, would Nixon have been elected president?", there is no question that we are still referring to Nixon, even though he might not have been president. We would still be using the proper name "Nixon" to refer to Nixon. The name refers to the same individual even when used in hypothetical discussions where important facts about the world and about the individual in question are changed.

Analysis of Natural Kind Terms

According to Kripke and Putnam, there are important analogies in the way that natural kind terms and proper names function. First, Kripke and Putnam argue that many of the properties that we may have taken to define a category term do not really do so. The claim is that the superficial properties that we use to identify natural kind categories do not function as necessary and sufficient criteria and that in fact each such property could be violated and yet we would still agree on the classification of the object. Putnam uses the existence of abnormal members of categories to demonstrate this point. As a way of describing the natural kind term "lemon," one might specify that lemons have an oval shape, yellow skin, and a sour taste. Yet one could imagine a change in some chemical in the atmosphere that would modify the pigment in the skin, causing lemons to become green. Similarly, a change in the nutrients in the soil could effect a change in the taste of lemons, causing them to be bitter, and so on. Yet, Putnam argues, despite all of these changes in the properties we have listed, we would still agree that these (green, bitter) objects are lemons. That is, the word "lemon" would still refer to lemons despite the changes that we would need to make in the description of the properties. To further illustrate this point, Putnam notes that what we currently take to be normal members of the category might, in fact, be abnormal members. Perhaps lemons were originally green and bitter but alterations in the chemical composition of the atmosphere and land have caused them to be yellow and sour.

On this causal theory of reference, the descriptions that we give for natural kinds function just like the descriptions we might give for a proper name. They are useful in identifying the objects in question, and they may effectively describe the stereotype we have of the object, but they do not qualify as criteria for the category. Even if the superficial properties change, the natural kind term will continue to refer to the same category.

Given this rejection of the traditional account of meaning, two questions naturally arise: How is the referent for a term established? and How can we tell whether or not the term is being used correctly—for example, how do we know that an object we call a "lemon" is in fact a lemon?

According to this theory, the reference of a term may be established by a causal chain, by analogy to the way the reference for proper names is established. While the object is present, someone labels the object, and that provides the first link in a causal chain in which subsequent speakers continue to use the label to refer to the same kind of object. For natural kind terms, speakers will typically select a prototypical exemplar to label at first, and they may provide a description of the natural kind to identify the relevant category. The description does not define the category, however, but serves as a way of helping speakers to fix the referent, that is, to identify what is being labeled. Tigers might be described as large, striped, ferocious, wild cats to enable someone to identify what objects are being referred to as "tigers." Yet under some circumstances we might readily agree that a small, albino, tame cat was, nevertheless, a tiger. First, Putnam points out that there is a "division of linguistic labor." Not everyone need acquire the methods for determining whether or not something is gold, for example. Instead, we may often rely on experts to make the final determination. But what do the experts rely on? Experts base their judgments on the best scientific knowledge that is available at the time—on the most well established empirical theory. In the case of gold, its atomic number will be the deciding factor; in the case of water, its molecular formula (H_2O); and in the case of lemons, their chromosomal structure. Here Putnam embraces a kind of essentialism. The assumption is that there are some "deep" properties, or hidden structural properties, that account for or determine what the more superficial properties will be. These structural properties establish the "essential nature which the thing shares with other members of the natural kind. What the essential nature is is not a matter of language analysis but of scientific theory construction" (Putnam 1977, 104).

Contrast this analysis of natural kind terms with a standard analysis of more arbitrary "one-criterion" terms, such as Mill's example of "white things." Here the properties we would give to describe the meaning of the term would function as a definition and not just as a useful aid to identifying the category. If the properties changed—for example, if pollution turned all white things a dingy grey—they would no longer be white things. We do not have a scientific theory of white things to rely on, nor do we expect there to be some deep, hidden structure that is common to all white things.

Each of these points—the unlimited richness of the categories, the search for more theory-relevant explanatory properties, the reliance on authority to distinguish exemplars of a category from nonexemplars, the acceptance of abnormal members, and the corrigibility of beliefs about categories—distinguishes natural kinds from other types of categories.

Natural Kinds and Induction

Susan Gelman and I (Gelman and Markman 1986, 1987) have argued that this analysis of natural kinds, especially the emphasis on the richness of the structure and the belief that unobservable properties are common to members of a natural kind, predicts that natural kinds will often be used to support inductive inferences from one category member to another. That is, if categories are structured so as to capture indefinitely rich clusters of information, then new features learned about one category member will often be projected onto other category members as well. In this way, natural kind categories should promote inductive inferences. Moreover, there are two ways in which the inductions are made without perceptual support. First, even if an object does not look much like other members of a given natural kind, knowing what kind it belongs to should lead people to assume that it will share relevant properties with other members of the category. Second, these properties, such as internal organs or chemical structure, are often unobservable by the average person.

Certainly, only some types of inferences within a kind are justified. Whether the inference is reasonable or not depends in part on what type of property is attributed to what type of natural kind. Among animal species, for example, we expect members of the same species to share methods of reproduction, respiration, and locomotion. We do not expect other kinds of properties to be common even to members of the same species. For example, if one poodle is 2 years old, we should not expect another poodle also to be 2 years old. Thus, at least implicitly, people have embedded natural kind categories in scientific or prescientific theories that limit what classes of properties are expected to be common to a given natural kind category.

Little is known about how expectations about natural kinds originate. How much exploration of categories or even explicit scientific training is needed before children come to expect that categories reflect more than superficial perceptual similarities? There is a large developmental literature suggesting that young children rely on superficial perceptual properties on cognitive tasks, including those involving classification, free recall, free association, and word definitions (see Flavell 1963, 1977; Mansfield 1977). Young children have often been characterized as "concrete" and as "perceptually bound," meaning that their cognition is captured by the appearances of things. A well-known example is the Piagetian conservation problems. In a task involving conservation of number, for example, two equal rows of objects—say, pennies—are lined up in one-to-one correspondence. Children judge that both rows have the same number of pennies. Then, while the child watches, one of the rows is spread out. Children now judge that the lengthened row has more pennies. One interpretation of this is that the children are unable to overlook the misleading perceptual cue of the length of the row. Their judgment of equality or inequality is presumably based on the available perceptual information rather than on the actual quantity. To take an example concerning categorization, Tversky (1985) has found that young children prefer to group objects together on the basis of color or shape rather than on the basis of common category membership. On one of her tasks, for example, a 4-year-old typically groups a fire engine with an apple because both are red rather than grouping a fire engine with a car because both are vehicles. In this task and others, children seem unable to override what are sometimes misleading perceptual cues.

Based on these findings, one might expect that young children would rely heavily on perceptual characteristics of objects for judgments of category membership. Young children may have no means of appreciating the rationale for grouping perceptually dissimilar objects together. Even for natural kinds, children might represent category members as sharing superficial properties and only later come to realize that they have deeper properties in common. Thus, according to this view, children, with their reliance on perceptual features and their limited scientific knowledge, should not rely on natural kind categories to support inductive inferences about objects.

On the other hand, given the importance of natural kind categories for human cognition, children might quite early on expect categories to have a richly correlated structure. Even with only rudimentary scientific knowledge, children might believe that natural kind categories are united by many unobservable properties. Children could be biased from the start to expect that categories they learn will share clusters of features, or such an expectation could be derived from experience. Even with only limited scientific knowledge, children could notice that natural kinds have many observable features in common. They could then extend this belief and expect natural kinds to be united by many unobservable properties as well. Any appreciation of natural kinds at this early age would probably reflect an unsophisticated, undifferentiated belief in the richness of categories. Children would lack the requisite scientific knowledge that could limit their inductions to categories and attributes that are appropriate.

One piece of evidence that children are not solely dependent on perceptual similarity for drawing inferences comes from work by Carey (1985). In one study she showed several groups of children between ages 4 and 10 a mechanical monkey, one that could move its arms to bang cymbals together. The mechanical monkey looked much like a real monkey. Children, who knew that real monkeys breathe, eat, and have baby monkeys, were asked whether the mechanical monkey could breathe, eat, and have babies too. All but one group of 4-year-old children denied that the mechanical monkey possessed these animate properties. In other words, despite the striking perceptual similarity of these two types of objects—mechanical and real monkeys—children did not generalize facts about one to the other. These children had differentiated living things from nonliving things and therefore refused to impute properties that characterize living things to nonliving things. It could be, however, that it is only at the level of such basic ontological distinctions (Keil 1979) such as living versus nonliving that children treat categories as natural kinds.

Gelman and I (Gelman and Markman 1986) questioned children about much more specific natural kind categories, from both biological (e.g., squirrel and snake) and nonbiological (e.g., gold and salt) domains. To determine whether children would induce new information from natural kind categories, rather than from perceptual appearances, we pitted category membership against perceptual similarity. Children were shown two objects and told a new fact abut each. They then had to infer which of the facts applied to a third object that looked very much like one of the first two objects but was given the same category label as the other one. These experiments test whether very young children are sensitive to the richness of natural kind categories and whether they use these categories, in the absence of perceptual support, to justify inductive inferences.

One of the main assumptions about natural kind categories that motivated our developmental work is that adults expect members of a natural kind to share many properties and will therefore use the natural kind category to support inductive inferences. In particular, adults should rely on the natural kind membership of an object more than on its superficial perceptual appearance to make inferences about its internal structure, behavior, and other theoretically relevant properties. Gelman and I conducted a preliminary study (reported in Gelman and Markman (1986) to establish that adults would use the natural kind category to support inductions for those categories that would later be used with children.

Undergraduates were presented with 20 problems. Each problem consisted of a set of three pictures. New information was given about two of the pictures, then a question was asked about the third picture. The correct answer could not be determined from the picture. The subject could arrive at one of two answers: either by making an inference based on category membership or by making a different inference based on perceptual similarity.

The three pictures for each problem were arranged on a card. Two pictures were at the top of the card, and the third (the target) was directly underneath, centered below the first two. Directly below each of the two topmost pictures was a sentence that labeled the picture and provided some new factual information about it. Directly below the target picture was a question asking which of two new attributes applied. For example, on one problem subjects saw a flamingo and a bat at the top of the card. Underneath the flamingo was written, "This bird's heart has a right aortic arch only." Underneath the bat was written, "This bat's heart has a left aortic arch only." Below these two pictures was a picture of a blackbird (which looked more like the bat than the flamingo). Underneath the blackbird was written, "What does this bird's heart have?" For each item, subjects were to choose one of the two answers. After each choice they were asked to justify their selection by responding to the question, "Why is this the best answer?" Finally they were asked to rate their confidence in their answer on a scale from "1" (very unsure) to "7" (very sure).

As predicted, adults based their inferences on the common natural kind membership of the objects. Overall, they concluded that the target picture had the same property as the other similarly labeled object an average of 86% of the time. Apparently subjects expected slightly more variation within a category for the biological categories than for the nonbiological categories. They inferred properties on the basis of common category 92% of the time for the nonbiological categories and 80% of the time for the biological categories. In addition, subjects were highly confident that their choices were correct (the mean rating was 5.8 on the 7-point scale). However, they were significantly more confident about their judgments for the nonbiological categories (mean = 6.0) than biological categories (mean = 5.5).

Young children might, like the adults, infer a new property of an object from its category, or they might instead be governed by the perceptual appearances of the objects. In study 1 from Gelman and Markman 1986 children were tested on the same categories as the adult subjects in the preliminary study. They were asked about different attributes, however, because they would not understand most of the ones that adults were questioned about.

Preschool children ranging in age from 4:0 to 4:11 (with a mean age of 4:5) participated in the study.

There were three conditions in this study. In the experimental condition children were taught information about each of two objects. They were then shown a third object that looked like one of the two training objects but was given the same category label as the other. Children were asked to infer which piece of information applied to the third object. This condition was designed to reveal whether children's influences are influenced by their knowledge of an object's category or by perceptual similarity.

A second condition, the no-conflict control, was designed to demonstrate that when perceptual similarity and category membership coincide, children readily draw the correct inferences. In this condition, like the first, children were taught properties of two objects. However, the third object not only looked like one of the training objects but also was given the same label as that object. This task provides a baseline measure for how often children will draw the correct inference when both perceptual similarity and category membership lead to the same conclusion.

A final condition, the attributes control, was designed to make certain that children did not already know the information we would be teaching them. Children saw only one picture at a time—the third item in the other two conditions—and were asked which of the two properties applied. Children were expected to perform at about chance level in this condition.

Since the experiment proper involved teaching children new properties about two objects and asking them to judge which of the properties applied to a third object, it was important to ensure that children did not already know the information to be presented. A preliminary study was conducted to select questions about various animals, plants, and substances to which children would not yet know the answers.

An item was selected for inclusion in the experiment proper only if children were unable to answer the question significantly above or below chance. Table 5.1 shows examples of items that were selected. Half of the items concerned biological natural kinds and half concerned nonbiological natural kinds.

In the experimental condition, children saw 20 sets of three pictures each. Information was given concerning two of the pictures in each set, and children were asked a question about the third picture. The third picture looked like one of the first two pictures but was

Table 5.1
Sample items and attributes used in Gelman and Markman 1986

Biological items
This squirrel eats bugs. (gray squirrel)*
This rabbit eats grass. (brown rabbit)
(Target:) squirrel (Kaibab, looks like rabbit)
This dinosaur has cold blood. (brontosaurus)
This rhinoceros has warm blood. (gray rhinoceros)
(Target:) dinosaur (triceratops, look like rhinoceros)
Nonbiological items
If you put this gold in a hot oven, it melts. (gold bar)
If you put this clay in a hot oven, it burns. (reddish blob)
(Target:) gold (brown blob; looks like clay)
This pearl comes from inside a sea animal. (seed pearl)
This marble comes from a big piece of rock. (round, pink)
(Target:) pearl (round, pink; looks like marble)

*Descriptions of the objects used are given in parentheses. These descriptions were *not* mentioned to subjects.

given the same category label as the other. Children could answer on the basis of either perceptual similarity or category membership. For example, children were shown a tropical fish, a dolphin, and a shark. In this case the shark was perceptually similar to the dolphin but was given the same label as the tropical fish. The experimenter labeled the three pictures, "fish" for the tropical fish, "dolphin" for the dolphin, and "fish" for the shark. Children were asked to repeat the names until they could name all three pictures correctly. (On 88% of the trials, children repeated all three names correctly on their first try.) The experimenter then pointed to the tropical fish and said, "This fish stays underwater to breathe." She pointed to the dolphin and said, "This dolphin pops above the water to breathe." Finally she pointed to the shark and said, "See this fish. Does it breathe underwater, like this fish, or does it pop above the water to breathe, like this dolphin?" Comparable questions were asked for each item in table 5.1. Figure 5.1 presents an example of another triad: bird, bat, bird.

In the no-conflict control condition, the picture triads and procedure used were identical to those used in the experimental condition, with one exception. In this case the labels of the two similar objects were made to agree rather than conflict. For example, children heard the tropical fish labeled "fish," the dolphin labeled "dolphin," and the third picture (shark) labeled "dolphin" (instead of "fish" as in the

Figure 5.1:
The bird, bat, bird triad from Gelman and Markman (1986).

previous condition). The children in this condition were provided with the same information about the two initial pictures—that is, that the fish breathes underwater and the dolphin pops above the water to breathe. The experimenter then pointed to the third picture and said, "See this dolphin. Does it breathe underwater, like this fish, or does it pop above the water to breathe, like this dolphin?"

In the attributes control condition children viewed only one picture at a time—the third item from each of the triads in the experimental condition. Without hearing any prior information, children were asked to judge which of the two properties applied. For example, children were shown the picture of the shark and asked, "See this fish. Does this fish breathe underwater or does it pop above the water to breathe?"

The main question that this study was designed to address is whether preschool children are willing to infer properties of an object based on its natural kind category. In particular, when category membership and perceptual similarity are in conflict, will children show any sensitivity to category membership, or will their inferences be based on the appearance of the objects? If children do use category membership as a basis for induction even in the absence of perceptual support, it is likely that they will do so for some conceptual domains before others. Therefore, we included both biological and nonbiological natural kinds, to test for generality. Table 5.2 presents the data according to condition and item type.

To address these questions, we first needed to establish that chil-

Table 5.2
Percent correct (category choices) from Gelman and Markman 1986

	Experimental condition	No-conflict control condition	Attributes control condition
Biological	67	89	59
Nonbiological	69	87	48

dren's inferences in the experimental condition were based on the information provided to them in the experiment rather than on preexisting knowledge. The results of the attributes control condition indicate that children were in fact unaware of the correct answers. When simply given the test question, with no extra information to guide their answer, children performed at chance level, answering a mean of 53% of the questions correctly.

On the other hand, when the perceptual similarity and category label coincided in the no-conflict control condition, children were capable of drawing the correct inference. When both the label and the appearance of the object led to the same conclusion, children were correct on 88% of the items.

In the experimental condition, where perceptual similarity and category membership were opposed, children preferred to use the category information 68% of the time, which is significantly better than chance, $p < .001$. Thirty-seven percent of the children consistently based their judgments on common category membership; that is, they inferred the property of the new object based on category membership on at least 15 out of 20 items. In contrast, no child showed a consistent preference for basing inferences on the perceptual similarity of the objects.

Thus, the children in the experimental condition were taking account of the training information in deciding about the properties of the new objects, as performance in that condition was better than in the attributes control condition. Although children in the experimental condition often based their judgments on the natural kind category of the object, they were in some conflict because of the divergence between category membership and perceptual appearances. Also, giving the category name may not be a perfect way of establishing category membership. That is, this procedure tests the power of the category in governing inductive inferences only insofar as the label successfully conveys the natural kind category. Some failure to respond to the category may reflect some degree of weakness in this for children, and not necessarily weakness in natural kind inductions per se. When category labels and perceptual similarity coincided (the no-conflict control condition), children answered more questions correctly.

Children were able to use category membership as often for the biological as for the nonbiological categories. Overall the mean correct was 67% for the biological and 69% for the nonbiological categories. However, there was a sex difference in the experimental condition. Boys performed better on the biological categories than on the nonbiological categories, whereas girls showed the reverse pattern. We could not explain this difference, although it is possible that boys and girls differ in which categories they find more familiar. Boys may be more familiar with such things as snakes, worms, bugs, and leaves (that is, the biological categories we tested), whereas girls may be more familiar with such things as sugar, salt, diamonds, and pearls (the nonbiological categories we tested).

In summary, even 4-year-olds realize that natural kind categories such as "squirrel" and "diamond" promote a rich set of inductive inferences. These young children have already come to expect new knowledge to be organized in accord with the categories named by their language, even in the stringent test case where the label conflicts with perceptual appearances. Using a simplified procedure, Gelman and Markman (1987), determined that this conclusion extends to 3-year-olds as well. For these young children, the procedure used in Gelman and Markman 1986 was too demanding. Instead of pitting objects against each other, we taught children a new fact about an object (as before) and then determined which objects it would generalize to: an object that (a) looked like the original, (b) had the same label as the original, (c) looked like the original and had the same label, or (d) differed from the original in both respects. The findings were that children drew more inferences based on category membership than inferences based on perceptual appearances. Thus, even 3-year-olds assume that categories named by their language will include more than superficial features.

Study 3 of Gelman and Markman 1986 addressed two questions raised by this finding. One question was whether identity of the linguistic information is necessary for children to use the common category as a basis for inductive inferences, or whether other means of indicating common category membership would be sufficient. To address this question, we designed a synonyms condition in which category membership was conveyed by means of synonyms rather than identical labels. For example, one triplet consisted of a target rabbit, another rabbit with a different appearance, and a squirrel that had long ears and looked like the target rabbit. The two rabbits in the synonyms condition were called "rabbit" and "bunny." If children infer that objects named by synonyms share the same properties, then their inferences cannot be based simply on identity of the labels.

Another question that was addressed in study 3 of Gelman and Markman 1986 was whether children would use the common category to make arbitrary decisions for which common category membership is not relevant. To test this, we designed an arbitrary decision condition in which children were asked to decide what color chip should go on a picture after witnessing the experimenter place a chip of one color on a perceptually similar picture and a chip of another color on a dissimilar picture with the same category label. For example, the experimenter placed a red dot on the picture of one rabbit (called "rabbit") and a yellow dot on the picture of the squirrel (called "squirrel"). The child then had to pick which color dot to put on the third picture, the other rabbit (called "rabbit") that looked like the squirrel. If children are distinguishing between the induction task, where category labels are relevant, and this arbitrary task, where they are not, then they should be at chance in this condition, having no real basis on which to make a decision.

The third condition in this study was the standard condition that replicated the procedure of the experimental condition in the first study using the items that appeared in the synonyms and arbitrary decision conditions.

In the standard condition children once again drew inferences to category members at an above-chance level (68%). As before, even when the category conflicted with perceptual appearances, children tended to base their inductive inferences on the common category membership. Moreover, as the results from the synonyms condition indicated, children do not need to hear common labels to use common category membership to draw inferences. When children heard synonyms to indicate common category membership, they still based their inferences on category membership at a level greater than chance (63% of the time). The results of this study further indicate that children have begun to differentiate between inferences where category membership is relevant and arbitrary decisions where it is not. When children were asked about arbitrary decisions such as what color chip should go on a given picture, they were no more likely to base that decision on the color chip they had seen placed on a common category member than to base it on a chip placed on a perceptually similar picture.

In summary, children's inferences were based on the category membership of the objects and not simply on how the pictures were labeled. Children drew inferences based on common category membership even when category members were not given identical labels. Moreover, when category members were given identical labels, children relied on these labels only when the task required them to draw inferences.

From these studies, we know that young children will infer that an object shares properties with another object from the same category, even when these inferences do not have perceptual support. With the exception of the completely arbitrary property, the properties that were examined were ones that in fact would be largely determined by the natural kind category of the objects. That is, we asked about the internal organs, method of respiration, feeding habits, behavior, and so on, of animals—all properties that typically are common to a species. Similarly, we asked about the internal structure and chemical and physical properties of the nonbiological categories—again, all properties that typically are common to a mineral, metal, or other substance.

There are cases, however, where inductive inferences based on category membership would be unwarranted. For some properties, the perceptual similarity of objects should be used as the basis for induction rather than the common category membership. The size of an object, for example, is a better predictor of its weight than is its category.

Study 4 of Gelman and Markman 1986 examined whether young children are selective in the kinds of inferences that they make based on category judgments. Preschool children have impoverished scientific knowledge, yet they believe that category members share unobservable properties. This implies that their beliefs about categories may be fairly general ones, not modulated by specific knowledge. In other words, such young children may not have sorted out which properties legitimately do and do not promote inferences within natural kind categories. They might, then, erroneously infer information on the basis of common category membership, even when asked about attributes that are more likely to be consequences of superficial perceptual properties. If attention to category membership dominates their judgments regardless of type of property, then children should assert, for example, that a rocklike chunk of salt will blow away in the wind as does fine-grained salt, and not remain in place as does a rock.

In this experiment children were taught a fact about each of two objects and then asked which of the properties applied to a third object. The third object was from the same category as one of the objects but was more similar in appearance to the other object. Unlike the previous studies, however, the properties were predicted more by perceptual similarity than by common category membership.

This study had two conditions, an experimental condition and a control condition. Children in the control condition were given the final test questions without any extra information. For example, they were shown a shark and were asked, "This is a fish. Do you think it weighs 20 pounds or 100 pounds?"

The procedure for the experimental condition was identical to that of the earlier studies, except that different attributes were being taught. Children viewed three objects, two placed side by side and one centered beneath them. Each object was labeled. A property was attributed to each of the two topmost pictures, and the children were then asked which of the properties applied to the third (target) picture. For example, after the pictures were labeled, children were told about a tropical fish, "This fish weighs 20 pounds." They were told about an object from a different category, in this case a dolphin, that, "This dolphin weighs 100 pounds." They were then asked about the target picture, a shark that looked more like the dolphin than the tropical fish, "See this fish. Does it weigh 20 pounds, like this fish, or 100 pounds, like this dolphin?"

In this study children were asked questions about perceptually based attributes: weight, visibility at night, and so forth. With no prior information on which to make inferences, children in the control condition selected the category choice no more often than expected by chance (48% of the time). In contrast to what happened in the earlier studies, fewer children in the experimental condition based their inferences on common category membership. They selected on the basis of common category an average of 49% of the time, which is not significantly different from chance or from the control group. However, the experimental condition, unlike the control condition, was markedly trimodal. Four of the 20 children consistently selected on the basis of perceptual similarity (that is, they chose the attribute of the perceptually similar picture on at least 15 out of 20 items); and 4 children consistently selected on the basis of common category membership even though that choice was unwarranted. The remaining 12 children did not seem to know which answer to choose, with a mean of 47% categorical choices. This condition contrasts with the control condition, in which none of the 20 children had a consistent preference.

Children who based their inferences predominantly on common category membership were overgeneralizing the importance of the category label. It was unwarranted to assume, for example, that a legless lizard can run as quickly as a four-legged lizard, or that a large pearl weighs as much as a smaller pearl. These children understood the importance of category names to promote induction but were not yet selective in their inferences.

Overall, however, children in this study who were asked about these perceptually based properties relied less on the category than did children in the earlier studies. Many of the children were sensitive to the differences between attributes such as weight that are consequences of perceptual properties and attributes such as means of respiration that are common to the members of a species. Of all the studies presented in Gelman and Markman 1986, this was the only one in which subjects chose predominantly on the basis of shared appearance. In this study of attributes derived from perceptual information, 20% of the children consistently based their judgments on perceptual similarity compared to only 1% of the children asked about attributes common to natural kind categories.

Summary of the Findings from Gelman and Markman 1986, 1987

On each of a series of problems, children had to decide whether a given object possessed one or the other of two attributes. On hearing the question alone, with no prior information to guide them, children had no basis for forming an induction and, as expected, simply guessed at which property applied. In two other conditions children were first told which attribute applied to each of two training objects. In the simple case where one of the training objects matched the target object in both appearance and natural kind category, 4-year-old children almost always drew the appropriate inference. Their performance was excellent, and establishes that the simple inferential problem is well within the capacity of young children.

The most informative condition was the one in which perceptual appearance and the natural kind category of an object led to divergent conclusions. Children relied on the shared category to promote inductions, even in this stringent case where perceptual similarity would lead to a different conclusion. Moreover, children's inferences were based on common category membership and not just on identity of labels. When members of the same category were given synonymous labels children still preferred to draw inferences within the category, at an above-chance level.

These results are at odds with a widely held view that children's thinking is strongly influenced by perceptual appearances. On this view, if young children draw inductions at all, they should rely more on perceptual characteristics of objects than on their category membership. Several of our findings suggest that children are not dominated by appearances either in their conception of the structure of categories or in their use of categories to support inductions.

First, most children accepted our label for the third object even though it looked more like a member of the other category. For example, one object was a squirrel with very long, rabbitlike ears. Overall, it looked more like a typical rabbit than a squirrel. Some children noted the discrepancy (remarking, for instance, "funny rabbit") and some even mildly objected to the label, but, for the most part, they accepted the labels for these abnormal category members. This finding is consistent with work by Flavell, Flavell, and Green (1983) on the development of the appearance-reality distinction. Flavell, Flavell, and Green showed 3- to 5-year-olds fake objects (for example, a sponge that looked like a rock) and then let them feel the objects to discover their true identity. On later questioning, children tended to say not only that the object was a sponge, rather than a rock, but also that it looked like a sponge. Like our subjects, these children accepted the category label even in the face of discrepant appearance.

Second, only 1 of 69 children in this condition consistently generalized properties on the basis of perceptual similarity between objects. Even though the rabbit and the rabbit-eared squirrel looked very much alike, children did not assume that they both ate grass. Whatever perceptual biases children have, they are overridden by the belief that members of a natural kind share many other properties as well.

Third, in each of the studies (studies 1–3 of Gelman and Markman 1986) children in the standard condition reliably used the category of the object to support inductive inferences, even when this conflicted with the appearance of the objects.

Children drew these inferences when asked about properties that were reasonable to project from one category member to another. We asked about the eating habits, means of respiration, and internal organs of the biological categories and about chemical and physical properties of the nonbiological categories. Young children, able to answer these questions correctly, might overgeneralize the importance of the natural kind category. That is, even when it is unwarranted to do so, they may use categories more than appearances to support inductions. The results of subsequent studies indicate ways in which children have begun to limit the importance of the category. First, when the task involves making an arbitrary decision, children are not biased to infer on the basis of category membership. Second, children have at least begun to distinguish some kinds of properties from others as a basis for induction. To test this, we asked children about properties that should generalize on the basis of superficial perceptual similarity rather than on category membership. In answering such questions, children did not reliably use the category to support the inductions. Across several studies, those children who were asked about perceptually based properties were the only ones to reliably use the perceptual appearances of objects to support their inductions.

By age 3 and 4 children expect natural kinds to have a richly correlated structure that goes beyond superficial appearances. They use category membership to support inductions, even in the stringent test case where perceptual appearance and category label lead to different conclusions. Moreover, children have begun to differentiate between the kinds of properties that can justifiably be projected to other category members and those that cannot. Despite all these accomplishments, however, there is much left for children to learn about natural kind categories.

The Problem of Determining Which Properties Support Inductive Inferences

First, children must sort out which properties are likely to be common to members of different types of natural kinds. Although they have begun to work out this problem by age 4, their distinctions on even a crude level are imperfect. Even with properties that for adults are blatantly determined by superficial perceptual features (such as weight), some children based their inductions on the category—claiming, for example, that a large fish weighs the same amount as a little fish, because both are fish. Furthermore, there are constraints on inferences that no one has yet been able to characterize (Goodman 1955). Even for adults, we do not have good theories to explain how inferences are constrained.[1] A predicate may or may not promote inductions, depending on the level of abstraction of a category (all dogs bark, but not all animals bark) or the scientific domain (density at room temperature is important for metals but not animals). Nisbett, Krantz, and Kunda (1983) have shown that adults are quite willing to infer new information from one category member to other members of the same category, but they do so selectively, depending on the property involved. Our studies have not tested the limits of children's

---

1. Sternberg (1982) has found that familiarity and complexity of a predicate affect how quickly adults can process it. However, familiarity and complexity alone cannot characterize the sorts of inferences we draw. Certainly, some simple and familiar predicates (say, "has a fever" or "is 3 days old") are not projectable. For example, just because one poodle is 3 days old, we do not expect the next poodle we see also to be 3 days old. Hence it is not clear how to extend Sternberg's findings to the problem of what confirms some inductions and not others.

abilities, but even so it is clear that children must develop more finely tuned distinctions among predicates and learn not to overgeneralize to obviously inappropriate predicates.

The Problem of Determining Which Categories Support Inductive Inferences

A related issue is how to constrain which kinds of categories support inductions. Some categories, such as "artifacts," do not pick out objects in nature that have indefinitely many properties in common. We do not assume, for example, that all forks or all saws will have unlimited numbers of properties in common. It is possible that children could very early on notice the natural kind–artifact distinction and use categories to support inductions mainly for natural kinds. It is also possible that children would begin by expecting most categories named by language to promote inductive inferences. That is, they would assume for a variety of conceptual domains that category members share many features with each other. Only after learning more about various domains would they restrict their inferences.

To address this question, Gelman (1984) draws several distinctions between types of concepts. Natural kinds are expected to share many features besides the obvious ones, whereas artifacts are not. This is not a strict dichotomy, however, as some complex artifacts (computers and cars, for example) are probably similar to natural kinds. Building on findings from Rips (1975) and Nisbett, Krantz, and Kunda (1983), Gelman argues that in addition to the complexity of the category, assumptions about its homogeneity also may well affect how likely it is to support inductive inferences. For example, adults will infer that other samples of a metal conduct electricity, given that one sample of the metal does, but they will not infer that other people within a geographical region are obese, given that one person in that region is (Nisbett, Krantz, and Kunda 1983). Adults rely on their conception of how variable the property is within the domain being questioned (for instance, conductivity for metals) to make their inferences. Gelman suggests that natural kinds tend to be more homogeneous than artifacts and therefore support more inferences. Another possibility, however, is that it is homogeneity of the category per se, rather than its natural kind status, that predicts which categories are more likely to support certain inductions.

In a series of studies Gelman had adults rate categories in various ways to determine whether they perceive natural kinds and artifacts as differing in homogeneity. One procedure was to ask subjects to predict what percentage of the category members would be expected to have a given characteristic. Another was to ask subjects directly to rate on a scale from 1 to 9 how similar the members of a given category were to each other. The results using both of these procedures were comparable, indicating that natural kinds on the whole tend to be seen as more homogeneous than artifacts. Although on some of the measures minerals were seen as less homogeneous, natural kinds were in general thought of as homogeneous, regardless of complexity. This difference held up for superordinate level categories, as well as for basic level categories. The main exception was that, as expected, complex artifacts such as machines were perceived as being more like natural kinds.

Gelman then went on to determine what kinds of distinctions children have made between categories. Four- and 7-year-old children were taught a new fact—for example, that a rabbit has a spleen—and then had to decide whether the fact applied to a similar object (a similar rabbit), a different object from the same category (another rabbit), an object from the same superordinate category (a dog), and an unrelated object (a telephone). As evidence that the children were taking the task seriously, Gelman found that children virtually always drew inferences to a similar looking object and rarely drew inferences to an unrelated object. Only for the two intermediate levels of generality does it make sense to ask whether there is a natural kind–artifact distinction. Seven-year-olds clearly distinguish between natural kinds and artifacts. They drew more inferences from natural kinds than from artifacts at both basic and superordinate levels of categorization. The results from 4-year-olds are not so clear. These children may have begun to draw such a distinction, but it is unstable. They are more likely to draw inferences from categories that adults perceive as homogeneous. Thus, Gelman argues that the natural kind–artifact distinction is not used by preschool children but that it may evolve from an earlier distinction based on homogeneity.

Another way in which young children are likely to be limited is that they may not be able to look much beyond perceptual features of objects when they form categories on their own. In the studies reported here children were told the category labels and then asked to infer information from one member to another. This task is simpler than the converse problem of having to form the category in the first place, without knowing beforehand which properties are relevant. When initially forming a category, children are likely to be much more susceptible to perceptual appearances. Most standard classification procedures (see Inhelder and Piaget 1964) require children to divide objects into categories where many bases of classification are possible. Given the complexity of this problem (see Gelman and Baillargeon 1983; Markman and Callanan 1983), children often find the superficial perceptual appearances of objects to be an easier basis on which to organize the material.

As for natural kinds, Keil (in press) found young children to be more dependent on perceptual similarity than on deeper biological properties when they are asked to classify anomalous objects. he asked children to classify artifacts and natural kind objects, given conflicting information. For example, one object looked exactly like a skunk but its biological structures (heart, bones) and lineage (parents) were supposed to be that of a raccoon. The youngest children believed for both natural kinds and artifacts that appearance determined category membership. For example, they would say that the animal that looked like a skunk was in fact a skunk, even though they had been told it had a raccoon heart, gave birth to raccoon babies, and so forth. Not until about second to fourth grade were children willing to say that internal structure was an important criterion for categorizing natural kind objects. But these children probably have no way of knowing whether internal structure or external structure is more important. Another way of stating the difference between Keil's task and ours is that children were asked to make different sorts of comparisons in the two studies. On Keil's task children had to compare two different kinds of attributes: perceptual appearance versus biological properties. On our task children had to compare attributes (perceptual appearance) to membership in a category. The category label may be considered a more powerful source of information than a few biological properties such as having a particular heart or set of parents. Gelman, Collman, and Maccoby (1986) found that inferring properties on the basis of categories was easier than inferring category membership on the basis of properties for one category: namely, gender.

Primitive Theories as Possible Constraints on Induction

Finally, as Carey (1985) has argued, children must learn how natural kind categories are related to one another in a system of theory-based knowledge. Carey has found that children initially organize biological knowledge around humans as a prototype. Inferences about the biological properties of other species are based both on what children believe about humans and on how similar the other species is to humans. For example, children in Carey's study were taught that humans have an omentum and were asked whether various animals and artifacts also have an omentum. Children generalized in accord with a rough similarity gradient from most to least similar to humans. What is most striking about Carey's findings, however, is how depen-

dent children are on the category of humans to organize new biological knowledge and to trigger inferences. Children draw inferences
about biological categories primarily when the property is known to
be true of humans. They are more likely to infer that a biological
property of *humans* will generalize to bugs than they are to infer that
a property of *bees* will generalize to bugs, despite the far greater similarity of bugs to bees than to humans. This marked dependence on
humans as the prototype changes with age: adults generalize from
one species to another based on how similar the two species are to
each other (Rips 1975).

Carey discusses this work in terms of developmental changes in
the scientific theories in which these natural kind terms are embedded. One of the roles of scientific theory is to constrain the kinds of
inductive inferences that are made. The marked asymmetries in pro-
jection found at age 4 (that 4-year-olds generalize more from human
to bug than from bug to bee, for example) disappear by about age 10.
This change reflects a major restructuring in the organization of children's biological knowledge. The biological knowledge of 4-year-olds
is focused on humans. Biological properties are fundamentally properties of humans and only secondarily properties of animals. New
biological knowledge must be related to humans in order for 4-year-
olds to project the properties to other animals. By age 10 the special
status of humans as biological creatures has diminished. Now humans are only one of many mammals as far as biological properties
are concerned.

Conclusions

At age 4, then, children still have much to learn about natural kind
categories. Yet, at an age when children are known to find perceptual
appearances compelling, they nevertheless expect rich similarities
among natural kind objects with the same name. Perhaps 4-year-olds
have learned enough information about natural kinds for them to
have reached this conclusion about the structure of categories. It is
also possible that children are initially biased to interpret category
terms this way, independent of experience. Other expectations about
the structure of natural language categories appear quite early. When
children as young as 18 to 24 months hear an object labeled with a
common noun, they assume the term refers to the object as a whole
rather than to one of its properties (Macnamara 1982). By the age of
3 or 4 and possibly earlier, children expect a noun to refer to objects
that are taxonomically related (e.g., a dog and a cat) even though in
the absence of a label they are likely to group objects on the basis of

thematic relations (e.g., a dog and a bone) (Markman and Hutchinson 1984). The assumption that categories will be structured as are natural kinds could be another early bias, one that helps children acquire category terms rapidly, organize knowledge efficiently, and induce information to novel exemplars of familiar categories. By expecting unforeseen nonperceptual properties to be common to members of a kind, children could go beyond the original basis for grouping objects into a category and discover more about the category members than they knew before. Children might start out assuming that categories will have the structure of natural kinds. With development, they would then refine these expectations, limiting them to properties, domains, and category types that are appropriate.

Chapter 6

Language and Richly Structured versus Arbitrary Categories

In this chapter I will make two separate but related arguments. First, I will argue that there is a continuum between natural kind and arbitrary categories that depends mainly on the richness of information categories convey, and that several psychological implications follow from this difference in the correlated structure of categories. Second, I will argue that there is a correlation, in English, between richly structured and arbitrary categories, on the one hand, and nouns and adjectives, on the other. The correlation is admittedly rough and imperfect, but it may be important nonetheless.

Recall Mill's contrast between a natural kind category such as "bird" and an arbitrary category such as "white thing." Knowing that an object is a member of a natural kind results in an enormous gain in information. Once we know that something is a bird, we know that in all probability it flies, has feathers, wings, two legs, claws, and a beak, lays eggs, and so on. The "and so on" here is important. Scientists devote their careers to studying birds, mammals, plants, and so forth, just because these natural kinds have so many (as yet unknown) correlated features. Properties such as the internal structure, behavior, and origin of natural kinds are so rich and complex that we believe further study will continue to reveal new truths about these categories.

An arbitrary category such as "white thing" contrasts with a natural kind category in being much less rich and less predictable. It is an arbitrary basis for classifying an object whereby, although some property has been attributed to the object, little else can be predicted about it with any confidence. Given that an object is white, we do not know whether it is living or not; nor do we know what size it is, what shape it has, or what function it serves.

On the basis of this distinction, one might be tempted to conclude that arbitrary categories do not accomplish much. They do, however, serve an important function. Natural kind categories point to relatively permanent, rich clusters of information. This allows for the mushrooming of information based on a small amount of initial input. But in devising categories, humans could not have had the fore-sight to anticipate every possible element. For example, when first forming the category "bird," people may not have expected there to be birds that cannot fly. Moreover, an efficient taxonomy, by its very nature, cannot specify every detail of the individual members. Thus, arbitrary categories work with natural kinds to allow for the updating of information, the modification of categories, and the devising of new categories, when existing ones are insufficient. Moreover, we do many things with language besides categorizing, such as picking out particular individuals. Arbitrary categories provide unlimited amounts of idiosyncratic, unpredictable information about individuals that natural kinds must by their very nature omit. Together, nat-ural kinds and arbitrary categories function as an adaptive, versatile system.

A Continuum from Natural Kinds to Arbitrary Categories

The examples of "bird" and "white thing" represent two very differ-ent kinds of classification. They should be viewed as endpoints on a continuum from natural kind categories, which have a rich correlated structure and are embedded in scientific theories, to arbitrary cate-gories, which have an impoverished correlated structure. Many other categories fall somewhere between these two extremes. "Chair," for example, is an intermediate type of category. Once we know an ob-ject is a chair, we know a fair amount about its physical appearance, construction, and typical function. It is unlikely that we would have a science of chairs, however; nor do we expect new discoveries and truths about chairs to emerge. The continuum from natural kinds to arbitrary categories is defined, at least in part, by the richness of in-formation obtained by the classification.

Further Implications of Differences in Richness of Category Structure

Given the large differences possible in the structure of categories, and especially considering both endpoints of the continuum, people are very likely to treat these kinds of categorization as quite different. In fact, there is some sense in which arbitrary categories do not even seem to qualify as "categories." The dramatic differences in the amount of information contained in these two types of concepts should generate other powerful intuitions about how they differ. I hypothesize that the following six differences should obtain between richly structured and arbitrary categories:

1. Based on their experience with different kinds of categories,

people should come to expect that richly structured categories will support more inferences than arbitrary categories. A person's expectations about a given category will probably determine how likely that person is to look for or infer additional properties about the objects in the category. When people believe that an object is a member of a natural kind or other richly structured category, they should be more likely to draw inferences than when they believe it is a member of an arbitrary category.

2. Because of the richness of information and the special explanatory power of natural kinds and other richly structured categories, they will be viewed as capturing something of fundamental importance about an object, whereas arbitrary categories may be viewed as providing less essential, more detailed information.

3. Natural kind categories may come to be viewed as central to the identity of the object—identifying what the object *is*—whereas arbitrary categories specify what the object *is like*.

4. The natural kind membership of a category will be seen as something relatively enduring and permanent. Because richly structured categories specify so many properties of an object, in some cases including properties that are embedded in a scientific theory, such as an animal's genetic code, it is unlikely that enough of these properties could change to bring about a shift in which richly structured category the object belongs to. In contrast, arbitrary categories, which specify much less information, may be seen as relatively more transient.

5. Richly structured categories may be more likely than arbitrary categories to be organized into taxonomies of subordinate, superordinate, and coordinate classes. One of the main functions of taxonomies is to help organize large amounts of information. Where the information is limited, as is the case with arbitrary categories, taxonomies are less likely to develop.

6. People may further constrain natural kind and other richly structured categories, viewing them as mutually exclusive or unique. This derives both from the amount of information and from the special status of the information conveyed by natural kinds. If so many properties are implied by a given natural kind category, it is unlikely that an object could qualify for membership in two unrelated natural kinds. For example, an object cannot be both a bird and a cat. If this intuition is exaggerated and overextended in children, as I will argue it is, then they would find multiple category membership very confusing—perhaps even contradictory—because it would be interpreted as giving an object two separate identities. In contrast, people should be less reluctant to view an object as a member of multiple

arbitrary categories. It is easy to understand, for example, how an object could be red, and square, and large. Arbitrary categories are viewed as less informative descriptions of an object, many of which could be mutually compatible.

The Role of Language

I will argue next that there is some association—not perfect, but strong enough to matter—between whether a category is richly structured or arbitrary and whether it is referred to by a noun or an adjective. First, a caveat. English is flexible in what kinds of concepts can be referred to by nouns, adjectives, verbs, and so on. A simple rule such as "Nouns refer to things and adjectives to properties" or "Nouns refer to categories and adjectives to attributes" is bound to fail. Maratsos (1982, 1983) gives many examples of how very similar concepts can be represented by different grammatical form classes. Nouns can refer to natural kind categories such as "bird," to arbitrary categories such as "square," to abstract categories such as "danger," and so on. Adjectives can refer to simple properties, such as "round," but they can also refer to extraordinarily rich, densely structured concepts such as "uxorious."

Despite the diversity of concepts that are encoded by nouns and adjectives, there is some relation between whether the word is a noun or an adjective and whether it refers to a richly structured or an arbitrary category. An adjective is more likely to refer to an arbitrary category than to a richly structured one, and a richly structured category is more likely to be referred to by a noun than by an adjective. Even with exceptions, the grammatical form class can still have considerable semantic force, especially if it is the familiar, frequently used nouns and adjectives that conform to the hypothesized pattern (Grimshaw 1981; Lyons 1966). There is also some research suggesting that people tend to exaggerate moderate correlations and perceive greater regularity than actually exists, as long as it fits with some prior expectations (Jennings, Amabile, and Ross 1980). Finally, in his interesting book on language development, Macnamara (1982) argues that children rely on the semantic basis of grammatical form classes in order to learn them.

As a consequence of this correlation, the form class of a word may come to carry surplus meaning. That is, that fact that the category is referred to by a noun instead of an adjective (or vice versa) will lead people to make certain assumptions about the category.

Related correlations between nouns and adjectives and types of concepts have been presented in various views of linguistics and philosophy. In traditional grammar, nouns were said to denote persons, places, or things, and adjectives were said to refer to properties. This definition has been accused of being circular, however, since abstract nouns (such as "justice") are considered to denote things only because they are known to be nouns (Lyons 1966). Nouns have sometimes been taken to be those terms that refer, whereas adjectives describe. Nouns point to, refer to, or designate objects, whereas adjectives characterize the objects in some way.

Although these distinctions are related to the one I am making, my claim is somewhat different. I am suggesting that people may expect nouns to refer to concepts that have considerable inferential depth. In particular, I suggest that people will be led to form assumptions based on the six intuitions listed above. When a concept is encoded by a noun, people will expect that it will support more inferences, that it will provide fundamental, essential information about the object, that it will provide information about the identity of the object, that the information will be relatively enduring and permanent, that the category might be more readily placed in a taxonomy, and perhaps that the category is difficult to combine with richly structured categories.

All of these judgments are relative, of course, and tempered by the meaning of the term. If the term refers to a category that is obviously at one or the other end of the continuum between a natural kind and an arbitrary category, then the form class of the word will probably have little impact. But if the term refers to a category that is intermediate between these two extremes, then the choice of form class may influence people's perception of the category.

Indirect Evidence for the Difference between Nouns and Adjectives

For many different theoretical reasons, psychologists have designed experiments to contrast nouns and adjectives. Although the results are not entirely consistent, these studies typically show that nouns and adjectives function differently in the way people organize and retrieve information in memory. For example, in paired associate learning, English-speaking subjects learn noun-adjective pairs better than adjective-noun pairs, even though this violates the normal word order of English (Lambert and Paivio 1956; Paivio 1963). Nouns have also been found to serve as better retrieval cues regardless of whether adjective-noun or noun-adjective pairs were learned originally (Lockhart 1969).

English-speaking subjects have also been found to be faster at verifying that an object has a property when the noun referring to the object precedes the adjective. For example, they are faster at verifying that an apple is red when they are presented with the phrase "apple-red" than when they are presented with "red-apple" (Tversky, Havousha, and Poller 1979). Again, this occurs despite the fact that the adjective-noun ordering is correct in English. Similarly, subjects can generate instances of a concept more readily when they are first given the noun and then the adjective than when they are given the standard English adjective-noun ordering (Freedman and Loftus 1971). For example, they are better able to respond "apple" when presented with "fruit-red" than when presented with "red-fruit." The present interpretation of these findings is that nouns that typically refer to rich categories allow people ready access to much related predictable information. Some of this information will consist of related category instances or more specific instances of a concept. According to Collins and Loftus (1975), since nouns (in this case "fruit") are so tightly interconnected to other concepts, much more so than adjectives (in this case "red"), processing must be delayed until the noun designating the appropriate category is presented.

In summary, evidence from studies of paired associate learning and semantic memory suggest that nouns may have some privileged status in memory, allowing more accurate, quicker access to information and being more effective as memory cues than adjectives. Comparisons between nouns and verbs support this interpretation.

Evidence for the Distinction between Nouns and Verbs
Huttenlocher and Lui (1979) have reported differences in memory for nouns and verbs that they interpret as reflecting different principles of organization. Across a wide age range and a variety of paradigms, they found that the effect of semantic relatedness was greater for nouns than for verbs. Concrete nouns, according to Huttenlocher and Lui, are closely related and organized into hierarchical class-inclusion relations. Verbs, in contrast, have a more matrixlike organization. This analysis fits with the present one in the following way. The organization of concrete nouns into hierarchies follows from the richness of information arguments (see point 5). Given that one knows the category, one will be able to move up and down the hierarchy, generating subordinate and superordinate categories, as well as other properties and relations to other categories. Huttenlocher and Lui's characterization of verbs as matrixlike refers to the relative lack of correlated structure among verbs. Given that one knows one feature of a verb, one may not be able to predict much else. For example, whether or not an act is intentional is encoded across many different semantic fields, including "murder" versus "kill," "chase" versus "wander," "throw" versus "drop," "steal" versus "take."

Gentner (1978, 1982) has demonstrated a variety of ways in which nouns and verbs differ and argues that these stem from a basic difference between object reference (nouns) and relational meaning (verbs). She argues that the representation of nouns is more "dense" than that of verbs, where density refers to the ratio between the number of internal links and the number of components linked (including external links). This implies that the meanings of nouns are more redundant, more overdetermined, than the meanings of verbs. This notion of density is consistent with the claim that nouns refer to concepts that have richly structured correlated features. Verbs are relational terms and are more likely to alter their meanings as a function of context than are object terms, whose meanings seem to be more stable. The evidence from which Gentner draws these conclusions comes from a variety of studies. In one study the number of word senses was tallied for each dictionary entry for the 20 most frequent nouns and verbs. As predicted, there were more senses per verb than per noun. In a second study subjects were asked to paraphrase metaphorical sentences such as "The lizard worshipped." In their paraphrase subjects were more likely to change the meaning of the verbs than the nouns. In a third study bilingual subjects were asked to translate English sentences into their second language, and other bilingual subjects then translated those sentences back into English. More of the original nouns than the original verbs reappeared in these second translations. On a variety of measures, nouns were found to be recalled more accurately than verbs. Finally, children acquire nouns before verbs.

Adjectives may contrast with nouns in some of the same ways that verbs do. They are less dense in meaning and have a less correlated structure. Although the research is yet to be done to confirm this, intuitively it seems likely that adjectives too may be more prone to adjusting their meaning according to context than are nouns. For example, the meaning of "good" is adjusted to fit the category it modifies ("good person" versus "good knife") (Katz 1964). "Large" interacts with what it modifies ("large house" versus "large mouse"), as does "red" ("red hair" versus "red apple"). Bolinger (1967) argues that in general, the interpretation of an adjective varies, sometimes dramatically, depending on the noun it modifies. For example, "criminal" means roughly 'defending criminals' in "criminal lawyer" but 'committed by criminals' in "criminal act." In these examples the noun refers to a category of objects; the adjective presupposes that category for its interpretation.

Analogously, adjectives adjust their form in some languages, depending on the noun they modify. For example, adjectives in French and Latin must agree in case, number, and gender with the noun they modify. In fact, it is a language universal that, of all languages in which the adjective follows the noun, "the adjective expresses all the inflectional categories of the noun [whereas] the noun may lack overt expression of one or all of these categories" (Greenberg 1966, 113). Again, this implies that nouns have a fixed form independent of any modifier they receive, whereas adjectives presuppose a noun and must adjust their form to correspond to the inflections of that noun.

In sum, there are semantic, formal, and conceptual distinctions between nouns and adjectives. Whereas nouns can stand alone, adjectives depend on or presuppose nouns. It may well be that, in general, adjectives adjust their meaning according to the noun they modify more than nouns adjust their meaning according to the adjective that modifies them. Thus, nouns and adjectives should differ in many of the same ways that nouns and verbs differ.

More Direct Evidence for the Correlation between Grammatical Form Class and Type of Category
A few studies have been conducted that provide a more direct test of the hypothesis that people are likely to expect nouns to have greater inferential depth than adjectives.

Richness of Structure in Common Nouns and Adjectives.   In this study I tested the prediction that nouns should have greater inferential depth than adjectives. The main argument is that because relatively frequent common nouns and adjectives tend to correlate with richly structured and arbitrary categories, respectively, speakers tend to extrapolate beyond the particular words and establish differences in the form class. Presumably it is because this correspondence is strong for common nouns and adjectives that the form class itself comes to convey some of this meaning. The important assumption in this argument is that common nouns do tend to convey richer information than do common adjectives. I was not trying to demonstrate that words such as "bird" convey more information than words such as "red." That is already obvious. The important point was to demonstrate that common, frequently used nouns would turn out to be richly structured, like "bird," and that common adjectives would turn out to be less richly structured, like "red." Because there are many exceptions to this correlation among nouns and adjectives in general, it was important to determine whether it exists for the common terms.

In this study 17 college students were asked to list information that they knew about the categories described by nouns and adjectives.

Common nouns and adjectives that referred to objects were obtained from the Thorndike and Lorge word list (1944). The 50 most common nouns and the 50 most common adjectives were selected for use in the study. From the list of 50 nouns and 50 adjectives, 9 nouns and 9 adjectives were randomly selected for each subject who participated, and the order of presentation of the 18 terms was randomized.

The instructions to the subjects were modeled after those used by Rosch and Mervis (1975). Subjects were told that this was a very simple experiment to find out what attributes people feel are common to and characteristic of ordinary, everyday objects and people. They were told that they would be given some information about the object or person and asked to list other relevant characteristics. They then heard two examples:

> For example, for a "bicycle," you might think of things like: two wheels, a handlebar, you ride on it, it doesn't use fuel, etc. As another example, for "henpecked," you might think of things like: a man who is married, who is dominated by his wife, who may be nagged by his wife, or who might be weak-willed.

Subjects were asked to write down all of the relevant characteristics they could think of but to try not to free associate or write down personal experiences.

The data were scored in two ways. First, because subjects listed characteristics on separate lines, we simply counted the number of lines a subject used for the nouns and the adjectives. On this measure, the results were as expected. Subjects listed more information for nouns than for adjectives. They listed an average of 6.4 items per noun compared to 4.9 per adjective, paired $t = 4.81$, $p < .001$. The second measure took into account exactly what the subjects wrote on each line. Sometimes they wrote more than one characteristic on each line, and sometimes the same characteristic would appear on two lines, in the form of synonyms, close paraphrases, and so on. On this measure, the difference between nouns and adjectives was even clearer than on the first, cruder measure. Subjects listed a mean of 7.4 properties for nouns compared to 5.4 for adjectives, $t(16) = 5.22$, $p < .001$.

The results of this study support the hypothesis that common nouns typically convey more information than common adjectives. Thus, on the basis of their experience with common nouns and adjectives, people could come to expect that a category denoted by a noun will have a richer correlational structure than a category denoted by an adjective.

Perceived Differences in Structure for Equated Nouns and Adjectives. Edward Smith and I have conducted two studies that address the main hypothesis that nouns refer to categories with a richer correlated structure. These studies test whether, on the basis of form class alone, people will infer that nouns tend to refer to richer categories than do adjectives. That is, if we can manipulate whether a noun or an adjective is used to refer to essentially the same category, we should find that people tend to treat a category referred to by a noun as conveying more information than the same category referred to by an adjective.

In one study 28 undergraduates were asked to rate which of two statements about a person seemed to be a stronger statement, in other words, which seemed to convey more information. In each statement the same word was used to describe the person, but in one case it was treated as a noun and in the other case it was treated as an adjective—for example, "John is a liberal" versus "John is liberal."

For this study, we needed identical noun-adjective pairs ("intellectual," "an intellectual") rather than pairs with derivational differences ("divorcee," "divorced"). To generate a list of such pairs, we listed the nouns and adjectives from sections of the Kucera and Francis (1967) word norms. Wherever possible, we generated an adjective or noun from the noun or adjective in the list. Then two judges rated the noun-adjective pairs on a 3-point scale, where 1 indicated that the terms were identical and referred to the same class of people and 3 indicated that they referred to only partially overlapping classes. The pairs that were included in the study received mean ranks of 1 or 1.5. As it turned out, all of the words that met the criteria referred to people. The 12 terms used were "adult," "American," "black," "Catholic," "gay," "German," "intellectual," "liberal," "male," "neurotic," "sexist," and "single."

For half the subjects the noun version of a given pair ("John is a sexist") was written first on the page, and for the other half the adjective version ("John is sexist") was written first.

Subjects were told that we were interested in their judgments about differences between very similar ways of describing someone. We asked them first to pick which of the two descriptions seemed to them to be a stronger or more powerful statement about the person. After they made that decision, we asked them to rate the difference on a 5-point scale. If they thought the statements were equally strong, they were to rate them as 1, and if they thought the statements were fairly different, they were to rate them as 5.

Once subjects had completed the judgments and ratings for all 12 items, they were asked to go back through the questionnaire and write down any ideas they had about what accounted for any differences they had perceived.

As predicted, subjects tended to select the nouns as conveying stronger information than the adjectives. Of the 28 subjects, 21 chose more nouns than adjectives, $p < .01$. The proportion of nouns selected was .68, which is significantly greater than the chance level of .50, $p < .005$. The overall mean rating of the nouns was higher than the rating for the adjectives, $p < .005$.

This tendency to find the nouns stronger held up over virtually all of the items. For 10 of the 12 noun-adjective pairs, the majority of subjects selected the noun as the stronger statement, $p < .025$.

In this study we compared nouns and adjectives that we equated to the greatest extent we could. The same word was used in each case, and the items were selected to be as close in meaning as possible. Yet subjects judged the nouns to convey stronger information than the adjectives. In their explanations for why they felt the nouns were stronger, these college students often mentioned that the noun form conveyed more information, conveyed more stereotyped information, and seemed to refer to a more central, permanent feature of the person. Here are some examples, all of which contrast "He's an intellectual" with "He's intellectual":

> "He's an intellectual" makes the person part of an elite group. "He's intellectual" just lists one trait of the individual.

> "He's an intellectual" implies it's a major part of his life. "He's intellectual" is a casual observation.

> "He's intellectual" says he's smart. "He's an intellectual" gives the feeling that he is a genius—studies all the time and wears glasses.

> "He's an intellectual" is stronger because there is something unusual about being *an* intellectual. It has certain connotations—being a bookworm, carrying calculators, etc.

> "An intellectual" is like a name tag or admittance to a select intellectual group. "He's intellectual" conveys he's intellectual sometimes but not always.

> "A" phrase makes me feel like person is a long-haired eggheaded type person—stereotype.

One subject summed up his intuitions as follows:

> I felt that the use of "a" created the stronger statement. It tended to label a person with a trait in such a way that one would think that's all that the person is or could be. It generates a stereotype. The other sentences use an adjective in a way which it seems that this particular trait is only one of many and not necessarily the predominant one.

Thus, even for these noun-adjective pairs that were virtually equated in meaning, subjects felt that the nouns made more powerful statements about the person they referred to than did the adjectives, sensing that nouns conveyed more information, more about the stereotype, than adjectives did.

Anecdotal evidence for this point can be found in literature. An author who wants to convey a prejudice about a person often uses a noun construction, just because it implies that a person has been categorized or stereotyped to a greater degree. For example, the following passage about prejudice uses this technique:

> "I said what if I couldn't think of a contemporary writer I wanted to talk about?"
>
> "Oh, for heaven's sake there must be dozens."
>
> She looked at me pretty stormily. It is her opinion that my distaste for many kinds of contemporary novelists, including the critic-intellectuals, the mythologizers, the fantasizers, the black humorists, the absurds, the grotesques, and the sexualizers, is as pigheaded as my prejudices against the young. (Wallace Stegner, *The Spectator Bird*, 156)

The study just described demonstrated that people judge that nouns convey more powerful information about a person than adjectives do. The next study, which also used identical nouns and adjectives, addressed whether subjects are likely to draw more inferences about a person if the person is described by a noun than if the person is described by an adjective.

Thirty-two undergraduates participated in this study. Half were given information about people using nouns ("an intellectual") and half were given information using adjectives ("intellectual").

Subjects were given 12-page booklets, each page blank except for a single sentence typed at the top. For the noun condition, the sentences were of the form "Suppose the person is an intellectual." For the adjective condition, the sentences were identical except for the omission of the indefinite article: "Suppose the person is intellectual." Subjects were asked to read the information provided for each person and to list what else might be commonly believed about the person, given that information. Subjects were told to list information even if they did not necessarily believe it themselves, as long as they thought most people would believe it.

The prediction was that subjects receiving noun descriptions should list more characteristics than subjects receiving adjective descriptions. Occasionally subjects skipped a page. This could have been an error, or it could be that subjects knew no characteristics to list (though this is unlikely); but in some cases it could be that subjects resented being asked to report on what they felt represented bigotry. However, it did not matter how we scored the blank pages. Whether we counted them as zero or treated them as missing data did not affect the results. Counting these skipped pages as "zeros," the mean number of attributes listed was 4.0 for nouns and 3.1 for adjectives, $t(30) = 2.06$, $p < .05$. The effect was not due to only a few items but could be generalized over the noun-adjective pairs, paired-$t(11) = 5.73$, $p < .001$.

Summary In summary, when subjects were asked to list properties of objects referred to by common nouns or adjectives, they listed more information for the objects referred to by nouns. Common nouns, then, refer to more richly structured categories than do common adjectives. Based on their experience with these highly familiar, often heard nouns and adjectives, people could come to expect that nouns will refer to categories toward the natural kind end of the continuum, whereas adjectives will refer to categories toward the arbitrary end of the continuum. This implies that even when the categories referred to are identical, people will draw different conclusions depending on whether a noun or an adjective is used to refer to the category. This is what Smith and I found in our studies that equated the stimulus nouns and adjectives to the greatest extent possible. Using noun-adjective pairs such as "a liberal" versus "liberal," "an intellectual" versus "intellectual," we found that subjects judged the noun of a pair to convey a more powerful claim about the individual than the adjective did and that subjects drew more inferences upon hearing the noun than upon hearing the adjective.

Developmental Studies

There is little developmental research that bears directly on the claims made in this chapter. There is, however, some indirect evidence that examines one of the consequences of the proposed distinction between nouns and adjectives. Namely, that nouns point to richly structured categories and adjectives point to arbitrary categories. Psychologically arbitrary categories—where a single property might be the defining characteristic—feel more like descriptions or depictions of objects than like categories. When one thinks of say, a red flower, one considers "flower" to be the category the object belongs to, and "red" to have singled out a particular property of the object that is not conveyed by the category term. One consequence of this difference is that people should expect that nouns and adjectives differ in their contrastive use.

Gelman and I (Gelman and Markman 1985) argued that adjectives imply a contrast between members of a single noun category, but nouns do not imply a contrast between members of the same adjective category. This means that adjectives imply contrast between members of a single category rather than between any two objects. Although adjectives make it possible to note countless contrasts between any two objects, speakers often constrain their use primarily to note contrasts between similar objects. In addition, it means that adjectives presuppose nouns in some way, whereas nouns do not presuppose adjectives. For example, "flower" (a noun) labels the contrast set, and "red" (an adjective) specifies the dimension of contrast, implying a contrast with "yellow," "pink," and so on. Logically, there is no reason why this must be the case; conceivably nouns could imply contrast within an adjective set. For example, "red" could label the class of red objects, and "flower" could specify one subset of the class "red," contrasting with "fire engine," "apple," and so on. However, this would be a highly arbitrary kind of classification. It seems much more natural for adjectives to specify divisions within a category. Thus, adjectives and nouns may serve different functions: adjectives, to pick out noteworthy properties or to suggest a relevant contrast with other similar objects; nouns, to focus on the name of a category or object per se. Again, this distinction between adjectives and nouns follows from the claim that adjectives tend to refer to relatively more arbitrary categories, whereas nouns tend to refer to more highly structured categories. Adjectives function to subdivide richer categories along many different dimensions.

This difference in the contrastive function of nouns and adjectives does not necessarily follow from the literal meanings of the terms. Rather, it seems to be a conceptual distinction deriving in part from the correlation of nouns and adjectives with richly structured versus arbitrary categories.

Because these differences do not follow from the literal meanings of the words, it is possible that children could acquire word meanings without noting these differences. It may require much experience in observing the communicative functions of nouns and adjectives before children can work out this distinction.

On the other hand, even quite young children may recognize that nouns and adjectives communicate different sorts of information. If so, then young children might be able to use this distinction to help them learn new words. That is, children may have noted the correlation between the form class of a word (noun or adjective) and the contrast that it implies. With this knowledge, children may be able to infer a new word's referent on the basis of its form class alone: an unfamiliar adjective should signal a contrast within an object category; an unfamiliar noun should not.

The first study reported in Gelman and Markman 1985 investigated whether very young children are sensitive to the different contrastive natures of nouns and adjectives and whether they can use them to interpret ambiguous messages. Children were asked a series of questions, each having two correct answers. The questions were designed so that children could answer correctly without showing any consistent preference for one response or another. However, if children are biased to assume that adjectives imply a contrast within a well-defined category, then they should consistently select one particular answer as described in the following paragraphs.

For each question, children were shown a set of four pictures and instructed to select one picture to match a familiar word (for instance, "ball" or "red"). Each word had two possible referents. For example, on one adjective trial children heard, "Find the red one," and could select either a red chair among other chairs or a red butterfly among the chairs. We predicted that children should prefer the red chair among other chairs, if they understand that adjectives imply a contrast between members of the same object category. The red butterfly, though just as obviously red, is not from the same category as the chairs and thus should not be chosen.

On one noun trial children heard, "Find the ball," and could select either a blue ball among other blue toys or a red ball among the blue toys. In this case we predicted that children would not have any bias to pick the blue ball and in fact might prefer the red ball because it is more distinctive. Thus, when given a noun, children should find the two pictures equally appropriate. Unlike adjectives, nouns should not imply a contrast between members of the same category.

Forty-two preschool children participated in this study. The children were divided into a younger group, with an average age of 2:11, and an older group, with an average age of 3:11. We included the youngest age that—based on diary studies (Bateman 1916; Bohn 1914; Boyd 1914; Brandenberg 1915; Gale and Gale 1900) and two observational studies (Bloom 1979; Nelson 1976)—we believed could be tested reliably on a range of adjectives.

Adjectives and nouns were chosen that were easily depicted and familiar to most 2½-year-old children. The eight adjectives used were "big," "blue," "broken," "clean," "dirty," "little," "red," and "wet." For each adjective, children could choose among four picture cards. Two of these pictures were "targets" that could be named by the test adjective. The other two were drawn from the same object category as one of the targets. For example, given the adjective "red," on one version children saw three butterflies (red, blue, and yellow) and a red chair. The word "red" could refer perfectly well to either the red butterfly or the red chair.

The eight nouns used were "airplane," "ball," "bed," "horse," "ice cream," "lollipop," "sock," and "spoon." For each noun, children could choose among four cards from the same category. The two target cards could be named by the test noun. The other two cards matched one of the targets in either color or size. Just as the adjective sets included an object category and a singleton (for instance, three butterflies and a chair), the noun sets included a perceptually salient adjective category (defined by color or size) and a singleton. For example, given the noun "ball," on one version of the test children saw three red toys (ball, kite, top) and one blue toy (ball).

Each child saw 20 sets of pictures, one at a time, corresponding to the 20 words being tested (8 adjectives, 8 nouns, and 4 filler items).

Each child was introduced to a puppet and asked to place the correct card in the puppet's mouth.

As predicted, when asked to interpret adjectives, children tended to focus on a contrast between members of the same object category (mean = 64%), more often than when they were asked to interpret nouns (mean = 45%). On hearing nouns, children selected the within-set member below chance. That is, nouns prompted children to select the more distinctive exemplar, at a level greater than chance. In contrast, children inferred that adjectives referred to the within-category contrast, again at a level greater than chance. There was, however, a developmental difference in children's interpretation of the adjectives. Only the 4-year-olds performed nonrandomly on the adjective trials taken as a whole: this older group selected the within-category member 73% of the time, whereas the younger group selected it only 51% of the time.

In this study we presented 3- and 4-year-old children with ambiguous questions. They could have resolved the ambiguity in a number of ways. For example, on the adjective trials children could have looked for the best exemplar, they could have looked for the most familiar object, or they could have chosen the most distinctive or salient picture; indeed, they could have shown any number or response biases. Instead, however, they relied on the conceptual distinction between nouns and adjectives to disambiguate the questions. Four-year-olds are sensitive to the different contrastive natures of nouns and adjectives and can use them to interpret ambiguous messages. On hearing a noun, children typically either chose the best or most distinctive exemplar of the category or showed no preference. In contrast, on hearing an adjective, children inferred that it presupposed a category of objects and pointed to a contrast within that category.

This study established that for well-known, familiar terms children can use information conveyed by the form class to help them disambiguate a word. When children know the meaning of a term, the sort of contrast it implies has also been represented. In particular, adjectives lead children to expect a prior relatively rich categorization and to look for a contrast within it. This raises the possibility that the word's form class alone can help children infer the meanings of unfamiliar words. Children may have a more abstract, general representation of the noun-adjective distinction, so that hearing an adjective leads them to search for contrast between members of a category. The next study, also from Gelman and Markman 1985, explores whether children can capitalize on the noun-adjective distinction to help them learn new words.

The materials for this study were constructed to be analogous to the adjective arrays in the first study, except that this new set depicted unfamiliar, imaginary objects and animals. Our main interest lay in whether children would choose differently depending on whether they were asked, for example, to find "the fep" (noun) or "the fep one" (adjective). Each question was designed so that children could select any one of four pictures and still be answering appropriately. However, if the form class alone provides semantic information, we predicted that children should choose one of a class of objects when asked for "the fep one" but should either show no preference or select a lone exemplar when asked for "the fep."

Fifty-seven children ranging in age from 2:7 to 5:8 participated in this study.

Children saw 12 arrays of pictures, each of which included three novel objects drawn from the same category and a fourth novel object drawn from a different category. An example of one array is shown in figure 6.1. The predictions were essentially identical to those in the first study: Given an adjective ("the fep one"), children should choose an object that contrasts with other members of the same category. However, given a noun ("the fep"), children should either

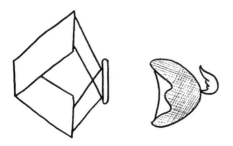

Figure 6.1:
An example of an array of objects used in Gelman and Markman 1985

show no preference or choose the most salient or distinctive picture. Because the words and pictures were both wholly unfamiliar, children were free to choose any picture.

In this study, where the category names and attributes were all unfamiliar, the same pictures were used for both kinds of questions. For example, when children were told, "Find the fep," they saw a blue machinelike object among other blue machines and a singleton furniturelike object. Since they did not know what "fep" meant, it could refer equally well to one of the machines or to the piece of furniture.

All pictures were drawn to represent imaginary objects and creatures, including food, furniture, clothes, toys, vegetation, animals, and miscellaneous artifacts. For any given array, three of the pictures formed a set: they had several features in common, including size, color, shape, and apparent function. One of the three set-members, the contrastive set member, differed from the other two along a single dimension (either color, size, or state). The fourth picture, the singleton, differed from the set-members on every important dimension. Thus, the set-members formed a perceptually salient group as distinct from the singleton.

On every experimental trial subjects heard a novel word, actually a nonsense syllable, to help direct their choice.

The four pictures for each question were arranged in big picture book. The children were given a smaller picture book that could hold only one picture per page. They were told to listen very carefully to the puppet, who would tell them what pictures should go in the book.

Children were told that some of the questions would be hard because they had never before seen some of the things, and that when the puppet talked about these things, he would use puppet talk. Children were asked to listen very hard to the puppet, to figure out what he wanted.

For each array of items, the puppet asked, "Find the X" or "Find the X one" (where X was the nonsense word). In all, there were 12 nonsense words, presented in blocks of 6 "nouns" and 6 "adjectives."

The major question of interest is whether young children were able to use form class alone as a clue to interpret unfamiliar nouns and adjectives. On the basis of the first study, we predicted that, given the opportunity to choose a single object or one of several objects, children would choose differently depending on whether they heard, for example, "Find the fep one" or "Find the fep." In the first study, the adjective (for instance, "red") led children first to find the category and then to look within the category to find the object with the relevant property. Here, since the words were unfamiliar, children did not know what the relevant property was, but they might still look for a contrast within a category. Thus, we predicted that the adjective ("the fep one") should help them focus on a category of objects and to pick the category member that contrasted with other members. Moreover, we predicted that the noun ("the fep") should not focus children's attention on the within-category contrast; instead, it might lead them to select the most salient or distinctive picture (the singleton).

As predicted, children tended to choose the singleton more on the noun trials than on the adjective trials, and they tended to choose the contrastive set-member more on the adjective trials than on the noun trials. However, there was a strong tendency for them to choose the singleton, regardless of the prompt they heard.

Given the unfamiliar pictures and the unfamiliar words presented as coming from puppet land, it is likely that some children may simply have been guessing. Even when given no information at all, children may be biased to select the singleton. This could mask any sensitivity that they have to the different contrastive natures of adjectives and nouns. To test the possibility that children have a bias to prefer the singleton, eight children were tested on the unfamiliar picture materials (as described above) but were not given clues for any of the trials. That is, they were told to find "the one that the puppet wanted" for each page, then usually not instructed further. In this control condition the singleton was again chosen most frequently. In essence, then, children who consistently opted for the singleton in the experimental condition may have been guessing.

We suspected that some of the children, when faced with these unfamiliar terms and pictures, were merely guessing, either by choosing the same corner repeatedly (as did the seven children who were dropped before the analyses were performed) or by preferring the same kind of picture (for example, the singleton).

Thus, to clarify what children were doing who did not rely on fixed strategies, we set aside the data from those children who chose either the same corner or the same picture type significantly above chance (that is, 10 or more times out of 12). This left us with 41 children.

The responses given by these 41 children were analyzed. As in the earlier analysis, children preferred the singleton over any other picture, across all items. However, these children clearly chose differently, depending on whether they had heard a novel adjective or a novel noun. Children focused on a category of objects and chose the contrastive member more on hearing an adjective (a mean of 1.7 times out of 6) than on hearing a noun (a mean of 1.2 times out of 6). They chose the singleton (rather than any category member) more on hearing a noun (a mean of 2.8 times out of 6) than on hearing an adjective (a mean of 2.2 times out of 6). The presence of a nonsense adjective helped children overcome their tendency to pick the lone exemplar and helped them focus instead on the category of the test objects.

In summary, children can use form class alone to interpret novel adjectives and nouns. Children were asked to match unfamiliar words to unfamiliar pictures. The study was designed in such a way that the form class of the nonsense words (for instance, "the fep one" versus "the fep"), was the only information available to guide the child's response. Given the absence of semantic and contextual information and the unfamiliarity of the pictures and the words, it is not surprising that some children would resort to guessing on this task. Nonetheless, many of these very young children were able to use form class information as a clue. Children selected the contrastive category member more on hearing an adjective than on hearing a noun. They selected the lone exemplar more on hearing a noun than on hearing an adjective. These two studies demonstrated that preschool children are sensitive to the different contrastive natures of adjectives and nouns.

In the first study 2½- to 4-year-olds interpreted familiar adjectives and nouns, each with two possible referents. For example, the word "red" could apply equally well to a red chair or to a red butterfly. Despite this ambiguity, children inferred that each adjective named a contrast between members of the same object category. For example, they chose a red butterfly among other butterflies, rather than a red chair among butterflies. However, on hearing a noun, children did not search for a way of grouping objects together but instead tended to select the best exemplar.

The second study stripped away all semantic and contextual cues, to test whether children can capitalize on the noun-adjective distinction to help them learn the meanings of unfamiliar words. In this task the entire burden of communication was placed on the actual form class of the word. For example, "the fep one" and "the fep" should convey different meanings to the child. We found that, among those who did not show fixed response biases, children were more likely to select one of a category of objects when given an adjective phrase than when given a noun. Thus, even when there is no information to rely on except the grammatical form class, adjectives direct young children's attention to a contrast within a category of objects, somewhat more than do nouns.

In a natural word-learning situation, children undoubtedly are guided by all sorts of additional information to interpret new words (for instance, a parent pointing to the object in question, or the prior linguistic context) and thus do not have to rely on form class alone. The general constraint given by the form class of the word in conjunction with this rich contextual information could help simplify children's word-learning task.

Summary and Conclusions

In this chapter I proposed that there is a continuum that ranges from natural kind categories to highly arbitrary categories, a continuum defined mainly by the richness of the correlational structure of the categories. One way of thinking about the continuum is that it spans what people would consider good, natural ways of categorizing objects (for instance, "flower," "dog") to what they would more naturally consider descriptions of objects (for instance, "red," "heavy"). When these descriptions are used as the basis of categorization, as in "red things," the categories appear quite arbitrary.

On the basis of this distinction, I proposed six differences that should obtain between richly structured and arbitrary categories:

1. Richly structured categories should promote inductive inferences more than arbitrary categories.

2. Richly structured categories should be viewed as capturing something fundamental about an object, whereas arbitrary categories should be viewed as providing less essential information.

3. Richly structured categories may be viewed as specifying an object's identity, stating what it is, whereas arbitrary categories specify what it is like.

4. Membership in a richly structured category will be seen as relatively enduring and permanent, whereas membership in an arbitrary category may be seen as more transient.

5. Richly structured categories may be more likely than arbitrary categories to be organized into taxonomies of subordinate, superordinate, and coordinate classes.

6. People, including young children, may view richly structured categories as mutually exclusive. There should be less reluctance to view an object as a member of multiple arbitrary categories.

The second line of argument developed in this chapter was that there is a rough correlation between the richness of the category and grammatical form class. Nouns tend to point to richly structured categories, whereas adjectives tend to point to more arbitrary categories. Although this correlation is by no means perfect, people may nevertheless use it in interpreting nouns and adjectives.

Several lines of research were found to support this distinction. In one study adults were found to list more characteristics as following from common nouns than as following from common adjectives, supporting the hypothesized difference in the richness of information. In a second study Smith and I equated the nouns and adjectives used and found that adults rated the statements involving nouns ("He is an intellectual") to be stronger, to convey more information, than comparable statements involving adjectives ("He is intellectual"). A third study provided descriptions of people, using the same term either as a noun or as an adjective, and asked subjects to list all the characteristics of the person that they thought followed from the statement. The subjects listed more when given noun descriptions than when given adjective descriptions. Thus, even in the most stringent comparison, where the nouns and adjectives are identical, people perceive the nouns as conveying more information than the adjectives.

The last studies reported (Gelman and Markman 1985) tested an implication of this analysis for children's acquisition and understanding of nouns and adjectives. Adjectives should be viewed as providing information to distinguish one member of a category from another (say, a red from a yellow flower). In other words, adjectives provide unique, individuating information that does not follow from the category term itself. Although the comparable role is in principle possible for nouns (for example, "flower" could distinguish members of the red category from each other, such as fire engine and apple), this analysis predicts that this is unlikely. Instead, a noun should serve to pick out a richly structured category and to contrast it with other richly structured categories. To test whether children are sensitive to the differences in the contrastive use of nouns and adjectives, we presented children with an array of objects and asked them to select an object that was either described by an adjective or labeled with a noun. The array of objects was constructed in such a way that children could select a technically "correct" object that either was a member of the same category as another object in the array, or was a singleton. By 4 years of age, children were sensitive to this distinction between nouns and adjectives, treating adjectives but not nouns as implying a within-category contrast. In a second study modeled after this one, children heard novel nouns and adjectives instead of familiar ones. Although this task was difficult for the children and many simply guessed at the interpretation of the novel word, they still tended to treat adjectives, but not nouns, as implying a within-category contrast.

Thus, in both children and adults, there is evidence for the psychological reality of the distinction between richly structured and arbitrary categories. Moreover, there is evidence that people tend to treat nouns as referring to richly structured categories and adjectives as referring to arbitrary categories or descriptions.

Chapter 7
Systematization of Categories

The previous chapters have focused mainly on the acquisition of single categories, examining different types of categories, their internal structure, developmental differences in the strategies used to acquire them, assumptions children make about categories and category terms, and assumptions they make about the relation between grammatical form class and the kind of category referred to. In these discussions, the issues were framed mainly in terms of single categories—categories considered in isolation. Yet one of the most striking characteristics of human categories, and one that sets human categorization apart from animal categorization, is the systematic relation of categories to each other. This systematization is manifest in many ways. One, which will be discussed briefly in chapter 9, is the tendency for terms in a language to form semantic fields, such as color terms, or shape terms, or verbs of motion. Another, which will be the focus of this chapter and chapter 8, is the tendency for categories to be organized into class-inclusion hierarchies.

The Systematization of Categories: What Might Be Unique about Human Classification

Humans have an astonishing ability to classify objects—one that far outstrips what other animals are capable of. All animals must have some ability to classify objects in their world: they must be able to identify food, predators, and shelter, tasks that certainly require classification. Even pigeons, trained using discrimination learning procedures, appear capable of learning categories, including "trees," "oak leaves," "fish," "humans," and the letter "A" (Herrnstein 1982). Yet the ability to classify with originality, insight, and flexibility is a major intellectual advance, probably accomplished by no species other than our own. Some of the more primitive forms of classification of which nonhuman animals are capable may not undergo much development in humans. Other forms may be unique to humans. Although intuitively we can be impressed with our ability to classify, it is more difficult to specify precisely how human categorization differs from that of other species. One way in which humans are likely to differ from other animals is in the sheer propensity to classify. Although all animals classify to some extent, humans seem far more prone to do so.

Hierarchical Organization of Categories

The most dramatic way that human categorization differs from that of other animals is in the construction of systems of categories, including class-inclusion hierarchies. Class-inclusion hierarchies not only are prevalent in human categorization but in fact may be unique to it. Class-inclusion hierarchies are found in everyday, lay concepts such as "chair/furniture," "hammer/tool," and "car/vehicle." They are found in cultures and subcultures ranging from primitive societies to advanced, technical, scientific discourse. Assuming that hierarchical organization is a major intellectual achievement of humans, we need to consider what would count as evidence that someone has represented categories hierarchically. This is particularly relevant developmentally because of the many contradictory claims about whether or not young children are capable of representing hierarchically organized classes. Some of these contradictions can be resolved by recognizing that different definitions or criteria for hierarchical organization yield different conclusions. In this chapter I will consider some of the possible criteria for determining whether an individual has represented class-inclusion hierarchies. I will evaluate both the criteria themselves, with respect to whether they adequately measure class inclusion, and evidence bearing on whether children represent class-inclusion relations according to the various criteria.

Categorizing at More Than One Level.   The minimal criterion for determining whether an individual has represented class-inclusion hierarchies would be that the individual can recognize that an object that is a member of one level of a hierarchy (say, a chair) is also a member of a more general category (say, furniture). The problem with this criterion, as it stands, is that it is trivially fulfilled by any concept whatsoever. A minimal criterion for having a concept is that discriminably different objects be treated as similar. On this criterion, even very unsophisticated animals will, of course, have concepts. For example, a pigeon can learn to peck at circles to be rewarded with food. Since the pigeon can see the differences between large and small circles yet treat them equivalently, it would be said to have the concept of circle. This pigeon could be said to know that a given object is a large circle and that it is a circle and would therefore be credited with understanding inclusion on this criterion. Maureen Callanan and I (Markman and Callanan 1983) have argued that since this criterion is fulfilled by most primitive concepts, it should be rejected as evidence of hierarchical organization.

Another way of looking at this, however, is that by virtue of being able to have concepts at all, we are guaranteed a primitive form of hierarchical representation, such as viewing something as a large circle or a circle. A primitive capacity to represent categories hierarchically may be present from the start in all animals that can form categories. Perhaps such a primitive implicit representation of class-inclusion relations could form the basis for more explicit representation and knowledge of the relations to come. It is still true, however, that this minimal sense of representing categories hierarchically implies only the most trivial understanding of class inclusion, and we still need to determine how the human understanding of categories could develop from this primitive base.

Classifying on a Nonperceptual Basis.   In the example with circles, both levels of the hierarchy are perceptually apparent. That is, the fact that the object is a large circle and that it is a circle can both be seen by inspecting the object. Perhaps we should require that one level of categorization be nonperceptually based. This modification makes the criterion somewhat more stringent, and may be useful in deciding when children begin to have a more explicit notion of class inclusion. To recognize that an object is a chair and that it is a piece of furniture is not a trivial consequence of categorization ability itself, in the way that recognizing that a large circle is a circle could be. One could have the concept "chair" in the sense of thinking that discriminably different chairs are nonetheless exemplars of the category "chair," without having the category "furniture." Thus, multiple categorization when one of the categories is not defined by obvious perceptual features, as with "chair/furniture," is not tantamount to multiple categorization that is a consequence of categorization itself, as with "large circle/circle." It may be, then, that the introduction of this type of categorization, which often occurs at the superordinate level rather than the basic level of categorization, is evidence that children have begun to represent more explicit class-inclusion relations.

There are problems with this criterion, however. One problem is that one could learn nonperceptual categories in rote fashion without really understanding anything at all about them. A child (or even an adult; see Smith and Medin 1981) might be able to identify many instances of, say, furniture by simply memorizing their category membership; that is, the child could learn that tables, chairs, dressers, and couches are called "furniture" without understanding why. Thus, the nonperceptual basis of categorization fails as a criterion because it can be fulfilled in a trivial way. Another problem is that this criterion rules out perceptually based categories as being represented hierarchically when, in many cases, they may well be.

Understanding the Asymmetry and Transitivity of Class Inclusion. The clearest evidence that children represent class-inclusion hierarchies is that they understand the inclusion relation between the categories and not just that they can apply two labels to the same object. Someone who understands class inclusion should show some appreciation of what the relation entails. Inclusion is an asymmetric, transitive relation. The asymmetry of the relation means that if class A is included in class B, then all of the members of class A are members of the more general class B but not vice versa. To take a concrete example, a child who understands the relation between dogs and animals should know that all dogs are animals and that not all animals are dogs. The transitivity of the relation means that if class A is included in class B and if class B is included in class C, then class A is included in class C. A child who understands the transitivity of the relation should be able to conclude, from "all dachshunds are dogs," that all dachshunds are animals. Further, a child who knows that a property is true of the more general category (say, all dogs bark) should be able to conclude that the objects in the included class also have the property (all dachshunds bark). The converse, however, is not true; from "all dogs have claws," the child should not conclude that all animals have claws.

Studies of Hierarchical Organization in Children
With similar criteria in mind, Callanan and I (Markman and Callanan 1983) reviewed the literature. We found that only a very few studies have directly examined children's understanding of the asymmetry and transitivity of inclusion. However, an enormous amount of research has been conducted to study the conceptual organization of young children. These studies of conceptual organization may shed some light on how well children have represented class-inclusion hierarchies.

The Piagetian Class-Inclusion Problem. One frequent way of assessing whether children understand hierarchically organized class-inclusion relations has been to ask the Piagetian class-inclusion question. For this task, children are presented with a category of objects—say, flowers—that are divided into two mutually exclusive subsets—say, daisies and roses. In this case children would be presented with more daisies than roses and asked, "Are there more daisies or more flowers here?" According to Piagetian theory, children must be able to simultaneously add the subclass of daisies and roses to form the whole class of flowers ($B = A + A'$) and subtract daisies from the whole class ($A = B - A'$) in order to answer the question correctly. That is, in order to make the daisies-flowers comparison, they must be able to think of daisies as *daisies*—as subtracted from the class of flowers— while simultaneously thinking of daisies as *flowers*—as included in the class of flowers. This is an extremely difficult question for children, and until they are about 7 or 8 years old, they incorrectly claim that there are more daisies than flowers.

In devising this task, Piaget was concerned in part with children's ability to recognize the asymmetry of class inclusion, for example, that all daisies are flowers but not all flowers are daisies. More generally, Inhelder and Piaget (1964) were concerned with the systematic nature of classification, because their theory of concrete operational thinking specifies that the major developmental change from preoperational to concrete operational thinking is the acquisition of a system of reversible cognitive operations. This reversible system was thought to underlie much of cognition, including classification. Thus, the class-inclusion task was designed to assess whether children have the reversible system of addition and subtraction of classes.

According to Inhelder and Piaget, children must answer the question correctly before they can be granted a true understanding of classification. This is too stringent a criterion (Markman and Callanan 1983). First, the class-inclusion question involves many additional task requirements, beyond what it is trying to measure. It has been criticized for its confusing language and methodology, and many questions have been raised about what it is really measuring (see Gelman and Baillargeon 1983; Trabasso et al., 1978; Winer 1980 for reviews and discussions of the problems). But even if the class-inclusion question were a valid measure of class addition and subtraction, it still seems to be too conservative a measure of having a classification system. A child could understand the asymmetry and transitivity of class inclusion without being able to fulfill the additional requirement of simultaneously adding and subtracting classes.

Object Sorting.   Another common way of assessing children's conceptual organization has been to have them sort or classify objects. Inhelder and Piaget (1964), Vygotsky (1962), and Bruner, Olver, Greenfield, et al. (1966) have each used a variant of this task as a basis for their theories of conceptual development (see Gelman and Baillargeon 1983 for an insightful summary and comparison of these theories). As described in chapter 2, in the standard classification task children are presented with an array of meaningful objects (for instance, people, animals, buildings, and plants) or geometric figures of various shapes and colors. They are asked to put together the things that "go together" or that "are the same kind of thing." Bruner and his colleagues (see, for instance, Olver and Hornsby 1966) used a slightly different task: children were presented with a pair of objects and asked to say how they were alike, then another object was added and they were asked to say how the three were alike, and so on. In these tasks the youngest children seem to sort on the basis of thematic organization. With blocks, they form designs; with meaningful materials, they construct a scene or put together objects with which they can tell a story. In the second stage, children construct what are sometimes called "complexive" sorts. These groupings are based partially on similarity, but children are not consistent in the criteria they use within a category. For example, a child might put together a red circle and a green circle, then add a green triangle because it is green like the circle, and so on. In the final stage, by around age 7 or 8, children sort taxonomically as adults do.

Many of these studies—in fact, the great majority of studies with children 4 years old and older—examine children's ability to classify objects at the superordinate level of categorization. As discussed in chapter 4, the superordinate level of classification often includes objects that are perceptually quite diverse, such as a boat, airplane, car, and bicycle in the class of vehicles. We can safely assume, in many of these studies, that the children who participate can already classify the stimulus materials used at the basic level (for instance, they can recognize different boats as exemplars of the category "boat"). Thus, children who successfully classify at the superordinate level may then be credited with understanding that the objects can be multiply classified. For example, a child who sorts diverse vehicles together in a sorting task, including a boat and a car, must recognize not only that they are vehicles but also that one object is a boat and the other is a car. In fact, it may be fair to say that most studies of classification in preschoolers and elementary school children are really studies of multiple classification in this sense. Because children are being asked to sort objects at a superordinate level of classification, they are being asked to think of an object not just at its basic level (which they know well) but at a more general level as well. For this reason, many studies purporting to explore children's classificatory abilities have underestimated their ability to classify objects. What they have explored, instead, is children's ability to classify at the superordinate level, which in turn may be tantamount to studying, at least in part, children's ability to form explicit class-inclusion relations. In this chapter, then, we will be examining studies of children's classification of objects for what they might reveal about children's ability to represent class-inclusion hierarchies.

These tasks can underestimate whatever knowledge children do have of these object categories, even at the superordinate level. Children may have knowledge of these superordinate categories, but other factors prevent this category knowledge from being revealed.

One difficulty children have with the sorting task is that they may take the spatial nature of the task too literally. Children may interpret the spatial arrangement of the objects to be an important part of the task, and this may bias them to construct meaningful scenes or storylike groupings. Markman, Cox, and Machida (1981) attempted to reduce the salience of the spatial arrangement of objects by asking children to sort objects into transparent plastic bags rather than into spatially segregated groups on a table. Children displayed more taxonomic sorting when they sorted into bags than when they sorted the same objects on the table. Thus, the spatial demands of the task confuse children and mask some of their knowledge of categories.

A second problem children may have with the standard sorting task is that they have to cope with a very large number of objects. Children are typically faced with a scrambled array of 16 different objects, four each from four different categories. To successfully classify the objects, children must scan this bewildering array, find some of the categories salient enough to emerge from this confusion, and keep them in mind while trying to impose some order on the rest of the objects. In a variation of the standard task, the oddity task, children see only three objects and are asked to choose the two that are the same kind of thing (Daehler, Lonardo, and Bukatko 1979; Rosch et al. 1976). This task is much easier, and younger children appear to demonstrate knowledge of superordinate categories in this procedure.

A third difficulty with the standard procedure is that the children may not always be familiar with the categories used. If the category used by the experimenter in choosing objects to be sorted were not familiar to children, then it would not be surprising that they did not sort taxonomically. Given sets of objects that can be sorted into more familiar concepts, they should do better. The study by Horton (1982) described in chapter 4 addressed this question. Horton pretested children for their ability to explicitly describe the superordinate principle that united exemplars of a category. She later had children classify objects that came from categories they could explicitly state, compared to those they could recognize but not formulate. She found that a given child could more successfully classify objects from the superordinate categories that that child explicitly represented than objects from the categories that were less familiar. Mervis and Judd (cited in Mervis 1980) have shown that children are better able to sort groups of typical category members than groups containing typical and atypical members. They argue that atypical members may not be part of the child's representation for that category and that they may therefore be very difficult to sort correctly.

A fourth and final criticism of the standard classification procedure is that children's preferences for thematic sorts may conceal any categorical knowledge that they have. In a study mentioned in chapter 2, Smiley and Brown (1979) presented children of different ages with triads of items, including a standard object, a thematic associate, and a taxonomic associate. None of the children in their youngest age group (mean age 4:3) were able to consistently justify their original choices, nor were they asked to justify the alternatives. However, all of the other children were asked to justify the opposite pairing after they made their original choice on an oddity task. For example, a child who responded with the pair "cow and milk" would later be asked whether "cow" and "pig" could go together. Except for the youngest, all children were able to explain both types of groupings. Smiley and Brown conclude that the shift is due to differences in preference rather than capacity, since children were able to justify both types of groupings. It is not possible to evaluate this claim for the youngest children, however.

In a study with 2- and 3-year-old children Daehler, Lonardo, and Bukatko (1979) attempted to assess the early end of the developmental trend from thematic to taxonomic sorting. They presented their subjects with an object and then asked them to "find the one that goes with this one" from an array of four objects. They found that children were better at matching superordinate pairs than thematically related pairs and concluded that the thematic bias does not appear until after age 4. This would certainly be a very young age for superordinate classification to appear and might provide evidence that quite young children can represent hierarchical relations. However, the results are not as clear-cut as they seem (Markman and Callanan 1983). Several of the superordinate pairs were also thematically related (for instance, comb-brush). Children's good performance on matching these items may have been based on thematic relations rather than on common superordinate category membership.

In conclusion, there are many demands of the classical sorting task that may prevent children from demonstrating whatever incipient knowledge of categories they may have. To successfully solve the classification problems, a child must find the categories to be salient, explicitly represented, and readily accessible. Knowledge that is less explicitly available may be obscured by the procedure. The requirement to form spatial arrangements, the large number of objects to be sorted, the wording of the instructions, and children's relative unfamiliarity with the categories all pose problems for children and may interfere with their categorical knowledge. When these demands are minimized, children's ability to classify improves. However, even when some of the confusion is cleared up, young children do not exhibit overwhelmingly mature taxonomic performance. If there is a striking thematic option, young children are likely to take it. This preference to sort objects thematically, however, does not rule out the existence of taxonomic knowledge.

Studies of Categorization in Infants
No task that has been used to study categorization in infants or very young children has provided evidence about the transitivity or asymmetry of inclusion. However, there is a growing body of evidence about the categorization abilities of infants and extremely young children that at first sight appears to contradict findings with older children. That is, there is evidence for categorical structure in infants that needs to be reconciled with older children's failure to indicate categorical knowledge in the classification task. The procedures used with infants require much less explicit knowledge and have fewer extraneous demands than the standard classification task. These may be more sensitive measures of superordinate categorization and suggest that quite young children have begun to represent superordinate categories.

One of the main procedures for studying categorical knowledge in infants is the habituation paradigm. In this procedure, originally used to study infant perception, a given object is shown repeatedly until the infant's fixation time decreases. Once the infant has habituated to an object, a new object is shown that is either identical to the original object or different in some way. When infants look longer at the novel object than the familiar one, that is evidence that they have perceived the difference between the two objects. The logic of this design has been extended to studying concepts in infants and young children (Cohen and Younger 1981; Faulkender, Wright, and Waldron 1974; Ross 1980). Instead of showing the same object repeatedly, the experimenter shows different objects within the same category. If infants look longer at a new object from a novel category than at a new object from the familiar category, then that is taken as evidence for the infant's perception of the category. Taking dishabituation as a measure of having a concept, there is evidence for categorization abilities in infants, at least in those older than 6 months. Most of this evidence, however, is for infants' ability to form categories that are defined by perceptually available features. Cohen and Younger (1981) review many studies demonstrating conceptual abilities on the part of infants, but none of these studies used materials that would qualify as nonperceptually based or superordinate categories. The kinds of categories used—stuffed animals (as contrasted with a rattle) and faces—are most like basic or subordinate categories on Rosch et al.'s (1976) criteria.

One other study with 10-month-old infants is relevant (Husaim and Cohen 1981), because it comes close to examining the learning of superordinate categories by infants. The infants in this study were taught "ill-defined" categories, that is, categories that have no necessary and sufficient features but are defined instead by family resemblance structures.

Infants were trained to discriminate between two categories, both of which were cartoonlike animal figures. The figures could differ on several different dimensions: body size, length of neck, length of leg, and number of legs. For each of these dimensions, there were two possible values: a large or small body, a long or short neck, long or short legs, and two or four legs. One value on each dimension was selected to be characteristic of category A; that is, animals in category A were more likely to have these values. For example, although having a long neck was not necessary or sufficient for being in category A, an animal that had a long neck was much more likely to be in category A than in category B. The other value on each dimension was characteristic of category B. Each exemplar of category A had three of the four values characteristic of category A but one value characteristic of category B. Thus, no single value was necessary or sufficient, but the combination of features would be more typical of category A than of category B.

Ten-month-old infants were trained to turn their heads in one direction when they saw an animal from category A and to turn their heads in the other direction when they saw an animal from category B. When an infant made the correct response, an electronic toy animal was turned on to play a musical instrument. It was very difficult for these infants to learn the correct responses, and of the 63 who began the study, only 20 completed the learning session.

Once the infants learned the discrimination, they were given novel examples to see how they would transfer what they had learned. One of the novel examples was a prototype of the category. According to Husaim and Cohen, the results indicated that infants were able to learn the ill-defined categories, and their transfer to new examples and their exceptionally good transfer to the prototype supported this analysis.

If so, then there is a very puzzling developmental trend that needs to be explained. In a study already summarized in detail in chapter 3, Kossan (1981) taught first graders ill-defined categories—in fact, they were also cartoonlike animals that varied along several dimensions. One procedure involved presenting examples from each category to the children, who were to learn to discriminate between them. Although the first graders had to label the category instead of turning their heads, the procedure was essentially the same as that of Husaim and Cohen. The results were significantly different, however, since Kossan's first graders could not learn the categories under this type of training. The discrimination was too difficult for them. If we accept Husaim and Cohen's conclusion, then, we must figure out why the 10-month-old infants could succeed on a task at which the 6-year-old children failed.

Unfortunately, there is an artifact in Husaim and Cohen's study that could account for their results. Their categories were defined by selecting one value on each dimension to be characteristic of category A and the other to be characteristic of category B. The first thing to note is that all of the dimensions that they used had to do with size: length of neck, size of body, and so on. This differs from Kossan's study, where the dimensions included body pattern (for instance, stripes versus dots), shape of ears, and so on. Moreover, Husaim and Cohen did not select the values on a given dimension randomly. Instead, category A had a large body, long neck, long legs, and four legs. Category B had a small body, small neck, short legs, and only two legs. This unfortunate selection of dimensions and features probably explains why the 10-month-olds were able to solve the problem. The infants would not have to learn ill-defined categories at all; they could have solved the problem by a kind of "big versus small size" judgment. For further discussion of this study, see Kemler 1981.

Ross (1980) and Faulkender, Wright, and Waldron (1974) have presented evidence from studies with 1- to 3-year-olds that suggests some rudimentary perception of superordinate categories. Faulkender, Wright, and Waldron (1974) habituated 3-year-olds to animals, fruit, or environmental patterns. These children looked longer at an object from one of the other two categories than at an object from the category they had been habituated on. Since these categories differed so much perceptually, it could be some more superficial perceptual feature that accounted for these findings, though by 3 years of age one would expect that children would have begun to work out the animal and fruit categories at least. Ross (1980) presented 12-, 18-, and 24-month-old infants with the following categories: M's, O's, men, animals, food, and furniture. Over trials, children's looking times decreased for the M's and O's but not for the other categories. Nevertheless, for all categories, children looked longer at a new object from a novel category than at a new object from a similar category. Ross attempted to control for the superficial perceptual properties of the novel objects. Thus, 1- to 2-year-olds showed evidence of perceiving different kinds of food, different kinds of animals, and so on, as similar. These results suggest the possibility that sometime after the first year of life, babies begin to represent class-inclusion hierarchies.

These procedures differ from the traditional classification paradigm in several ways that might make the problem easier for children. First, of course, single objects are viewed one at a time, and a simple response measure is taken. The child is not forced to scan a jumble of 16 objects to determine explicitly which are most similar. Also, there is always only one contrasting category.

Another major difference is that no other response competes with the judgment of similarity. That is, for children asked to sort objects, their perception of similarity must be salient enough to dominate their perception of other relations between the objects. But in the method used for the habituation procedures no other relations are possible. For example, children are presented with pictures of babies over and over again until they have habituated to them. In the standard version of this procedure children are then shown either another baby or a totally unrelated object. There is never a comparison group in which a bottle, a crib, or some other strong associate of "baby" is shown and compared to an unrelated object. Thus, there is no way to assess the relative salience of similarity or category membership over other relations. Yet this is what the classification procedure measures.

It is not clear what would happen if thematic alternatives were given to infants. There might be a curvilinear developmental pattern. Young infants may not find thematic associations salient enough to interfere with the similarity between two objects. Some knowledge of the world, and of what causal, temporal events the objects participate in, is necessary before thematic responses are possible. So even if infants were presented with such alternatives, it might not interfere with their performance. In other words, infants could be more sensitive to categorical relations than older children, not because they know more about the categories, but because they know less about relations that compete with a categorical response. At an intermediate level of development thematic relations compete for attention with taxonomic relations and will often win, especially at a superordinate level where perceptual similarity is slight. At a more mature level the categorical similarity becomes salient enough that it will continue to be preferred to the thematic relation. It would be interesting to conduct studies with infants and very young children using thematic distractors, to test whether such a curvilinear developmental course exists. Thus far no thematic distractors have been used in studies of visual habituation or visual preference.

Thus, it is not hard to reconcile the claims that infants already have some knowledge of superordinate categories with the claim that elementary school children lack such knowledge. The tasks used in infancy are more sensitive measures of knowledge that eliminate some of the confounding factors present in the standard classification tasks. It might be fruitful to adapt some of the infancy procedures to use with older children. These tasks, however, may be overly sensitive to all sorts of relations other than taxonomic ones that exist between the objects.

Ricciuti (1965) introduced another procedure for studying conceptual development in infants that has been further developed by Starkey (1981) and Sugarman (1982). In this procedure young children are given objects to play with but are not told to group them in any way. Their spontaneous manipulation of objects is recorded. Ricciuti found that the order in which children touched the objects defined a temporal grouping and could be used to indicate that children perceived the similarity of the objects. Ricciuti used only geometric forms that differed on some dimension and were therefore very similar perceptually. Using sequential touching as the measure, Starkey (1981) found that 9- and 12-month-olds perceive several categories. By 12 months of age, children actually manipulated the objects into groups. However, the stimuli that Starkey used consisted of concepts such as red squares, red hooks, ovals, metal bottle caps, and toy plastic people. None of these categories is at a superordinate level of categorization; that is, none requires going much beyond a perceptual similarity. Moreover, thematic relations were unlikely with these materials. Sugarman (1982) also used only objects that were highly similar perceptually. However, because Sugarman argues that her findings reveal when babies begin to notice relations between classes, this work is relevant. Although the findings do not speak to superordinate classes per se, they are informative about the larger question of the systematization of categories.

Sugarman (1982) argues that because the final product of classification can be achieved by different routes, it is important to observe the procedures by which infants manipulate objects. Three object manipulation tasks were presented to children ranging in age from 12 to 36 months. Children were presented with eight objects, four each from pairs of categories such as plates and squares, spoons and cups, or dolls and circular rings.

In the spontaneous play task infants were given the objects and told to play with them. All children produced at least one construction that contained at least three out of four objects from one category. Sugarman does not report any data indicating how many of the constructions would have qualified as graphic or thematic constructions. We do not know, for example, how many times a child placed the spoon in the cup or put the doll in the ring. It would be interesting to compare the rate of production of such constructions to the classification data.

The percentage of constructions that sorted objects into two groups increased with age. Moreover, Sugarman argues that there is an important developmental difference in the way the two-class groupings were constructed. With one exception, all of the 12- and 24-month-old infants sorted objects one category at a time; for instance, they placed the dolls together before placing the rings together. The older infants were able to produce mixed groupings; that is, they shifted back and forth between categories, constructing them at the same time. It should be noted, however, that an extremely small percentage of the two-class constructions was produced in this mixed order, even by the oldest children. The percentage increased from 0% at 12 months to 2.6% at 36 months, a very small difference.

Although the rate of spontaneous production of mixed groups was very low, the developmental findings were substantiated in the other two tasks used. In the elicited grouping, a single object from one category was placed on a table, separated from a single object from the other category. Then the infant was shown another object and asked where it should go. This procedure was continued with the remaining objects from the two categories. Only the older children were able to alternate placement of an object from one category with placement of an object from the other. In the third task children were presented with two groupings, each containing three items from one category and one item from the other, and were asked to "fix them up." Again, only the older children could interchange the objects.

Sugarman argues that this developmental change indicates an ability to deal with relations between relations, or the coordination of relations. To construct a single category, children have only to decide whether an object is or is not in category A. In fact, construction of a single category can be accounted for by assuming increased salience of the category after selecting one member, without any explicit awareness of the categorical equivalence of the members. But according to Sugarman, to shift back and forth between categories, the child must consider whether that object is "A or B." Apparently Sugarman believes the disjunction implies a comparison between two similarity relations, and this relating of relations is a significant achievement.

This interesting analysis is consistent with data from other sources that Sugarman (1982) reports. However, the existence of mixed categorization strategies is rather weak evidence for the coordination of relations. The data reveal that older children are capable of simultaneously keeping both categories in mind. But this in itself is not evidence for any relating of the two categories. From the infant's point of view, the two tasks may be relatively independent of each other. The fact that two activities are conducted in alternation does not imply any conceptual link between the two. It implies the ability to shift attention from one task to another without interfering with the performance of either task. This is not necessarily evidence that the two categories are being coordinated in any conceptual way.

Hierarchical Organization of Ontological Knowledge

Some evidence that young children represent hierarchically organized categories comes from extremely interesting work by Keil (1979) on the development of ontological knowledge. In a somewhat indirect way, this work provides evidence that young children are capable of recognizing the transitivity of inclusion relations. Ontological knowledge refers to beliefs about what the basic categories of existence are. These are very general categories such as events, abstract ideas, physical objects, living things, and nonliving things. Building on a philosophical analysis by Sommers (1965), Keil (1979) argues that these ontological categories are organized into strict hierarchies; that is, there are no intersecting sets. One source of evidence for the hierarchical organization of ontological categories was obtained by determining what types of predication are permissible at different levels of the hierarchy. According to this view, if categories are organized hierarchically, then a predicate that is applicable to a category term at one level in the hierarchy should be applicable to all terms below it. The appropriateness of a predicate depends on whether or not it makes sense to apply the predicate to the term, and not on whether or not the predicate truthfully applies. In other words, the predicate must produce a sensible and not an anomalous sentence, but it need not produce a true one. Thus, "green" can be predicated of cows because, although cows are not green, we can make sense out of the sentence. In contrast, it makes no sense to say that a cow is an hour long. This is anomalous because terms denoting physical objects cannot take predicates such as "an hour long"; since a cow is a physical object, the sentence "a cow is an hour long" is not sensible. Thus, although it is applicability of a predicate rather than its truth that is at issue here, a transitive inference is involved.

The claim for hierarchical ordering implies that predicates that are sensibly applied to a category term at one level of the hierarchy will apply to all those below it. For example, the predicate "is red" can be sensibly attributed to physical objects but not to events. In accord with the hierarchical prediction, "red" can also be sensibly applied to all subsets of physical objects such as artifacts, plants, animals, and liquids.

The claim that ontological categories are hierarchically organized is not a trivial or vacuous one. Exceptions are certainly possible in principle, and in fact there do appear to be violations of this constraint (see Keil 1979 for discussion of why they may be only apparent exceptions). For example, the predicate "is rude" applies to nonphysical entities, as in "rude remark." It also applies to people, as in "rude person." However, it does not apply to other physical objects. For example, it is anomalous to speak of an orange being rude. But since "rude" refers to nonphysical entities high in the hierarchy (remarks) and to a physical object category low in the hierarchy (people), it should refer to the intervening physical object categories as well. Since it does not, it violates the hierarchical order.

Assuming, however, that most terms will obey the hierarchical ordering constraint, Keil (1979) investigated whether or not children's conceptual structure is hierarchical. Children as young as 5 years old were asked to make judgments about the appropriateness of a predicate for a term. The main difference found was that with development the ontological trees became more differentiated. That is, children appeared to collapse several nodes of the adult tree into one by, for example, allowing physical objects and events to share predicates that adults would have differentiated. Yet despite this difference, the children's categories still appeared to be ordered in a strictly hierarchical pattern. Children seem confused about the distinctions between abstract ideas, events, and physical objects and have not differentiated them as clearly as adults have. But the ontological categories children have established appear to be hierarchically ordered.

Keil's procedure probably overestimates the extent to which predicates follow a strictly hierarchical organization. The predicates that he tested are not a random selection of possible predicates. Rather, they often seem closely related to the criteria that define the ontological categories. For example, events, which have duration, form one ontological category. One predicate tested, which is closely related to having duration, was "is an hour long." Living things and sentient beings form two other ontological categories, and "is alive" and "is sorry" were two other predicates tested. Because the predicates are so closely related to the criteria that distinguish the ontological categories, they would be expected to conform to the hierarchical organization even if a more general sample of predicates might not.[1,2]

There are many differences between the work on ontological cate-

1. Gerard and Mandler (1983) have questioned the generality of Keil's procedure on other grounds as well. They suggest that pragmatic aspects of language use will influence how subjects decide whether or not a sentence is acceptable. The context in which sentences are presented as well as the instructions given may determine how subjects judge whether a sentence is sensible. To test this hypothesis, Gerard and Mandler asked subjects to judge the acceptability of sentences under several conditions. For some subjects, the target sentences were presented among filler sentences that were designed to be abnormal sentences. The prediction here is that against a background of bizarre sentences, subjects may judge supposed violations of the hierarchical ordering of predicates to be acceptable. Gerard and Mandler also varied the instructions. One group of subjects was warned not to allow any metaphorical interpretation of sentences to pass as acceptable. The other group of subjects was not so instructed. The results were as predicted. When not warned against metaphorical interpretations, and when presented with target sentences in a context of bizarre sentences, subjects judged more of the supposed violations as acceptable. There was a huge difference between Keil's results and those of Gerard and Mandler. Keil found virtually no violations of the hierarchical ordering in his studies, fewer than 1%. Gerard and Mandler found 40% violations. Even in the condition that most closely replicated that of Keil (1979), Gerard and Mandler found substantial numbers of violations of the hierarchical ordering. They suggest some minor differences in the instructions and subjects that may have accounted for these differences but conclude that pragmatic factors powerfully affect subjects' judgments.

2. Carey expresses a very different kind of concern about Keil's analysis. Although she does not dispute Keil's original findings, she offers several compelling counterexamples to the claim that a strict hierarchical ordering of predicates with respect to categories is possible. Carey considers the predicates "is long" and "contains gold" applied to mass terms such as "water" or "copper," to holes, and to shadows. No matter what arrangement of these kinds of categories and predicates we try, it is impossible to find a strict hierarchical organization that is not violated. Mass terms refer to "stuff" such as water or copper. But, Carey argues, "stuff" is inherently dimensionless, so it makes no sense to talk about water being "big" or "long." Thus, to maintain the hierarchical ordering of predicates, we could not place predicates such as "big" or "is long" at the node where physical objects are or where stuff is without producing this violation. The predicate "contains gold," although false, is applicable to water and so could be placed at a higher node. But this poses a problem when we consider shadows and holes. Since shadows and holes have extent, it makes sense to speak of them as being "big" or "long"; but since they are not made of anything, it makes no sense to speak of them as "containing gold."

gories and standard treatments of categorical knowledge. First, the level of generality of the two types of categories differs. Ontological categories consist of extremely general categories such as "physical object" and "abstract idea," whereas most studies of categories focus on more specific categories such as "vehicles," "dogs," "roses," and so on. Keil (1979) points out another difference: most studies of traditional categories specify which features are true of a given category rather than which features are sensible. For example, most analyses of categorization would emphasize that birds have feathers and bats do not. In contrast, from the ontological perspective, the predicate "having feathers" can be sensibly attributed to both birds (truly) and bats (falsely), so these two categories would not be differentiated in the ontological hierarchy. If we convert Keil's procedure to making judgments of truth rather than appropriateness of the predicate, it can be seen that the predicates, as well as the categories, are extremely general. For example, it is because ideas do not have color that "the idea is green" becomes anomalous. Because physical objects do have color, the sentence "the cows are green" is sensible. Thus, the predicates that are truly attributed to the terms are extremely general ones such as "has color," "has weight," "has duration." In sum, ontological knowledge can be expressed in terms of sentences attributing very general properties to very general categories such as "physical objects have weight."

The work on ontological categories reveals that 5-year-olds have the potential to organize categories hierarchically—that the representational capacity exists. But there is little systematic data on children younger than 5 concerning this kind of knowledge of ontological categories. Keil reports from preliminary work with young children, however, that their hierarchical tree is very radically collapsed—so much so that they may treat everything as a physical object. Thus, Keil's work would not provide evidence for the representational capacity of children younger than 5. It is also difficult to know how to generalize from Keil's work to ordinary categories in terms of what children actually accomplish. We cannot generalize from the way children represent ontological knowledge to the way they represent much more differentiated categories such as "poodle," "dog," and "mammal."

Children's Understanding of the Asymmetry and Transitivity of Inclusion
A study by Harris (1975) more explicitly addressed whether children appreciate the transitivity and asymmetry of class inclusion. In this study children ranging in age from 5 to 7 years old were told, for example, "A mib is a bird" and then were asked "Does a mib have

wings?" and "Does a mib eat food?" Children almost invariably responded "yes" to these questions, inferring that the properties of the category will transfer to a new subset or a new member of the category. It is possible, however, that children took the term "mib" to be a synonym for "bird" rather than a type of bird. Moreover, the children showed little evidence of understanding the asymmetry of inclusion. When told, for example, that a mib was a bird, a sizable proportion of the children were likely to conclude that it was a robin. The results are not reported according to age, so we do not know whether these invalid inferences came mainly from the younger children. The inappropriate inferences could be prevented by specifying a property that would be incompatible with the inference. For example, when told that a mib was a *white* bird, children no longer concluded that it was a robin. However, this could be because children know that robins are not white and not because they understand the asymmetry of inclusion.

The clearest evidence that young children have some appreciation of the asymmetry of inclusion comes from a study by Smith (1979) that improved upon the methodology originally used by Inhelder and Piaget (1967) to study this question. Inhelder and Piaget (1964) showed children a category of objects (say, flowers) divided into two subsets (daisies and roses) and asked quantified questions about them such as "Are all the roses flowers?" In their study children denied that all the roses were flowers, noting that there were daisies too. This finding suggests that children interpreted the inclusion relation as being symmetric (all the roses are flowers and all the flowers are roses) rather than asymmetric. However, the details of the methodology and data are not clear in Inhelder and Piaget's report, and the research has been extended in important ways by Smith (1979) and also by Carey (1978).

In Smith's (1979) study children ranging in age from 4 to 6, who had passed a pretest demonstrating their understanding of "all" and "some," were questioned about three consequences of inclusion.

One type of question was about class inference. Children were told, "A ___ is a kind of x." They were then asked, "Does a ___ have to be a y?" In one-third of the cases the conclusion was valid (where x was a subset of y), in one-third of the cases the conclusion was indeterminate (where x was a superset of y), and in one-third of the cases the conclusion was invalid (where x and y were disjoint). An example of a valid item is "A pug is a kind of dog. Does a pug have to be an animal?" Note that "pug" is unfamiliar to children, whereas "dog" and "animal" are familiar.

Children were also asked questions about property inferences.

They were told, "All x's have ____," and were asked, "Do all y's have to have ____?" As before, one-third of the inferences were valid, one-third were indeterminate, and one-third were invalid. An example of a valid inference is "All milk has lactose. Does all chocolate milk have to have lactose?"

The 6-year-old children were able to draw the appropriate transitive inferences very reliably, getting close to 90% correct. The 4-year-olds, though not performing nearly as well as the older children, did demonstrate an ability to draw the appropriate transitive inferences. For the class inference task and the property inference task, the 4-year-olds answered 64% and 66% of the questions correctly, which was above chance performance.

In addition to testing children's ability to draw transitive inferences from the class-inclusion relation, Smith tested children on their understanding of the asymmetry of inclusion. Children were asked questions using the quantifiers "all" and "some" for three types of set relations: where x is a subset of y, where x is a superset of y, and where x and y are disjoint. Half of the children heard questions involving the quantifier "some" first, and half heard questions involving the quantifier "all" first. The youngest children's ability to answer the questions correctly varied markedly as a function of the task demands. By the second half of the procedure, the youngest children were showing little sign of understanding the asymmetry of the relation. Similarly, when the questions involving the quantifier "some" were asked first, children showed little sign of understanding the asymmetry. In these "unfavorable" conditions, children sometimes responded in accord with Inhelder and Piaget's claim that children treat the inclusion relation as a symmetric one. However, on the first half of the trials for those children who answered questions about the quantifier "all" first, even the youngest children consistently honored the asymmetry of class inclusion. Though their ability to deal with it is fragile and easily disrupted, 4-year-old children are able to appreciate the asymmetry of the class-inclusion relation.

Macnamara (1982) has suggested a promising method for determining whether children understand the asymmetry of class inclusion. Suppose we present a child with a dog and an elephant and ask simple yes-no questions such as "Is this a dog?" and "Is this an animal?" If the child knows that the dog is "a dog" and agrees that it also is "an animal," and if the child knows that the elephant is "an elephant" and that it too is "an animal," and if the child denies that a dog is an elephant and that an elephant is a dog, then we could credit the child with knowing the inclusion relation. Unfortunately, not enough systematic work of this sort has been done (though there is some question how successful it would be since, as I will discuss in chapter 8, young children will not always agree that, for instance, a dog is an animal).

Some work has even been done on a chimpanzee's understanding of quantified relations (Premack 1976). Premack taught Sarah, the linguistically trained chimpanzee, the quantifiers "all," "none," and "one." Two sets of crackers were used in training. One set consisted of five round crackers and nothing else, the other set consisted of five square crackers and nothing else. Sarah had to note that "all" of the crackers were round when presented with the round crackers and that "none" of the crackers were round when presented with the square crackers. In the first attempts to train Sarah, her error rate was very high, on the order of 12 errors out of 20 trials. The training was then modified to include another set of crackers, triangular ones, and to ask separate questions about round, square, and triangular crackers instead of always asking about round ones. With this additional training, Sarah's performance was 74% correct. Thus, this advantaged chimpanzee seems capable of making simple quantified inferences.

However, there is no way of knowing whether or not Sarah understood the asymmetry of the relation. Recall that the error children make in interpreting quantifiers is to deny that (for example) all roses are flowers because there are some daisies too. For Sarah to be able to find the analogous error in this situation, the materials would have to consist of all round crackers plus some other round things, say, round cookies. With the current materials the relation between the two classes is in fact symmetric; that is, all the crackers are round and all the round things are crackers. Because Sarah was presented with a symmetric rather than an asymmetric relation, it is not possible to tell whether she understood the asymmetry of class inclusion.

Premack (1976) noted that in this training the relations being quantified were perceptually defined. Sarah could see that the crackers were round. The materials were extended to see whether Sarah could learn to quantify over conceptually defined relations. She was asked to quantify over part-whole or belonging relations. For example, she was asked to judge whether an apple wedge, apple skin, and an apple stem were all parts of an apple. Sarah could successfully quantify over this conceptual relation. One might be tempted to generalize from this finding to assume that Sarah could quantify class relations on a conceptual basis. However, as I will argue later, there are striking differences between part-whole and inclusion relations, and children are capable of solving problems with part-whole relations that they fail with class inclusion.

Summary and Conclusions

Human categories do not exist in isolation but instead are often related to each other. One widespread type of relation among categories is the class-inclusion hierarchy. To determine when children represent categories hierarchically, it is first necessary to define criteria for judging when someone has represented one category as being included in another. Simply being able to categorize the same object in two different categories (which are at two levels of a hierarchy) guarantees only a very primitive, implicit hierarchical organization. That criterion is trivially satisfied by any concept. A somewhat more stringent criterion is that one of the concepts be nonperceptually based, as in the case of superordinate categories. This criterion may much more often lead to correct diagnosis of a hierarchical organization, although it is not foolproof. What seems to be the clearest evidence for hierarchical organization is an understanding that the relation between the categories is asymmetric and transitive.

The literature on children's classification was reviewed with these criteria in mind. The Piagetian class-inclusion problem, where children need to make quantitative comparisons between included classes, is often not solved by children until age 6 or older. This task is an overly conservative measure of whether children represent class-inclusion hierarchies, however, even on a Piagetian account where it requires reversible operations. A large body of research on object sorting exists where children are asked to sort objects at the superordinate level. Good sorting by superordinate categories would not provide evidence for understanding the asymmetry and transitivity of class inclusion but would provide evidence that children can classify a single object into two categories: the object's basic level category and its superordinate level category. Children often do not perform well on these sorting tasks until they are 6 years old or older. Here again, though, the task is very conservative and suffers from many extraneous task demands, including having to cope with large numbers of objects and having to override competing thematic relations.

Research on classification in infancy depicts a very different developmental course. Using habituation procedures or simple selection tasks, researchers have found some evidence that children as young as 1 year old have begun to represent some common superordinate categories (Ross 1980; Faulkender, Wright, and Waldron 1974). These procedures eliminate the extraneous demands of the sorting tasks and may therefore provide a much more sensitive measure of children's knowledge.

Research on understanding the transitivity and asymmetry of class inclusion is quite rare, but the existing work suggests that children have the capacity to draw inferences based on these relations by age 4. Keil's (1979) research on children's hierarchical organization of ontological categories reveals that by age 5, children have the capacity to draw transitive inferences such that if a predicate is applicable to one ontological category, it is applicable to all the categories included in it. Smith's (1979) work, which is one of the few studies to directly test children's understanding of the asymmetry and transitivity of class inclusion, also indicates that by age 4 children have the capacity to represent these relations and that by age six the representation of asymmetry and transitivity is quite robust.

In conclusion, on the weaker criterion for class inclusion, there is evidence that the ability to represent class-inclusion hierarchies exists in 1-year-old babies. This primitive representational ability of babies presumably becomes more explicit and more readily accessed by children, such that by age 4 children have begun to understand the asymmetry and transitivity of class inclusion.

Chapter 8

Collections versus Classes: Indirect Evidence for the Mutual Exclusivity Assumption

Class inclusion is one way of systematizing categories. Another very simple way in which categories are related to each other is that many categories are mutually exclusive; that is, an object can be a member of only one of them. This is especially apparent at the basic level of categorization, where an object cannot be both a cat and a dog, a cat and a bird, and so on. I will argue more extensively in chapter 9 that very young children assume that category terms are mutually exclusive and that this assumption, along with the assumption of taxonomic organization discussed in chapter 2, helps them acquire word meanings. One problem that arises for children is that these two ways of systematizing categories—class inclusion and mutual exclusivity—are in conflict. If children are biased to treat category terms as mutually exclusive, then class-inclusion relations should be more difficult to learn because class inclusion violates mutual exclusivity. In a class-inclusion hierarchy, one category is included in another, and both category names can refer to the same object. That is, the subordinate and superordinate categories are not mutually exclusive in such a hierarchy.

From the child's point of view, then, class inclusion poses special problems. The child knows that a particular object—say, a doll—"is a" doll. Now the child hears that the object "is a" toy. On the assumption of mutual exclusivity, the child will have difficulty understanding how a given object can both be a doll and be a toy.

In addition to helping to explain why children have difficulty with class-inclusion relations, the mutual exclusivity assumption may help to explain why children find the part-whole organization of collections easier to represent than inclusion hierarchies. Collections are the referents of collective nouns (for instance, "forest," "pile," "family," "army") and are structured into part-whole hierarchies (a tree is part of a forest, a block is part of a pile, a child is part of a family, and so on). In the past I have offered several distinctions between classes and collections and argued that these distinctions contribute to the differences in children's abilities to deal with these two kinds of relations (Markman 1981, 1984). What I want to emphasize now is the possibility that collections are easier for children because, unlike class-inclusion hierarchies, they do not violate mutual exclusivity. In a collection structure a particular object is not given two labels. Something "is an" oak, for example, but it "is part of" a forest. Hence, mutual exclusivity is maintained.

Children have several choices when confronted with a label (say, "animal") for an object for which they already have a label (say, "dog"). I consider two of these choices here, though I will discuss more in chapter 9. One possibility, the correct choice in this case, is to violate mutual exclusivity and to recognize that one of the categories ("dogs") is included in the other ("animals"). Another possibility is to erroneously treat the more general term as though it referred to a collection rather than a class. By imposing a collection structure on the class-inclusion hierarchy, children would be able to salvage the mutual exclusivity assumption and begin to work out the hierarchical structure between the two categories. The part-whole structure of collections provides a potential substitute for class inclusion that does not violate mutual exclusivity. The studies to be reviewed next address whether children might impose part-whole structures on class-inclusion hierarchies.

Learning Hierarchical Relations

If children prefer the structure of collections to that of class inclusion, then they might organize objects into collections rather than classes when they need to construct a hierarchy. If so, this would run counter to what one would expect based on the familiarity or frequency of words in English. Class terms are far more frequent in English than collective nouns, and children must have encountered many more of them. Nevertheless, it could be that the collection hierarchy is easier for children to construct. When children are relatively free to impose their own structure on a novel hierarchy, they might prefer a collection to a class-inclusion organization.

This hypothesis was tested by contriving a situation in which children were presented with only minimal information about a hierarchical relation (Markman, Horton, and McLanahan 1980). This study was designed to see how children would spontaneously interpret the relations when given relative freedom. Novel class-inclusion relations were taught to children using drawings of novel objects that were referred to by nonsense syllables. Four different categories were used, each consisting of two lower level categories. Figure 8.1 presents one exemplar from each of the lower level categories for all four

ANIMATE – SIMILAR

ANIMATE – DISSIMILAR

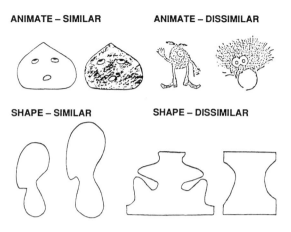

SHAPE – SIMILAR

SHAPE – DISSIMILAR

Figure 8.1
Illustrations of the exemplars of each category used in Markman, Horton, and Mc-Lanahan 1980

categories. The category terms were taught through ostensive definition (pointing and labeling: "These are wugs," "These are bifs," "These are daxes"). This allowed us to specify the inclusion relation in a minimal way. To clarify the procedure, I will illustrate it using a familiar class-inclusion relation. Imagine that oaks and pines are lined up in a row. The experimenter would point to the oaks, saying, "These are oaks"; to the pines, saying, "These are pines"; and to the trees (the oaks and the pines), saying, "These are trees." In English, when objects are labeled using a plural noun ("These are trees"), it means that each individual object is an exemplar of the category (each individual tree is a tree). Thus, the use of the plural establishes the class-inclusion relation. In contrast, a singular term, a collective noun, would have to be used in order to refer to a collection; in the setting just described someone would point to the trees, saying, "This is a forest." Although the ostensive definition provides only minimal information, it does establish that the objects presented form a class-inclusion hierarchy.

After the inclusion hierarchies were taught by ostensive definition using plural (nonsense) terms, children were questioned about single objects using singular (nonsense) terms. For a given category, children were asked a yes-no question for an object from each of the lower level categories and then were asked whether the singular category term for the upper level applied to one of the objects. Again, to illustrate with a familiar hierarchy, the questions were analogous to pointing to a pine and asking, "Is this a pine?", pointing to an oak and asking, "Is this an oak?", and pointing to an oak and asking, "Is this a tree?" The children were also asked to show the experimenter an example of the lower and upper level categories, again analogous to being asked to "Point to an oak," "Point to a tree."

Suppose children misinterpret the class-inclusion relation as a collection hierarchy. They should, then, erroneously believe that several of the items together form an instance of the concept at the higher level of the hierarchy (trees, in the example) but should not believe that any single item is an instance. To see why, consider what the correct response would be had children actually learned a collection, say, "forest." If asked to point to the forest, children should point to many trees but should deny that a pine or any other single tree is itself a forest.

Children from 6 to 17 years of age participated in the study. Each child learned four novel categories, one at a time, each composed of two subcategories. All of the category exemplars were small construction paper figures of novel shapes or novel animate creatures. Nonsense syllables were used as names for the novel figures.

The results of this study revealed that until a surprisingly late age children tend to misinterpret class-inclusion relations as collections when only minimal information is provided. When novel class-inclusion relations were taught by ostensive definition, children as old as 14 often mistakenly interpreted the relations as collections. The results are presented in table 8.1, which gives the number of errors children made out of a possible 8. The right half of the table presents the errors made on the lower level categories, divided into the yes-no questions ("Is this an x?") and the behavioral questions ("Show me an x"). Children hardly ever made an error on these novel lower level categories. When asked to "Show me a wug," children correctly picked up a single wug. When the experimenter, pointing to a wug, asked, "Is this a wug?" children correctly said, "Yes." The errors occurred almost exclusively on the upper level of the hierarchy (see the

Table 8.1
Mean number of errors for yes-no and behavioral questions by grade, learning condition, and hierarchical level, from Markman, Horton and McLanahan 1980

| Grade | Upper level | | Lowel level | | |
	Yes-no	Behavioral	Yes-no	Behavioral	Total
2	5.83	4.25	0.33	0.25	2.67
6	4.17	3.33	0.33	0.00	1.96
8	4.17	4.58	0.25	0.00	2.25
11	0.83	0.75	0.33	0.00	0.48

left half of table 8.1). With the exception of 11th graders, who rarely made an error, children gave collection interpretations to the categories around 50% of the time. When asked of the upper level categories to "Show me a dax," children often scooped up all of the daxes rather than just one. This is analogous to being asked "Show me a tree" and picking up all the oaks and pines rather than a single tree. For the yes-no questions about the upper level, children often denied that a single dax was a dax. This is analogous to children saying of an oak that it is not a tree. This is exactly as would be expected if children were answering questions about a collection.

At least in the somewhat artificial conditions of this study, children found it simpler to impose a collection structure on a novel hierarchy than to correctly interpret it as a class-inclusion relation. This is true despite the fact that children must certainly have more experience learning inclusion relations, since collective nouns are relatively rare. Because this was an unusual way to learn novel concepts, one might suspect collection errors to be unlikely in natural situations. However, certain anecdotal (Valentine 1942) and experimental (Macnamara 1982) evidence suggests that such errors may indeed be found in a naturalistic context.

Callanan and I (Callanan and Markman 1982) conducted a more controlled study to further investigate this possibility. We questioned 2-, 3- and 4-year-old children about five familiar hierarchies that consisted of an upper level category (for instance, toys) that was divided into two lower level categories (for instance, dolls and balls). If children interpret such hierarchies as collections, then they should believe that the upper level label applies only to a group of objects and not to any single individual. Children were asked two types of questions on which they could make collection errors: yes-no questions such as "Is this a doll?" and "Is this a toy?" and questions that required a behavioral response such as "Put a doll in the box" and "Put a toy in the box."

Each category and subcategory that we used was pilot tested to ensure that the objects and their labels were familiar to the young children in this study. Items were included in the study only if the children tested could correctly answer questions about the upper level label for the entire array ("Are these toys?") and about the lower level labels for individuals ("Is this a ball?"). The five categories and their subcategories were toys (balls and dolls), animals (horses and cows), drinks (milk and juice), children (boys and girls), and cars (racing cars and Volkswagens). Two small objects were used to represent each subcategory.

Overall, children's performance was very good. They answered questions correctly over 75% of the time. Yet children did occasionally interpret these hierarchies as collections. If children interpret these categories as collections, then it is on singular questions about the top level of the hierarchy that errors should dominate. This is what we found. Children made more errors on singular questions about the top level of a hierarchy (24%) than on singular questions about the lower level (16%). Children agreed, for example, that several animals were "animals" but would deny that a single animal (a horse, for example) was itself an animal and would pick up several animals when asked for one.

We were able to rule out several alternative explanations for these findings. One possibility is that if children were unfamiliar with the higher level category terms, the errors could have reflected their lack of knowledge rather than a collection interpretation of the term. As mentioned earlier, these category terms were pretested to ensure their familiarity to even very young children. Nevertheless, there were some errors in comprehension. To test this possibility, we examined children's responses only for those items on which they did correctly answer the upper level plural question. That is, children had to agree that the group of toys was "toys," that the group of animals was "animals," and so on. Having guaranteed correct use of the category term for plural questions, we still found children to be interpreting the terms as referring to collections. Children made more errors (22%) on questions about the upper level of the hierarchy ("Is this a toy?" or "Put a toy in the box") than on singular questions (15%) about the lower level ("Is this a ball?" or "Put a doll in the box").

Another possibility is that children's responses could have resulted from strategies induced by the experimental procedure. During the course of the procedure, children may have been influenced by labels that they had previously used or heard the experimenter use. Children may have been more likely to reject the upper level singular term for an object if they had already labeled the same object with a lower level term. For example, having said "yes" to "Is this a cow?", a child might be prone to say "no" when later shown the same cow and asked, "Is this an animal?" To test this possibility, we divided the upper level singular questions into two groups: those questions that were asked before the lower level question for each subcategory, and those questions that were asked after the lower level question. The error rates for these two groups were virtually identical. Regardless of the order in which labels were mentioned, children interpreted some of the categories as collections.

A final possible explanation for these findings is that children might pick the best label for a given array and then reject any other label. If so, they would deny that a doll is a toy because "doll" is a better label than "toy." To test this hypothesis, we asked children whether the superordinate label applied to a plural but homogeneous set of objects. For example, children were shown two dolls and asked, "Are these toys?" If the hypothesis were correct, then children should have denied that the dolls were toys because the best label for the two dolls would be "dolls," not "toys." The results argue against this hypothesis and support the collection interpretation. Children accepted the higher level labels for groups of homogeneous objects, with an error rate of 14%, as well as they accepted singular terms at the lower levels, with an error rate of 13%.

These findings suggest that in first acquiring natural language terms for superordinate categories, young children at least occasionally distort some class-inclusion relations into the part-whole structure of collections.

A second study using a somewhat different procedure was conducted to provide converging evidence that children sometimes treat natural language inclusion hierarchies as collections (Callanan and Markman 1982). Two- and 3-year-old children played a game with a puppet who needed help in deciding whether certain statements were "okay" or "silly" things to say. The sentences were analogous to the yes-no questions of the previous study. It was predicted that a child who has imposed a collection organization on the hierarchies should judge as "silly" sentences in which a singular upper level term (say, "toy") is applied to a single object (say, a doll).

As in the previous study, children made relatively few errors. As before, however, they made the largest number of errors when they were judging sentences about single objects at the top level of the hierarchy—for example, judging the sentence "This is an animal" (said of a cow) to be silly.

However, in this sentence judgment task, unlike the previous study, children did prefer the best labels for the objects. That is, children judged sentences such as "These are animals" to be silly when said of two cows. To some extent, then, they may have interpreted their task as being to help the puppet decide on the preferred thing to say.

In summary, in both of these experiments children were capable of working out the appropriate class-inclusion relations for highly familiar categories. When they did make errors, however, they tended to impose a collection organization on these categories. Thus, even in naturally occurring contexts, very young children may find it simpler to impose a collection structure on what are actually inclusion hierarchies they are trying to learn. In order to make this incorrect collection interpretation, children in the natural setting must disregard many linguistic and nonlinguistic cues. In addition, collective terms are rare relative to class terms in English, and 2- and 3-year-old children are unlikely to have many in their vocabularly or to hear them used very often by adults. Because these factors work against the imposition of a collection structure, its occurrence suggests that in some ways it is a simpler or preferred organizational principle for young children. I argued earlier that one reason collection hierarchies should be preferred to class-inclusion hierarchies is that collections do not violate mutual exclusivity, whereas class inclusion does.

The Role of Language in Helping Children Construct Hierarchies

These findings suggest that if superordinate category terms were represented by collective nouns, then children would find them easier to learn. But collective nouns cannot themselves serve as superordinate terms for the very reason that they express a different relation. And this difference is extremely important when one considers the function of taxonomies. One of the main purposes of taxonomies is to support inductive and deductive inferences. For example, if I know that something is true of all mammals (that they breathe, eat, are warm-blooded, and so on), then once I learn that a previously unfamiliar animal is a mammal, I can transfer all of this knowledge to the newly introduced animal. Collections do not support inferences in the same way. Properties true of a forest may not be true of individual trees. Nor will properties shared by the trees allow an inductive inference that they will also be true of the forest. Thus, although the part-whole organization of collections is simpler for children to learn, it is not a useful substitute for the inclusion relation that defines taxonomies. I will argue, however, that mass nouns may provide an appropriate substitute for collective nouns.

Many superordinate category terms in English are mass nouns (for instance, "furniture," "jewelry," "money"), even though conceptually they refer to diverse, discrete, countable objects. This violates the common intuition that mass terms refer to masslike homogeneous substances, such as milk or clay, or to substances made of small, virtually identical particles, such as sand or grass. That is, the homogeneity of the substance and the difficulty of individuating elements of the substance characterize the semantic basis of many typical mass terms. Yet "furniture," for example, refers to heterogeneous, readily individuated objects. I will argue for a functional explanation for this violation of the semantic basis of mass terms. However, many other exceptions to this oversimplified semantic rule (see Gordon 1981) may reflect only unprincipled vagaries of English. For example, some (but not all) abstract concepts are referred to by mass nouns (for instance, "justice"); some seemingly countable objects are referred to by mass nouns ("toast," "paper"); and some substances are referred to by mass nouns ("gravel") whereas other very similar substances are referred to by count nouns ("pebbles"). There may not be any cogent explanation for all of these idiosyncrasies. I will argue, however, that the exception for superordinate categories is a principled one.

By using mass nouns to refer to superordinate categories, languages may help speakers learn hierarchical relations between the superordinate and lower level categories. Like collective nouns, mass nouns may help children represent a hierarchy; unlike collective nouns, however, they may be able to accomplish this while still maintaining a taxonomic organization. I have argued (Markman 1985) that in a sense mass nouns can be viewed as a compromise between collections and classes or, to be more precise, as a compromise between "part-whole" and "is a" relations. Consider a typical mass such as clay. A piece of clay is part of the whole mass of clay. This is similar to the part-whole organization of collections, where each tree, for example, is part of the forest. On the other hand, each piece of clay is itself clay. This is more like the "is a" relation of class inclusion, where each oak is a tree. Another way of thinking about these distinctions is that mass nouns could provide a purely linguistic rather than a conceptual advantage over count nouns, in constructing hierarchies. By designating inclusion in the higher category by "piece of" or similar phrase, one may circumvent the problem of having two "is a" relations, which clearly violate mutual exclusivity. Instead of having to say that a given object, for example, "is a" chair and "is a" furniture, one says it is a "piece of" furniture. This linguistic differentiation of the way relations at the lower and higher categories are specified may itself be helpful.

Thus, for conceptual reasons, linguistic reasons, or both, by referring to discrete objects with mass terms, a language might be able to provide some of the advantages that the part-whole organization of collections would have achieved, yet remind the speaker that an inclusion relation is still involved.

This analysis predicts that this peculiarity should not be limited to English. Other languages with a count-mass distinction should also have this type of aberration. Further, if these aberrations serve the purpose of helping to give stability to hierarchically organized categories, then such "inappropriate" mass terms should occur mainly

on superordinate or relatively high levels of the hierarchy, not on relatively low levels. That is, languages should contain terms that require a speaker to say "a piece of furniture" or "a piece of vehicle" in
order to refer to a single piece of furniture or a single vehicle. But
they should not require a speaker to say "a piece of chair" or "a piece
of car" in order to refer to a single chair or a single car. I tested this
hypothesis in Markman 1985 by asking native speakers of various
languages to judge whether terms were count nouns or mass nouns
in their language.

All of the participants in this study spoke English as a second language. They were asked to translate 25 higher level category terms
that are relatively common in English into their native language and
judge whether or not the terms could be used in a phrase in which
the objects were counted directly, such as "two pencils," or whether
they required a quantificational phrase, such as "two cups of sugar."
All of the object categories used by Rosch et al. (1976) and Rosch
(1975) that fulfilled Rosch's criteria of superordinate categories were
used in this study. Several other high level categories were added.
The left-hand column of table 8.2 presents these categories. For each
category, two lower level terms were also selected to be translated:
one a very common, high-frequency exemplar, and the other a somewhat lower-frequency exemplar. For example, for the category "veg-
etable," informants would judge whether "carrot" and "onion" were
mass or count nouns in their native language. (Due to an error, two
terms were omitted, leaving 48 rather than 50 lower level judgments.
Thus, there were almost twice as many opportunities for lower level
terms to be judged as mass nouns as there were for superordinate
terms. Table 8.3 presents the 48 lower level categories used, arranged
to correspond to the higher level categories of table 8.2.

Table 8.4 presents the languages that were included in this study,
classified according to their language family and subgroup. Eigh-
teen languages, at least 11 different subgroups, and 7 different
language families were represented (Katzner 1975; Voegelin and
Voegelin 1977).

American Sign Language was included in the sample. It should be
noted that the superordinate terms in ASL are not finger-spelled English terms. Quite often they are compound signs, such as "knife-
fork" for "silverware" (Newport and Bellugi 1978).

The results of this study strongly support a functional explanation
for the fact that superordinate terms are often mass nouns. As can be
seen in table 8.4, in every language family, every language subgroup,
and, in fact, every language, some superordinate categories are represented by mass nouns. In marked contrast, lower level category

Table 8.2
Number of languages (n = 18) treating each superordinate term as a mass noun, from Markman 1985

Term	Number of languages
Money	17
Food	16
Clothing	13
Furniture	11
Reading material	11
Sports equipment	11
Jewelry	10
Silverware	9
Fruit	9
Vegetable	9
Footwear	6
Headgear	6
Linen	5
Weapon	6
Human dwelling	6
Tools	5
People	5*
Toy	2*
Building	1
Musical instrument	2
Flowers	1
Vehicle	1*
Tree	0
Animal	0
Bird	0

*One additional language had an optional mass usage.

Table 8.3
Number of languages (n = 18) treating each lower level term as a
mass noun, from Markman 1985

Term	Number of languages	Term	Number of languages
Dollar	0	Towel	0
Penny	0	Gun	0
Egg	0	Sword	0
Shirt	0	House	0
Belt	0	Apartment	0
Chair	0	Hammer	0
Mirror	0	Saw	0
Book	0	Man	0
Magazine	0	Woman	0
Ball	0	Doll	0
Racquet	0	Church	0
Ring	0	School	0
Bracelet	0	Piano	0
Fork	0	Guitar	0
Spoon	0	Rose	0
Apple	1	Daisy	0
Melon	1	Car	0
Carrot	2	Airplane	0
Onion	2	Oak	1
Shoe	0	Palm	0
Skate	0	Dog	0
Hat	0	Pig	0
Scarf	0	Robin	0
Sheet	0	Eagle	0

Table 8.4
Percentage of superordinate and basic-level terms that are mass nouns in
each language, from Markman 1985

Family	Subgroup	Branch	Language	Higher level category	Lower level category
Indo-European	Germanic	Western	Afrikaans	44	0
Indo-European	Germanic	Western	Dutch	48	0
Indo-European	Germanic	Western	English	48	0
Indo-European	Germanic	Western	German	40	0
Indo-European	Romance		French	36	0
Indo-European	Hellenic		Greek	16	0
Indo-European	Slavic	Eastern	Ukrainian	16	0
Indo-European	Indo-Iranian		Urdu	44	0
Uralic	Finno-Ugric	Finnic	Finnish	16	0
Uralic	Finno-Ugric	Ugric	Hungarian	24	0
Altaic	Turkic	Southwestern	Turkish	44	0
Independent			Japanese	28	0
Independent			Korean	24	0
Afro-Asiatic	Semitic	North Arabic	Arabic	44	2
Afro-Asiatic	Semitic	Camanitic	Hebrew	20	0
African			Guro	32	8
African			Nzema	20	0
			American Sign Language	68	4
Mean percent				34	.7

terms are almost always represented by count nouns. Overall, languages represented an average of 34% of the superordinate categories as mass nouns. In marked contrast, languages represented an average of less than 1% of the lower level terms as mass nouns. Every one of the 18 languages studied encoded more superordinate terms than lower level terms as mass nouns.

Table 8.2 presents the number of languages out of 18 that represented each of the 25 superordinate categories as a mass noun. With the exception of "tree," "animal," and "bird," every superordinate category was represented by a mass noun in at least one language. In contrast, as can be seen in table 8.3, of the 48 lower level category terms, only 5 were treated as mass nouns in any language.

There is one aspect of the procedure that may have exaggerated the extent to which informants judged terms from their language to be mass nouns. Informants were asked to translate the English category term into their native language and then judge whether it was a count or mass noun. Languages may have more than one way of referring to a given category. Hearing the English mass noun might bias informants to select a mass noun category term over a count noun term when both options are available. A second study was carried out to test this possibility. In this study informants were given lists of objects and asked to generate the appropriate category terms that referred to the lists in their language. (Speakers of a few languages that were not represented in the first study were also included.) The English superordinate terms were never presented. To take two examples, the informants were asked what word in their language referred to (1) coat, dress, shorts, and skirt, and (2) knife, gun, bomb, and spear. The results indicated that the original procedure did not exaggerate the extent to which superordinate category terms are represented as mass nouns. The results of the second study replicated the finding of the first study that a substantial proportion of these superordinate category terms are represented by mass nouns.

In summary, these findings reveal a striking tendency for languages to refer to higher level but not lower level categories with mass nouns. Moreover, the procedure used probably underestimated the magnitude of the effect. Although the 25 category terms selected were familiar to English-speaking cultures, they were not always important in other cultures. For example, there were 13 categories with no translation into Nzema, 10 with no translation into Ukrainian, and 7 with no translation into Turkish. Thus, the proportion of superordinate categories that were denoted by mass nouns is greater when considered as a proportion of the easily translatable categories than when considered as a proportion of the total number of categories. If superordinate categories had been selected that were more frequent in these various cultures, even more of them may have been referred to by mass nouns.

This study established that it is not just English that refers to superordinate categories with mass nouns. There is a systematic tendency across languages to use mass nouns to refer to these categories. This finding provides indirect support for the hypothesis that hearing superordinate categories referred to by mass nouns should help speakers learn the categories. A third study reported in Markman 1985 tested the hypothesis more directly by comparing how well children learn a new category when it is labeled by a mass versus a count noun. Preschool children were taught a new superordinate category for familiar objects. For example, they were taught the new category "vehicle" for a bicycle, a boat, a plane, and a fire truck.

There were two training conditions. In one the category was referred to with a mass noun, in the other with a count noun. Otherwise the training procedures and categories taught were identical. The prediction was that children who hear, for example, "A car is a piece of vehicle," "This (a boat, a plane, a bicycle, and a fire truck) is some vehicle," and "How much vehicle is here?" should be better able to learn the category than children who hear "A car is a vehicle," "These (a boat, a plane, a bicycle, and a fire truck) are vehicles," and "How many vehicles are here?"

Three- and 4-year-olds were selected to participate in the study because the procedure was feasible with them and because there is evidence that children this young can learn the count-mass distinction even when it is taught as a syntactic distinction, that is, without semantic support (Gordon 1985).

Children were taught one of three categories: "sports equipment," "vehicles," or "bathroom supplies." Four exemplars were used to teach the category. For example, for the category "sports equipment" children were shown a racquet, a helmet, a hockey stick, and a baseball mitt. In the subsequent tests children were shown new exemplars and distractors for each category. Some of the exemplars were very similar to the training exemplars (for example, a different helmet). Some of the exemplars were novel (for example, a soccer ball). Some of the distractors were designed to be simple to reject (that is, they were quite distinct from the category exemplars), whereas some were designed to be more difficult to distinguish from the exemplars.

Children were introduced to a puppet and told that the puppet was going to play a game with them in which she would teach them a special puppet word for some of the pictures they would see. They were given training to learn the new category and were tested on their ability to distinguish category exemplars from distractors; they were then retrained and retested. The only difference between the two conditions was that children in the mass noun condition always heard the new term (a nonsense syllable) used as a mass noun, whereas children in the count noun condition always heard it used as a count noun. To illustrate, if the new word was "veb" and the category was "bathroom supplies," some of the training items for the two conditions were as follows: (1) The puppet pointed to the four exemplars (soap, shampoo, comb, and toothpaste) and said, "This is veb" (for children in the mass noun condition) or "These are vebs" (for children in the count noun condition). (2) The puppet pointed to several of the items, saying, "Here are some pieces of veb" (for children in the mass noun condition) or "Here are some vebs" (for children in the count noun condition). (3) The puppet asked, "How much veb is here?" (for children in the mass noun condition) or "How many vebs are here?" (for children in the count noun condition).

In general, the 4-year-old children in this study found these superordinate categories difficult to learn. This is to be expected given the well-known difficulty that young children have with superordinate categories and given that this procedure provided only minimal training. Nevertheless, having the categories encoded by mass nouns rather than count nouns helped children learn them. Although the effects were small, children in two studies who heard mass nouns were significantly better able to discriminate category exemplars from distractors, especially after the second training session. The pattern of responding was quite different for children in the two conditions. Children who heard the categories labeled with count nouns did not learn very much about the categories. In fact, the majority of these children tended to respond in a highly stereotyped manner. Fifty-six percent of the children hearing count nouns answered at least seven out of eight questions in the same way; that is, they showed an extreme bias to say "yes" to everything (or, in some cases, "no"). Not one of the children hearing mass nouns responded in such a stereotyped manner. Thus, children hearing count nouns seemed bewildered by the task, perhaps confused about the violation of mutual exclusivity—about how the new word related to objects whose labels they already knew. Instead of becoming involved and trying to learn the category terms, they gave up and resorted to stereotyped responding. In contrast, children hearing mass nouns seemed to understand that they were to learn the new category terms and focused on the task at hand, at least trying to figure out what the new term referred to.

Taken together, the results from these three studies indicate that languages tend to use mass nouns to refer to superordinate categories because this way of encoding the categories helps children to learn them. In other words, children can capitalize on their knowledge of the count-mass distinction to help them organize categories into hierarchies.

The Piagetian Class-Inclusion Question

In addition to being a simpler relation than class inclusion for children to acquire, the structure of collections may be simpler for children to explicitly analyze or reason about. Several well-known Piagetian tasks require children to consider quantitative relations between one class and a class it is included in. As discussed in chapter

7, young children find the asymmetry of class-inclusion hierarchies difficult to maintain. For example, children find questions such as "Are all the roses flowers?" difficult (Inhelder and Piaget 1964). They often incorrectly answer "no" because there are daisies and other flowers around. This suggests that they are answering a question about the total identity of the classes, a symmetric relation, rather than a question about the asymmetric relation of inclusion. Even adults can become confused and treat inclusion as a symmetric relation. In syllogistic reasoning tasks, for example, when adults hear a premise such as "All As are Cs," they erroneously infer that "All Cs are As" (Ceraso and Provitera 1971; Chapman and Chapman 1959; Revlis 1975). With abstract or unfamiliar material, adults fail to treat inclusion as asymmetric.

Because it does not require learners to cope with two "is a" relations, the asymmetry of part-whole relations should be easier to maintain than the asymmetry of class inclusion. That is, the two levels of a collection hierarchy are clearly distinct, whereas the levels of a class-inclusion hierarchy are more similar and thus more confusable. For class inclusion, both levels of the hierarchy involve the same "is a" relation. A poodle "is a" dog and "is an" animal. This may contribute to the child's confusion of levels and difficulty in keeping track of the asymmetry. If there is less confusion between part and whole than between subclass and superclass, then the asymmetric relations of collections will be easier to maintain.

Since collections are predicted to help children maintain the asymmetry of the hierarchy, one might think that collections should also help children appreciate transitivity. This does not follow, however, because the part-whole relations of collections are not transitive. A property true of the whole will not necessarily be true of the part. For example, if we know that a family is large, it does not follow that a child in the family is large. If we know that a pile of bricks is U-shaped, it does not follow that the bricks in the pile are U-shaped. Because the two levels of the collection hierarchy are defined by different relations, transitivity is violated, but the asymmetry should be simpler for children to establish and maintain.

One task that requires quite explicit knowledge of class-inclusion relations is the Piagetian class-inclusion problem (Inhelder and Piaget 1964). This task requires, among other things, that children be able to keep both levels of a hierarchy in mind to compare them. For this reason, children are asked to make a quantitative comparison between a superordinate set and the larger of its subordinate sets. For example, a child might be shown pictures of four baby pigs and two adult pigs and asked, "Are there more baby pigs or more pigs?" Although children are asked to make a part-whole comparison (baby pigs versus pigs), they make part-part comparisons (baby pigs versus adult pigs) instead. In devising this task, Inhelder and Piaget were concerned, in part, with children's ability to recognize the asymmetry of class inclusion, for example, that all baby pigs are pigs but that not all pigs are babies. To answer the class-inclusion question correctly, children must keep the whole class in mind while simultaneously attending to its subclasses. This division of the superordinate class into subordinate classes strains children's ability to keep the whole class in mind. If part-whole relations of collections are easier for children to represent, then children should be better able to keep the whole class in mind even while focusing on the parts.

In several studies children have consistently revealed a superior ability to make part-whole comparisons with collections as opposed to classes (Markman 1973; Markman and Seibert 1976). Each study encompassed two conditions. The objects children viewed and the questions they were asked in the two conditions were identical. The only difference between the two conditions lay in the description of the higher level of the hierarchy. For instance, for the "baby pigs–pigs" comparison in the class condition, children were told, "Here are some pigs. These are the baby pigs and these are the big pigs and these are the pigs." They were then asked, "Who would have more pets, someone who owned the baby pigs or someone who owned the pigs?" As usual, young children often answered incorrectly, claiming that there were more babies (when there were more babies than big pigs). The collection condition version of this question was identical except that "pigs" was changed to "pig family": "Who would have more pets, someone who owned the baby pigs or someone who owned the pig family?" With this kind of change in how the higher level category was labeled, children became better able to solve the part-whole comparisons that they usually find so difficult.

An alternative explanation for these findings has been proposed by Dean, Chabaud, and Bridges (1981). They argue that collective nouns in English can connote large numbers of objects. For example, terms such as "bunch" and "pile" refer to large numbers of objects. If children are sensitive to this aspect of collections, Dean, Chabaud, and Bridges argue, it may provide them with a strategy for answering the collection question that does not require knowledge of the logic of part-whole relations. In other words, it may be that children think collective nouns mean "a lot" of something and that they choose the collective term in the class-inclusion task for this reason. If so, this would mean that the collection advantage on the class-inclusion task would be an artifact of the procedure—collections always label the

most numerous set of objects (the whole array), and the correct answer is always to choose the collection. Under the large number
interpetation, then, children should choose the referent of the collective noun, even when it is not the correct answer. For example, if the
smaller subject of objects is labeled as "a family" or "a bunch," children who are responding on the basis of the semantics of the collective terms should incorrectly respond that the small subset has more
objects. Dean, Chabaud, and Bridges set out to test this hypothesis,
by comparing children's responses to standard collective whole questions with their answers to class-inclusion questions in which the
smallest subpart was labeled as a collection. They found some tendency for children to incorrectly choose the less numerous subset
when it is labeled as a collection. Unfortunately, problems with the
design of the study, ranging from failing to counterbalance important variables to confounding the kind of instructions children were
given in the class versus collection conditions, make these results
inconclusive.

Although it is possible that children are to some extent sensitive to
the large number interpretation of collective nouns, Callanan and I
(Callanan and Markman 1985) have evidence that this interpretation
cannot account for the results reported by Dean, Chabaud, and
Bridges. Several of the problems with their procedure would have
seriously confused children about what was being asked of them.
First, children always viewed the same array of objects, and the same
collective noun was used to refer to different parts of the array from
one question to the next. For example, in order to answer one question about green and brown frogs, a child might be told to suppose
that the green and brown frogs were a family. On the next question
the child might be told to suppose that the green frogs were a family
but the brown frogs were not a family. This continual shifting of referents for the collective noun is quite confusing, especially for young
children. Second, the wording of the questions was problematic.
Whenever a collective noun was used, the questions were worded in
a hypothetical manner. Children were asked to "suppose" that one
group of frogs were a family and then asked, "Do you think that
there are more frogs or more in the family?" This use of hypothetical
language for the collection questions is likely to encourage children
to answer the question based on the meaning of the term rather than
on the basis of the objects in front of them. Third, to ensure that
children would remember which group of objects was currently
being labeled with the collective noun, the experimenters repeatedly
tested them, asking, for example, "Which one is the family?" Children were given feedback until they could respond correctly. This

testing and feedback occurred only for the collection conditions, never for the class conditions. This procedure would have made the collective referent very salient to children and could well have biased them to give collective responses.

Children in this study, then, could have been biased to make collective responses, both by their confusion about shifting reference and by the experimenter's repeated emphasis on the collective noun. Particularly when they are confused about what they are being asked to do, young children are apt to rely on some response bias. Because this study was inconclusive, Callanan and I conducted another study to test the large number hypothesis. We followed the logic of the procedure suggested by Dean, Chabaud, and Bridges but eliminated the confounds and other problems we noted with their experimental procedure. In this study 48 children were divided into four groups of 12 children each. Each child was asked five questions about five different arrays. One group was asked the standard class-inclusion question, namely, to compare the whole class to the larger of its subparts (the class-whole condition). Another group heard the whole set labeled as a collection and was asked to compare the collective whole to the larger of the subparts (the collection-whole condition). These two conditions were the same as those in the original Markman and Seibert (1976) study, and Callanan and I expected to replicate the finding that hearing the whole set described as a collection should help children solve the problem. A third group was asked to compare the whole class to the smaller subclass (the class-subset condition). We predicted (as had Dean, Chabaud, and Bridges) that children should rarely select the smaller class here. The fourth group was also asked to compare the whole class to the smaller subclass, but now the smaller subclass was labeled with a collective noun (the collection-subset condition). We predicted that if the large number interpretation is correct, then children should be likely to pick the collective noun in this condition. If, on the other hand, collections help children answer correctly because they better understand the part-whole structure of collections, and not for a superficial reason, then children hearing the smaller subset labeled as a collection should, like their class-inclusion counterparts, be unlikely to pick the smaller subset as having more.

The main question is whether children will select the set described by a collective noun as having more, even when that is not the correct answer. If so, then children hearing the less numerous subset described by a collective noun should select the less numerous subset as having more objects more often than children hearing the less numerous subset described by a count noun. The number of times chil-

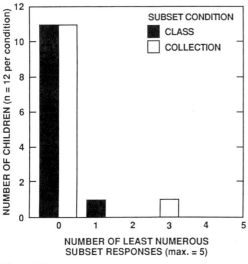

Figure 8.2
Number of Children selecting the least numerous subset as having more from 0 to 5 times, from Callanan and Markman 1985

dren selected the less numerous subset as having more is presented in figure 8.2, according to whether children were in the collection-subset or class-subset condition.

Children could select the less numerous subset between 0 and 5 times. The histogram shows the number of children who chose the less numerous subset 0, 1, 2, 3, 4, and 5 times. It is obvious from this distribution that there was no tendency for children to choose the subsets that were labeled as collections. The median number of subset choices was 0 across the collection-subset and the class-subset conditions. In fact, only two children made any responses in which they chose the less numerous part: one child in the class-subset condition and one child in the collection-subset condition. In contrast to the findings of Dean, Chabaud, and Bridges (1981), there is clearly no difference between these two conditions.

If children's good performance on collection-whole questions could be accounted for by a bias to say that collections had more, then there should be no difference in the number of children saying that the collection had more depending on whether it referred to the whole set or the subset. Yet, in contrast to Dean, Chabaud, and Bridges, we found a marked difference between the two collection conditions. Children could make from 0 to 5 collection choices in the collection-subset condition, which is shown in the white bars of figure 8.2. They could also make from 0 to 5 collection choices in the collection-whole condition, which is shown in the white bars of figure 8.3. Children who heard the whole array labeled as a collection were much more likely to respond with collective nouns than were children who heard the less numerous part labeled as a collection (Mann Whitney $U = 14$, $z = -3.62$, $p < .0005$). Therefore, children's correct responses on collection-whole questions cannot be explained by an overall bias to make collective responses.

We also replicated the original finding that treating the whole sets as collections helps children solve the part-whole comparison problems (Markman 1973; Markman and Seibert 1976). This can be seen in figure 8.3, which presents the distribution of responses in which children in the collection-whole and class-whole groups selected the whole set as having more. The mean number of "whole" responses by children in the class-whole condition was 1.67, compared to 3.58 for children in the collection-whole condition. Children hearing the whole set described by a collective noun were better able to answer the questions than children hearing the whole set described by a count noun, $p < .02$, by a median test.

In sum, the results are very straightforward and provide no support for the large number hypothesis. As in the original work demonstrating children's improved ability to solve part-whole comparison problems on collections (Markman and Seibert 1976), children were

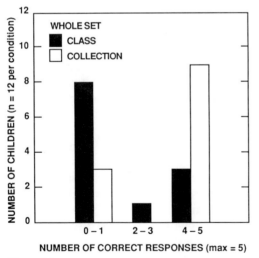

Figure 8.3
Number of children correctly selecting the whole set as having more from 0 to 5 times, from Callanan and Markman 1985

more likely to choose the collective whole than to choose the whole array labeled with a class term. Moreover, children almost never chose the less numerous part of an array, whether it was labeled by a class or a collection term. For example, children who were shown an array of trees labeled as a forest of oak trees and some Christmas trees did not say that there were more in the forest than there were trees. These results contradict the prediction of the large number hypothesis. When the problems of Dean, Chabaud, and Bridges's (1981) procedure are eliminated, it is clear that children do not show a bias to choose small arrays labeled with collective nouns. Thus, the large number hypothesis is not a viable alternative explanation for the collection advantage on the Piagetian class-inclusion problem.

Empirical versus Logical Solutions to Part-Whole Comparison Problems

I have just summarized evidence that children unable to solve part-whole comparison problems with classes are able to solve them with collections. The studies to be reported next (Markman 1978) addressed whether children have an even more explicit understanding of the logic of class inclusion.

Given a part-whole relation, it follows logically that the whole is larger than any one of its parts. Children could, however, correctly answer the Piagetian class-inclusion question on empirical rather than logical grounds. They could take the greater numerical size of the superordinate set as compared to its subordinate set to be an empirical fact about the class rather than a logical consequence of the inclusion relation. Given the hypothesized abstractness of the part-whole relation of class inclusion, children might be expected to have difficulty examining the relation in order to assess its logical consequences.

There are several ways of determining whether children understand the logic of the problem. First, when empirical means of judging the relative numerical size of the classes are withheld from children, they should still be able to answer the question. Second, children should realize that no addition or subtraction of objects could result in the subordinate set having more members than its superordinate set. Third, if a new, unfamiliar class is said to be subordinated to another class, then children should be willing to make the part-whole comparison without any additional information about the classes. A child who does not solve the part-whole comparison problems in these situations can be said to be treating the answers as empirical rather than logical consequences of the classes.

All the second through sixth graders who particpated in the studies reported in Markman 1978 could consistently solve the traditional class-inclusion problem. Based on results from these subjects, the first study established that when children initially solve the class-inclusion problem, they do so on empirical rather than logical grounds. Children below the age of about 10 or 11 did poorly on class-inclusion problems when empirical means of quantification were not available, and they often allowed for the possibility that a subordinate class could be made larger than its superordinate class. Thus, children who could consistently solve the traditional class-inclusion problem treated the quantitative relationship between the subordinate classes as an empirical fact.

The more literal part-whole relation that characterizes collections should promote an explicit appreciation of the logic of the problem. The hypothesis was tested in a replication of the first study that included a condition in which children heard objects described as collections. As before, children from grades two through six participated, and only children who demonstrated competence in solving standard class-inclusion problems were included in the study. The findings from the first study were replicated. Again, children failed to appreciate the logic of the class-inclusion problems. In contrast, the collection questions produced superior performance. Although the materials used and the questions asked were identical in all respects except for the collection-class difference, children solving collection problems better appreciated that empirical confirmation of the part-whole comparison is not needed.

Summary and Conclusions

In this chapter I have suggested that one simple way in which children relate categories is by assuming that they are mutually exclusive. Mutual exclusivity and class inclusion are two ways that children have of systematizing categories—of organizing them with respect to each other. The problem for children is that these two organizing principles conflict with one another because class inclusion violates mutual exclusivity. Children's bias toward treating categories as mutually exclusive should make it more difficult for them to work out class-inclusion relations. In addition to helping explain why children have difficulty with class-inclusion relations, the mutual exclusivity assumption may also help explain why children find the part-whole organization of collections (such as "forest," "family," "pile") easier to represent than class-inclusion hierarchies. In a collection structure a particular object is not given two labels. Something "is an" oak, for example, but "is part of" a forest.

One consequence of this hypothesis is that children should tend to distort class-inclusion hierarchies into collections. By imposing a collection structure on the class-inclusion hierarchy, children would be able to salvage the mutual exclusivity assumption and begin to work out the hierarchical structure between the two categories. Two lines of evidence support the prediction that children should mistakenly interpret class-inclusion relations as collections. One comes from a study of children learning artificial categories, where even early adolescents distorted class-inclusion relations into the part-whole structure of collections (Markman, Horton, and McLanahan 1980). Another comes from a study of very young children learning natural language hierarchies. Two- and 3-year-olds sometimes misinterpret superordinate category terms as though they referred to collections. A child who agrees that a set of dolls and balls are "toys" will deny that a single doll is a toy and, when asked to "Show me a toy," will pick up all the dolls and balls rather than just one (Callanan and Markman 1982).

Given that children prefer collections to class inclusion as a means of forming hierarchies, then if superordinate categories were represented by collective nouns, children would find them easier to learn. Because collective nouns do not readily allow for the making of transitive inferences, they would not be suitable as superordinate category terms. I have argued, however, that mass nouns could provide an appropriate substitute for collective nouns. That is, languages could capitalize on the fact that, like collections, mass nouns have a kind of part-whole organization, but that, unlike collections, they allow transitive inferences to be made. Many superordinate category terms in English are mass nouns, for example, "furniture," "jewelry," "clothing," "food," "money." If there is a functional explanation for why these category terms are mass nouns, then superordinate category terms in other languages should also show some tendency to be represented by mass nouns. Evidence from bilingual speakers of over 20 different languages supported this hypothesis (Markman 1985). Further, children who are taught new superordinate category terms as mass nouns should learn them better than children taught them as count nouns. Children who are taught, for example, "A car is a piece of vehicle," "This is some vehicle," "How much vehicle is here?" should find it easier to learn the category "vehicle" than children who are taught "A car is a vehicle," "These are vehicles," "How many vehicles are here?" This hypothesis was supported in two studies of young children learning new categories (Markman 1985).

Collections may help children reason about hierarchies as well as learn them. Evidence for this came from studies in which children were asked modified versions of the standard Piagetian class-inclusion question, which asks for a quantitative comparison between a subset and the whole set. In several different studies children were better able to make part-whole comparisons on collections than on classes (Markman and Seibert 1976; Markman 1978).

Thus, both in terms of the learning of hierarchical relations and in reasoning about hierarchical relations, collections are easier for children to deal with than is class inclusion. One reason why collections may be easier for children is that they do not violate mutual exclusivity as class-inclusion relations do. These findings provide implicit support for the argument that children are biased to assume that category terms are mutually exclusive. Chapter 9 examines this mutual exclusivity assumption in more detail and provides more explicit evidence in support of it.

Chapter 9
Mutual Exclusivity

In this chapter I present a more complete discussion of the mutual exclusivity assumption, compare it to other similar assumptions, provide more direct evidence that children expect terms to be mutually exclusive, and draw some of the implications of the mutual exclusivity assumption for language acquisition.

The Mutual Exclusivity Principle

In chapters 7 and 8 I discussed one aspect of systematizing categories and organizing them in relation to one another, namely, the construction of category hierarchies. This kind of systematization focuses on overlap and inclusion among categories. There is also a complementary aspect of systematizing categories concerned with the relationships among catgories in general, but most especially with the relationships among categories at the same level of a hierarchy. This aspect focuses on differences or separation among the categories—exclusion rather than inclusion. The most extreme form of this emphasis on distinguishing categories from each other is to treat them as mutually exclusive. In this chapter I will examine the mutual exclusivity principle primarily with respect to word meanings (although at the end I will consider whether it is more properly viewed as a general principle of category formation and not just as a principle related to language).

Given the nature and function of category terms, they will tend to be mutually exclusive. Categories, especially the richly structured categories and natural kinds discussed in chapters 5 and 6, provide much correlated information about an object. Given an object's basic level category, for example, many properties are implicitly attributed to it. To be a member of more than one such category requires that two or more such richly structured sets of properties be attributable to the same object. A single object cannot be both a chair and a dresser or a table. A single object cannot be both a cow and a bird or a dog. Thus, in order for categories to be informative about objects, they will tend to be mutually exclusive, especially at the basic level of categorization. Of course, there are exceptions: categories can overlap, as do "dog" and "pet," and they can form inclusion relations, as do "poodle" and "dog." The point here is that mutual exclusivity is a reasonable, though not infallible, assumptions to make. By assuming mutual exclusivity, children would avoid redundant hypotheses about the meanings of category terms, and in many cases would be correct.

Sometimes, of course, children would be led astray by assuming terms to be mutually exclusive. Adhering to this assumption, as I argued in chapter 8, would explain why children find class inclusion difficult (because it violates mutual exclusivity) and why the part-whole relation of collections is simpler (because it maintains mutual exclusivity). We expect, however, that children's lexicons will eventually include many violations of mutual exclusivity. To acquire class-inclusion relations, for example, children must override their initial tendency to assume that terms are mutually exclusive. With enough evidence to the contrary, children will allow multiple labels for the same object. Thus, violations of mutual exclusivity in children's lexicons are not necessarily evidence against this principle. The claim is that children should be biased to assume, especially at first, that terms are mutually exclusive, relinquishing that assumption only when confronted with clear evidence to the contrary.

Related Principles

Three closely related principles have been hypothesized to account for other aspects of language acquisition. I will briefly discuss two of these: Slobin's (1973) principle of one-to-one mapping and Pinker's (1984) uniqueness principle. Since the third—Clark's (1983, 1987) contrastive principle—is the most closely related to mutual exclusivity, I will consider it in greater detail.

One-to-One Mapping
One of Slobin's (1973, 1977) operating principles of language acquisition is that children expect the organization of language to be clear. That is, underlying semantic relations should be marked clearly and overtly. One way of accomplishing this is for languages to establish a one-to-one mapping between the underlying semantic structures and the surface forms. The one-to-one mapping principle was originally formulated for morphemes in a sentence. Extending this principle to category terms, however, would be tantamount to positing mutual exclusivity of the terms. That is, each category would be referred to

by only one category term. Mutual exclusivity is consistent with the one-to-one mapping principle and therefore would also be consistent with expectations that the organization of the lexicon would be clear.

Extending Slobin's principles of overt and clear marking of relations to the category domain provides another way of seeing why class-inclusion relations are difficult for children, relative to part-whole relations. As mentioned earlier, class membership and class inclusion are described by the "is a" relation regardless of the level of the hierarchy. For example, a particular object "is an" oak and "is a" tree. For the part-whole relation, a different relation is used at each level. A given object "is an" oak but "is part of" a forest. Using two distinct relations should be a clearer and more overt way of marking the relation and should be simpler on Slobin's criteria.

The Uniqueness Principle
The uniqueness principle (Pinker 1984; Wexler and Culicover 1980) is another related principle that has been hypothesized to help account for the acquisition of language. The motivation for this principle is to help explain how children can acquire grammatical rules in the absence of negative feedback. If children are not informed that a given grammatical rule they have hypothesized is wrong, how can they reject erroneous hypotheses and settle on the correct grammar for their language? Following Wexler and Culicover (1980), Pinker (1984) argues that the need for negative evidence in language acquisition can be eliminated if children assume the uniqueness principle. That is, when children are faced with a set of alternative structures fulfilling the same function, they should assume that only one of the structures is correct unless there is direct evidence that more than one is necessary. This principle allows children to reject structures even when there is no negative feedback indicating that they are ungrammatical. Languages do violate the uniqueness principle to some extent. According to Pinker, however, children require more evidence to accept a construction that violates the principle than one that does not.

Mutual exclusivity is consistent with the uniqueness principle as applied to category terms. Further, as Pinker argues for the domain of syntax, if children start out biased to assume that terms are mutually exclusive, then they should require more evidence to accept a construction such as class inclusion that violates mutual exclusivity than to accept one that is consistent with it. There is one major difference between the rationale for the uniqueness principle and the rationale for mutual exclusivity. The major impetus behind postulating the uniqueness principle is the problem of lack of negative evidence in language acquisition. There is very little evidence that parents or other adults explicitly correct children's ungrammatical sentences, and even some evidence that they do not (Brown and Hanlon 1970). A theory of the acquisition of syntax cannot depend on children being explicitly corrected when their constructions are wrong. Moreover, even when children do receive negative feedback, there is a serious problem of interpreting what aspect of an utterance is being criticized (Bowerman 1987; Gleitman 1981). The situation is, I believe, quite different in the acquisition of vocabulary. Children are frequently corrected when they use wrong labels for objects or mistakenly use other terms: for example, "It looks like a dog, but it's a wolf," "That's not a dump truck, it's a fire truck." How widespread such corrections are for children at various stages of language acquisition and how children make use of these corrections has not yet been investigated to any great extent, but the situation is clearly different from that of the acquisition of grammar. Nevertheless, children may still be able to make use of the mutual exclusivity principle in a way that is analogous to their use of the uniqueness principle, thus enabling them to reject certain hypotheses about a word's meaning because it would violate mutual exclusivity, even if no negative evidence were provided.

The Contrastive Principle
Clark (1983, 1987) postulates a third related principle to help account for semantic acquisition. Following Bolinger (1977), she argues that every word in a dictionary contrasts with every other word and that to acquire words children must assume that word meanings are contrastive. Mutual exclusivity is one kind of contrast, but many terms that contrast in meaning are not mutually exclusive. Terms at different levels of a class-inclusion hierarchy, such as "dog" and "animal," contrast in meaning in Clark's sense, since obviously the meaning of "animal" is different from that of "dog." Yet these terms violate mutual exclusivity. Mutual exclusivity is one specific way in which terms could contrast in meaning, but only one way among many. Mutual exclusivity is a more specific and stronger constraint than the contrastive principle. Moreover, evidence in favor of one of these principles is not necessarily evidence in favor of the other. Children could act in accord with the contrastive principle and yet violate mutual exclusivity, as just described. On the other hand, children could assume that terms are mutually exclusive but not assume the more general contrastive principle. Some of the evidence that Clark (1987) cites for the principle of contrast is, in fact, evidence in support of mutual exclusivity as well and thus is helpful in considering the latter.

The contrastive principle states that every two forms contrast in meaning. From this principle, Clark (1987) develops three predictions: (1) there are no synonyms; (2) established words have priority in the expression of meaning; and (3) innovative words fill lexical gaps and therefore may not be used in place of established words from the same meanings. Clark (1983, 1987) provides an extensive review of the literature from both linguistics and language acquisition in support of the lexical contrast theory.

As for the first prediction, Clark argues that apparent synonyms are in fact not synonymous. Some, such as "sofa" and "couch" or "autumn" and "fall," mark differences in dialect. Others, such as "cop" and "police," mark differences in register, where terms are marked according to whether they are colloquial, polite, pretentious, and so on. Others differ in connotation, such as "skinny" and "slim," where one has a negative and one a positive connotation. Still others differ in their collocations, such as "rancid" (which can be said of butter and fat) versus "addled" (which can be said of eggs and brains).

According to this argument, then, apparent synonyms do not conflict with the contrastive principle because they are not genuinely synonymous. Any given pair of apparent synonyms actually marks some difference in meaning.

Although Clark's examples are often compelling, there are problems with this line of argument. First, what may be true of a given language is not necessarily true of a given speaker of the language. That is, linguistic facts are not necessarily psychological facts. For example, although the pairs "sofa/couch," "pail/bucket," "autumn/ fall" differ in terms of which dialect of English introduced them, it is not clear that they differ in meaning to any given speaker who knows them both. Speakers might use both "pail" and "bucket" equally naturally without having any sense that one is more a part of their dialect than the other, and without having any sense of a difference in their meanings. Thus, there may be cases, perhaps only a few but perhaps more, where for a given speaker terms are genuinely synonymous.

A second problem is that, to preserve the claim that all apparent synonyms really provide contrasts in meaning, differences in register count toward differences in meaning. On this view, "cop" and "policeman" differ in meaning. There are two difficulties with this argument. One is that notions of "formality," such as whether a term is polite versus colloquial, are not on a par with other components of meaning. To see why, consider the more usual kind of semantic feature, such as "animate" or "human." Suppose I know that a given term includes the feature "human." I can then conclude that any term that is subordinate to that term also includes the feature "human." This same transitivity of features is not true of register differences. Although a captain is a kind of cop, "captain" is not a slang term. So differences in register are not the same as differences in meaning, or, not to prejudge the issue, as other differences in meaning. A second problem with counting register differences as differences in meaning concerns the postulated advantages of the mutual exclusivity principle and presumably the contrastive principle. One advantage of such assumptions is that they prevent a person learning a language from making many redundant hypotheses. Given the contrastive and mutual exclusivity principles, meanings for a given term can be rejected on the grounds that the language already contains a term with the same meaning. Even without negative evidence, many hypotheses can be rejected because they would be redundant. If differences in register can count as differences in meaning, however, then the hypothesis space is markedly increased. On this view, numerous redundant hypotheses could be considered as long as the learner suspects a minor difference in dialect or register could be possible. One way out of this problem might be to rank order certain hypotheses that learners, including children, would consider, and to claim that dialect and register differences are among the last to be considered, and only when the contrastive principle seems otherwise ready to fail.

The second prediction to be made from the contrastive principle is that established forms take priority, whenever an innovative term and an established term would be synonymous. Although we can say "to bicycle," "to skate," and "to ski," we cannot say "to car" or "to airplane" because the terms "to drive" and "to fly" already exist in the English lexicon.

The third prediction to be made from the contrastive principle is that speakers coin new words to fill lexical gaps. That is, new terms are coined when no term exists to convey a particular meaning.

Clark (1987) provides a parallel line of argument to demonstrate that young children first acquiring language assume the contrastive principle. Clark (1983) reinterpreted the data on overgeneralization of terms in light of this view. Her analysis revealed that children narrow down the domains of a previously overextended word by contrasting a newly acquired term with an old one. Children will not overextend a term to cover a new object when they already have a name for that object. Although Clark interprets this observation as evidence for lexical contrast theory, it actually supports the mutual exclusivity hypothesis and raises a problem for the contrastive principle rather than supporting it. To take an example from Clark 1987, suppose a child starts out by overextending the word "dog" to cover not only dogs but also cats, sheep, and other four-legged mammals. Once having acquired the word "cat," the child stops overextending "dog" to cover cats. Given the mutual exclusivity principle, it is obvious why this should be the case: the child cannot have two category labels for the same object, so one or the other must be dropped. It is much less clear why this should happen according to the contrastive hypothesis. On this account, the word "cat" would refer to cats, whereas the word "dog" could continue to refer to dogs, cats, sheep, and so on. "Dog" (meaning four-legged mammal) and "cat" (meaning feline animal) would still clearly contrast in meaning. Thus, the contrastive principle alone does not explain why overextension should be narrowed in this way. Similarly, the contrastive principle does not explain why children will not overextend a term to cover a new object when they already have a term for that object. Since one term would be more general than the other, as the normal uses of "dog" and "animal" are, they would contrast in meaning and should, therefore, be legitimate.

Another piece of evidence that Clark (1987) cites for the contrastive principle, which again supports the mutual exclusivity principle, is that 2- and 3-year-olds appear to reject multiple labels for objects. A child told that something is an animal, for example, replied by saying, "It is not an animal, it's a dog." I will return to this source of evidence later when I summarize the best evidence we have for mutual exclusivity per se.

Thus, some of the evidence Clark (1987) cites actually supports the mutual exclusivity hypothesis and not the contrastive hypothesis. Children's rejection of terms is somewhat puzzling on the contrastive assumption alone. Since words can contrast in many different ways, not just by being mutually exclusive, specific and general terms applying to the same object would conform to, not conflict with, the contrastive principle. One way of dealing with this problem would be to supplement Clark's (1987) argument with the added assumption that mutual exclusivity is a favored way of adhering to the contrastive principle.

More support for the contrastive hypothesis comes from bilingual children. Early on (for the first 50–150 words) children acquiring two languages simultaneously tend to learn only one label for a given category even though they are exposed to a label from each language. The argument here is that children start out believing they are learning a single language, and therefore the contrast and mutual exclusivity principles would prevent them from learning two terms in this language. Later, when they become aware that they are dealing with two languages, they can allow these cross-language synonyms. It is interesting that these constraints on language acquisition are relative to a given language.

One problem with this evidence is that it comes almost entirely from production data. Although we know, for example, that a young child first acquiring French and English who has learned "bird" will not say "oiseau," we do not know whether or not the child might comprehend "oiseau." There may be many reasons why beginning language learners are limited in the amount they can produce, a limitation that would prevent them from expending valuable resources on redundant information. This limitation on production could thus have a very different basis from a constraint on the lexicon such as "Every two forms contrast in meaning." A lexical constraint, if it is operating, should be apparent in comprehension as well as production. In fact, the best evidence for the contrastive or mutual exclusivity hypothesis would come from comprehension, not production.

Clark (1987) reviews other very interesting sources of data that provide more support for the contrastive principle. Children should assume that unfamiliar words fill lexical gaps, and fast-mapping studies such as those of Carey and Bartlett (1978), Au (1987), Au and Markman (1987), and Dockrell (1981) do show that children expect novel terms to map onto unnamed objects or properties. Further, children's word coinages should fill lexical gaps. Children invent new words to supplement their relatively small vocabularies (such as "plant-man" for "gardener"). Because their limited vocabularies contain many gaps that the adult lexicon does not, young children must decide what to do when confronted with a conventional form that is synonymous with one of their innovations. According to Clark (1987), it is because children realize that the two forms do not contrast in meaning that they give up their innovation in favor of the conventional form.

Evidence for the Mutual Exclusivity Principle

As noted, a fair amount of the evidence that Clark (1987) cites for the contrastive principle is in fact evidence for children's adherence to the mutual exclusivity principle.

Another source of evidence for mutual exclusivity can be found in children's early vocabularies. Among the earliest words children acquire are labels for objects—usually labels for objects at the basic level in Rosch et al.'s (1976) sense. For the most part, basic level category terms such as "dog," "apple," and "car" are mutually exclusive. Inspection of the first words in children's vocabularies (see, for example, Goldin-Meadow, Seligman, and Gelman 1976; Gillham 1979) reveals that they consist of object category labels that are largely mutually exclusive, with no subordinate or superordinate categories.

Part-whole terms do not violate mutual exclusivity, so they should be learned before class-inclusion terms. In fact, although children's early vocabularies do not contain hierarchically organized category terms, they do contain many terms that can be organized into part-whole relations. Even children's early vocabularies contain a number of words referring to parts and wholes of the same object. For example, Gillham (1979) studied the early vocabularies of 14 babies by asking their mothers to record the first 100 words they produced. I found no words in Gillham's data that referred to superordinate categories. In contrast, there were nine that referred to body parts ("eye," "ear," "hair," "hand," "knee," "mouth," "nose," "toe," and "teeth"), as well as some that referred to a whole person ("baby," "boy"). Children also had a few other terms referring to what might be seen as parts of a house or other object ("door," "drawer," "gate," "button"), as well as for the whole objects that would correspond to these parts ("house," "home," "shoe," "coat"). Thus, even very young children acquire terms for both parts and wholes considerably before they acquire subordinate-superordinate terms.

There is also some anecdotal evidence suggesting that children revise their interpretation of words in order to avoid violating mutual exclusivity. Grieve (1975) cites data from an unpublished study by Curtis (1973). A 2-year-old child used the term "car" to refer to all cars. Eleven days later the child used "car" to refer to cars and "Cadillac" to refer to Cadillacs. The child now denied that a Cadillac was a car. When asked, "What's this?", the child replied, "Cadillac." When asked, "Is that a car?", the child replied, "No, Cadillac." Later the same thing happened for "taxi" and for "Rover." When asked, "What's this?", the child replied, "Rover." When asked, "Is it a car, too?", the child said, "No, Rover." Later in the same session the experimenter pointed to the Rover and asked whether it was a car. This time the child said, "Yes, car." But now when asked, "Is it a Rover?", the child said, "No, car." This anecdote suggests that the child was unwilling to allow two different terms to apply to the same object in immediate succession. Clark (1987) presents other examples, such as "Not a plate, it a bowl" (from a child who was asked to take a plate off the table). Related anecdotes have been reported by Valentine (1942) and Macnamara (1982). My daughter Erin has argued with great conviction about a number of such cases. For example, she insisted that she was not her grandparents' granddaughter, emphasizing, "I'm *not* a granddaughter, I'm a girl." What is so compelling about these reports is the child's explicit denial of the applicability of a term, often in the face of an adult authority labeling the object. It is tempting to interpret the emphatic denials as stemming from a powerful assumption of mutual exclusivity. It is as though the child finds two labels for the object contradictory.

The problem with most of the evidence reviewed so far is that either it is anecdotal, possibly reflecting an interesting, noticeable aberration in the learning of category terms rather than a general principle, or it comes largely from production data. As noted earlier, limitations on production (that is, on mastering the phonology of words, recall of words, and so on) may limit a child's productive lexicon without any constraint from mutual exclusivity. Thus, if evidence for a child's having only a single category term for each object were found only in production and not in comprehension, then the mutual exclusivity principle would not be supported. There are certainly cases in which apparent support of the principle from production data alone would have to be rejected once comprehension data were taken into account. My daughter Erin produced two such examples when she was about 11 months old. Erin's word for duck was "quack quack" and her word for truck was "brmm brmm." At that time she never produced either "duck" or "truck" yet it was very clear that she understood both of these terms. For example, if I asked her to "Find the duck" or to "Find the truck," she had no trouble doing so. Similar pairs were "cow/moo moo," "cat/meow," "coffee grinder/brr brr." Faced with my daughter's lack of filial loyalty in generating violations of mutual exclusivity, I vainly attempted to distinguish between "routines" and "words," hoping that words would adhere to the mutual exclusivity principle and that routines might not. No matter what criteria I came up with at the time to distinguish routines and words, however, "quack quack" and "brmm brmm" functioned as words. For example, if Erin wanted her truck when it was out of reach, she would extend her arm in a reaching motion toward the truck and repeat "brmm brmm, brmm brmm" until someone handed her the truck—exactly the same way she would request other objects using more conventional terms. In this case, then, I was forced to conclude that these were genuine counterexamples. Erin's productive vocabulary contained only one category term per object at this stage, but, in these few cases at least, she could comprehend more than one. At about the same time I noticed one other violation of mutual exclusivity. Erin normally used the term "orange" to refer to oranges, but on a couple of occasions—for instance, after she kicked an orange and watched it roll—she also used the term "ball."

All of these potential counterexamples except the last one have the same character. Erin comprehended the conventional label for the object but produced an interesting sound the object made instead. Although to my knowledge adults never labeled the objects with the sound, adults quite often provided the sound effects after labeling the object—for example, "Here is a duck and it goes quack quack." Because the sounds are so interesting and because they were repeatedly associated with the objects, these may be special cases where the child is given considerable information early on and uses it to overcome mutual exclusivity.

In summary, evidence from a number of sources suggests that children adhere to the mutual exclusivity principle, but the evidence is either largely anecdotal or solely based on production data. Experimental studies of children's comprehension of terms would provide the clearest test of whether they widely assume that terms are mutually exclusive.

Experimental Tests of the Mutual Exclusivity Hypothesis

The simplest situation where the mutual exclusivity principle could be applied is one in which two objects are presented, one that already has a known label and one that does not. If a new label is then mentioned, the child should (1) on the taxonomic assumption, look for an object as a first hypothesis about the meaning of the label; (2) on the mutual exclusivity assumption, reject the already labeled object; and (3) therefore, assume that the novel label refers to the other object.

Three studies have found support for this hypothesis (Golinkoff et al. 1985; Hutchinson 1986; Markman and Wachtel 1988). In a study with 12 subjects, Golinkoff et al. found that 2½-year-olds would pick a novel object over several familiar objects when they heard a novel noun. In general, children presented with four objects—three familiar and one unfamiliar—and told to select one, might prefer to select the novel one whether or not it was labeled. If so, then the results could not be interpreted as revealing a constraint on word meaning but would instead have to be interpreted as a response bias to attend to the novel object. Golinkoff et al. argue that such a bias could not account for their results because children handled both the novel and familiar objects before the start of the session, which, they claim, would make the familiar and novel objects equally salient. It is not clear, however, that the short time spent handling the objects could have achieved this effect. Golinkoff et al. further point out that in a subsequent trial when children were presented with the same novel referent—this time grouped with two familiar objects and one unfamiliar object—they continued to select the original referent when the label was repeated. They argue that this finding rules out a general preference for picking the novel object. Moreover, when the original object was presented along with another unfamiliar object and a different novel label was mentioned, children now selected the second novel object.

Hutchinson (1986) dealt with this novelty problem by conducting preliminary trials in which children were presented with novel and familiar objects, paired as they would be in the experimental session. The children were asked to select one. If a child preferred the novel object of the pair on two trials, then that pair was dropped from that child's analysis. As it turned out, very few pairs of objects had to be dropped. Hutchinson's study was extensive, comparing children from a broad age range and comparing normal to retarded children. She found that, when a novel label was spoken, normal children as young as 2 years old reliably selected a novel object over a familiar object.

Study 1 of Markman and Wachtel 1988 was a modified replication of these studies that used a control group to ensure that if children select a novel object when they hear a novel label, then it is due to the labeling per se and not just a response bias to choose the novel object. To control for this possibility, the children in one group were simply asked to select an object.

Three-year-olds were presented with six pairs of objects, one member of each pair being an object that they could label (for instance, banana, cow, spoon) and one an object for which they did not yet know the label (for instance, a lemon wedgepress, a pair of tongs).

In the control condition each child was shown the six pairs of objects and asked by a puppet to "Show me one." In the novel label condition the procedure was identical except that the child was asked to "Show me the x," where x was a nonsense syllable, randomly assigned to the object.

Children who heard a novel term applied in the presence of two objects, one of which was familiar and one of which was unfamiliar, had a striking tendency to select the novel object as the referent for the novel term. They selected the novel object in almost 5 of the 6 pairs, mean = 4.90. The tendency to select an unfamiliar object as the referent for a novel label does in fact reflect children's adherence to the mutual exclusivity principle because they do not have such a bias when no labels are provided. In the control condition children perform at chance, selecting a mean of 3.30 unfamiliar objects out of 6.

In summary, in this very simple situation where it is possible to map an unfamiliar word to an unfamiliar object, 3-year-old children use the mutual exclusivity principle in figuring out the meaning of a new word. Note also that in this situation the child can simultaneously satisfy the principles of taxonomic organization and mutual exclusivity. Study 2 from Markman and Wachtel 1988 examined what happens when this simple mapping strategy is no longer possible, and the taxonomic assumption and mutual exclusivity may conflict.

Suppose a novel word is used to describe a single object. As argued in chapter 2, according to the taxonomic assumption (Markman and Hutchinson 1984), a child should first hypothesize that the new word refers to the object as an exemplar of a category of similar objects, and not to a part of the object, the object's substance, and so on. Suppose, however, that the object described by the novel term is an object for which the child already has a label. In this case, in order to adhere to the mutual exclusivity principle, children must reject the novel term as a label for the object. Then, however, they may not have any clear alternative as a possible meaning for the term; that is, since no other object is around to label, the simple novel label–novel object strategy cannot be used. Under these circumstances several options are available. Children could decide to abandon mutual exclusivity in these cases and interpret the novel term as a second label for the object. Another possibility is that they could reject the term as a label for the object without coming up with an alternative meaning. Rejecting one meaning for the term, however, leaves them with a term that is not yet attached to any referent. This in itself may be a motivation for children to try to find some meaning for the novel term. The mutual exclusivity principle does not speak to the issue of how children select among the potential meanings, but one possibility is that they might analyze the object for some interesting part or property and interpret the novel term as applying to it. Such an analysis is considerably more difficult than the simple novel label–novel object matching strategy, and there may be many candidate meanings for a term. The remaining studies examine whether children can use mutual exclusivity, in this more difficult situation, to learn part and substance terms.

Study 2 of Markman and Wachtel 1988 addressed whether children can use mutual exclusivity to reject a novel term as a label for an already labeled object, and whether that motivates them to search for another salient aspect of the object to label. In this study we attempted to teach children labels for objects with prominent parts. The children heard a novel noun attributed to either a familiar or an unfamiliar object. The term could thus refer either to the object itself or to a salient part of the object.

Three- and 4-year-olds heard either familiar or unfamiliar objects labeled with a novel term and were then tested to see whether they thought the term referred to the object as a whole or to a salient part of the object. The set of familiar and unfamiliar objects, along with their relevant parts, is presented in table 9.1.

Children were assigned to one of two conditions, the familiar condition (where the children knew a label for each object) or the unfamiliar condition (where they did not). In both conditions children were taught a label applied to an object with a noticeable part. The labels used were in fact adult labels for the part. In neither condition did children already know a label for the part being taught. For example, children in the familiar condition were taught "boom" as the part of a (familiar) firetruck and "dorsal fin" as the part of a (familiar) fish. Children in the unfamiliar condition were taught "finial" as the part of an (unfamiliar) pagoda and "trachea" as the part of an (unfamiliar) lung. The prediction was that children would interpret the label as referring to the object itself for unfamiliar objects but as referring to a part for familiar objects.

In order to ensure that children understood the questions about parts and wholes, children in both conditions were asked about familiar objects and their parts using known labels. For example, all children were shown a pencil with an eraser and asked whether the eraser was the whole object or just a part, and whether the pencil was the whole object or just a part. They were shown a cat and asked whether the tail was the whole object or just a part, and whether the cat was the whole object or just a part. These well-known objects and labels are presented in table 9.2.

For the experimental items, the experimenter mentioned what the child was about to see by providing the label, and placed the picture on the table. Then she asked the child, "Which one is the ____? This whole thing (the experimenter circled the object with her index finger), or just this part (the experimenter pointed to the part)?"

The predictions from this study can be summarized as follows. First, children in both conditions should understand the known labels for parts and wholes, and all children should do well on these items. Namely, they should think that a known term for a whole refers to the whole object and that a known term for a part refers to the part. Most important, the predictions for the experimental items differ depending on the condition. Children hearing a label applied to an unfamiliar object should assume that the label refers to the object itself and not just a part of it. Thus, they should give few part re-

Table 9.1
Experimental items for study 2 of Markman and Wachtel 1988

Familiar condition		Unfamiliar condition	
Object	Novel label for object	Object	Novel label for object
Fish	Dorsal fin	*Current detector	Detector
Fire truck	Boom	Pipe tool	Damper
Hammer	Claw	*Ritual implement	Crescent
Camera	Focusing grip	*Pagoda	Finial
Telephone	Receiver	Microscope	Platform
Race car	Air foil	*Lung	Trachea

*These items were used in study 3 as well.

Table 9.2
Known objects and parts for study 2 of Markman and Wachtel 1988 (used in both familiar and unfamiliar conditions)

Known label for whole	Known label for part
Cat	Tail
*Wagon	*Handle
Bird	Beak
*Flower	*Stem
*Pencil	*Eraser
*House	*Chimney

*These items were used in study 3 as well.

sponses. Children hearing a label applied to a familiar object should, on the basis of mutual exclusivity of labels, reject the term as a label for the whole and assume that it refers to the part instead. Thus, these children should give more part responses. The actual results in terms of number of part responses given are shown in figure 9.1.

Children in both conditions were expected to perform quite well on the familiar baseline items, giving part responses for known part terms ("tail") and object responses for known objects terms ("cat"). As can be seen in figure 9.1, children in both conditions performed as expected when known labels were used to refer to parts and wholes.

As predicted, children interpreted a novel term quite differently depending on whether the object was familiar or not. Children gave a mean of only 1.2 out of 6 part responses (20%) in the familiar condition, compared to a mean of 3.4 part responses (57%) in the unfamiliar condition. Thus, as expected by the mutual exclusivity hy-

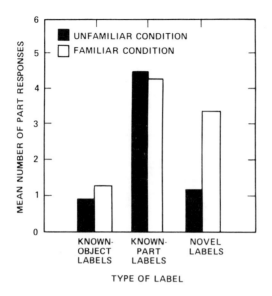

Figure 9.1
Number of part responses (out of a maximum of 6) given by children in the familiar and unfamiliar conditions to known labels for objects, known labels for parts, and novel labels

pothesis, children hearing a novel term in the presence of an object with a known label were less likely to think the novel term referred to the whole object than were children who heard the term in the presence of an object with no known label.

One rather stringent test of the strength of the taxonomic and mutual exclusivity assumptions is to compare children's interpretation of novel terms to their interpretation of the well-known words. The taxonomic assumption predicts that children in the unfamiliar condition should treat the novel terms similarly to the way they interpret known object labels and differently from the way they interpret known part terms. Conversely, the mutual exclusivity assumption predicts that children in the familiar condition should treat the novel terms differently from the way they interpret known object terms and similarly to the way they interpret known part terms.

By and large, the results were in accord with even this stringent test. In the unfamiliar condition children treated the novel label much as they treated known labels for objects and quite differently from the way they treated known labels for parts. Moreover, in the familiar condition children gave more part responses to novel labels (such as "receiver") than to known object labels. This is what one would expect on the mutual exclusivity hypothesis. On the other hand, they gave fewer part responses to novel terms than they gave for known part terms. The bias to interpret novel labels as labels for objects (as well as the assumption of mutual exclusivity) may have been affecting children in the familiar condition, leading them to make an intermediate number of part responses.

In summary, the results from this study support the mutual exclusivity hypothesis. When shown an unfamiliar object—that is, an object for which they do not yet have a label—young children interpret a new noun as a label for that object. In this study children interpreted new terms as labels for whole objects just as frequently as they interpreted known terms as labels for whole objects. When they are shown a familiar object, however, then by mutual exclusivity children should reject the term as a label for the object and look for some other meaning for the term. In this study, although there was some tendency to interpret the term as labeling the object, children were less likely to interpret the new noun as a label for a familiar object and interpreted it as referring to a salient part of the object instead.

In study 2 the parts and wholes that children were questioned about in the experimental items differed for the familiar and unfamiliar conditions. Study 3 was designed to equate the items in the two conditions. Only unfamiliar objects were used in this study, but some of the children were provided with labels for the objects before the experimental labels were taught. In this way, the same item could be unfamiliar for some children and "familiar" (or at least previously labeled) for other children.

There were two conditions in the study, the familiarization condition and the unfamiliar condition. The labeling procedure and the method of asking children whether the object referred to the part or the whole were virtually identical to those used in study 2. The main difference was that in the familiarization condition children were first taught a label for the object. They were shown a picture of the object (for example, the lung), told what it was called ("This is a lung"), and given a short description of its function ("We all have two lungs in our chest and use them to breathe"). After they were familiarized with the experimental objects in this way, they participated in the standard procedure.

In both conditions children were asked about four of the six unfamiliar objects that had been used in study 2. These are indicated in table 9.1 They were also asked about four objects whose labels and parts were familiar. These are indicated in table 9.2. As before, the experimenter told the children what they were about to see (for example, "Here is a finial"), presented the picture of the object, and asked what the label applied to: "Which one is the finial, this whole thing (the experimenter circled the object with her index finger) or just this part (the experimenter pointed to the part)?"

In summary, the design of study 3 was very similar to that of study 2. The main difference was that, instead of a familiar condition in which children were taught a term for a familiar object, study 3 included a familiarization condition in which children were first familiarized with a previously unfamiliar object and then were taught the new term.

As in study 2, children's responses were scored according to whether they said that the label referred to the whole object or its part. The results, which are plotted in figure 9.2, replicated those of study 2. As predicted, children interpreted a novel term quite differently in the two conditions. Children in the unfamiliar condition, who heard the term in the presence of an unfamiliar object, more often interpreted it as referring to the object and not its salient part. For example, children who simply saw a picture of a lung interpreted "trachea" as referring to the object (the lung) and not its salient part (the trachea). They gave a mean of 1.27 part responses out of 4 (32%). In contrast, children in the familiarization condition interpreted the novel labels as referring to parts of the object. For example, children who had just heard the picture of a lung labeled "lung" interpreted "trachea" as referring to the salient part (the trachea) and not the object (the lung). They gave a mean of 3.4 part responses out of 4 (85%).

In summary, study 3 again provides evidence for the mutual exclusivity hypothesis. When a novel term is used in the presence of an object that already has a label, children tend to reject another label for the object and, in this case, assume that the term refers to a part of the object instead. This was true in this study, even though the label for the (previously unfamiliar) object was provided only a few moments before another novel label was taught.

In study 1 of Markman and Wachtel 1988 children could use a simple strategy of mapping an unfamiliar label to an unfamiliar object to preserve mutual exclusivity. Because only one object was presented at a time in studies 2 and 3, this simple strategy was precluded. Children still adhered to mutual exclusivity in this case, using it to learn terms for salient parts of objects. Parts of objects are themselves objects or at least objectlike, however. Thus, learning parts of objects may be as close to the simple mapping strategy as one can get using a single object. The next three studies from Markman and Wachtel 1988 examined whether children avail themselves of mutual exclusivity when the experimenter refers to an object made of a

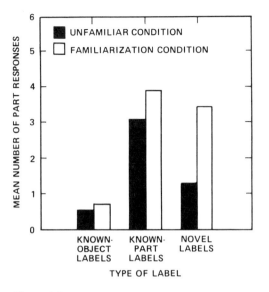

Figure 9.2
Number of part respones (out of a maximum of 4) given by children in the familiarization and unfamiliar conditions to known labels for objects, known labels for parts, and
novel labels

salient substance, using an adjective or mass noun. This procedure
differs in two ways from that of the studies on learning labels for
parts. First, instead of depicting objects with salient parts, we selected objects made of a metallic substance that we thought would be
salient and that young children have not yet labeled. Second, in these
studies the object was referred to by an adjective or a mass noun:
"See this? It's pewter." This is not the typical way, in English, of designating objects. It therefore provides a strong test of the taxonomic
assumption. When an unfamiliar object is labeled, the bias to look for
object labels may be strong enough to override grammatical form
class information. So even when an adjective or mass noun is used
to describe an object, children may interpret it as the label for the
object. A commonly heard anecdote, for example is that young children think that "hot" is the label for stoves, for example, because
parents refer to stoves by the term "hot" before they label them as
"stoves": "Don't touch that, it's hot."

Study 4, then, was designed to examine these two issues: First,
following the taxonomic assumption, will children interpret even a
novel adjective as a label for an unfamiliar object? Second, following
the mutual exclusivity assumption, will children reject a novel term
as a label for a familiar object made from a salient substance?

In study 4 3- and 4-year-olds heard a puppet refer to an object as "pewter." Half of the children heard the term attributed to a familiar object: a metal cup. Half of the children heard the term attributed to an unfamiliar object: a pair of metal tongs. To introduce the novel term "pewter," a puppet showed the child the object (either the metal cup or the metal tongs) and said, "See this? It is pewter."

If the tendency to expect an object label is strong enough to override form class cues, then children hearing "pewter" ascribed to the metal tongs should interpret "pewter" as the label for tongs. They should then agree that a different pair of tongs, made from a different substance and of a different color—a pair of wooden tongs—is also pewter. In contrast, when children hear "pewter" ascribed to a familiar object, if they try to adhere to the mutual exclusivity principle, then they should reject "pewter" as the label for the cup. They should deny that a cup made from a different substance and of a different color—a ceramic cup—is pewter. The main prediction, then, is that when the children see an object that is similar in kind to the original object but of a different substance, they should agree that it is "pewter" when the object referred to is unfamiliar (the metal tongs) but deny that it is pewter when the object is familiar (the metal cup). Thus, children should agree that a pair of wooden tongs is pewter but deny that a ceramic cup is pewter.

This prediction was confirmed. Of the 12 children who were taught that a metal cup was pewter and then asked whether a ceramic cup was pewter, only 1 child thought that it was pewter. The other 11 children denied that it was pewter. Thus, even in this more difficult situation, children adhered to the mutual exclusivity principle, denying that a new term could be a label for an object even when it might not be clear what else the term referred to. In contrast, of the 12 children who were taught that metal tongs were pewter, 7 of the 12 thought that wooden tongs were also pewter.

The results also indicate that at least to some extent 3- and 4-year-olds are willing to override form class clues in order to interpret a novel adjective or substance term as a label for an unfamiliar object. That is, about half of the children considered "pewter" to be the label for tongs and agreed that wooden tongs were pewter.

Study 5 was a modified replication of study 4 that used a within-subjects design. Each child heard a novel substance term applied to a familiar object and a different novel substance term applied to an unfamiliar object. The two substance terms were "chrome" and "rattan."

The findings from this study replicated those of study 4. First, the bias to assume that a novel term refers to a novel object was again strong enough to override discrepancies in grammatical form class. Seventy-five percent of the children who heard the term "chrome" or "rattan" attributed to a novel object treated the term as a label for the object. Second, children were less likely to think that the novel term was a label for the object when they already knew a label for it. Only 40% of the children who heard "rattan" and "chrome" attributed to familiar objects treated the terms as labels for the objects; 60% rejected the terms as labels.

In studies 4 and 5 3- and 4-year-old children treated a novel term as a label for a novel object but tended to reject the term as a label for a familiar object. Although we know that children reject the novel term as a label for a familiar object, we do not know whether they have in fact accepted the term as a substance term. Study 6 attempted to get at children's hypotheses about the meanings of the terms more directly by giving children a forced choice between object labels and substance labels.

As in the previous studies, we labeled an object using a novel term: for instance, "See this (a metal cup)? It's chrome." Children were then shown a similar object made of a different substance (in this case a ceramic cup). They were also shown a chunk of the substance itself (in this case an unformed piece of chrome). They were then asked, "Which is chrome? This thing here or this stuff here?" (This is similar to the procedure used by Soja, Carey, and Spelke (1985) in their investigation of children's acquisition of count nouns and mass nouns.) Our question was, would children interpret a term as a substance term in the presence of an object as long as the object had a known label? In other words, would mutual exclusivity help children override their bias for object labels to interpret a novel term as a substance term?

As in studies 4 and 5, children heard a familiar object (a hat) or an unfamiliar object (an odd-shaped container) labeled as rattan. They also heard a familiar object (a cup) or an unfamiliar object (tongs) labeled as chrome. The experimental test for whether children interpreted the term as a label for the object or the substance was to give them a choice between a similar object of a different substance and the substance itself.

To ensure that children understood the questions and procedure, they were asked the same kinds of questions for two familiar objects and two familiar substances before the experimental items were shown. Each child was shown a wooden cat and a hunk of wood and asked, "Which one is the wood, this thing here (pointing to the cat) or this stuff here (pointing to the wood)?", "Which one is the cat, this thing here (pointing to the cat) or this stuff here (pointing to the wood)?" The same procedure was used for a sand-filled car and a pile of sand.

The two experimental items were then presented. For the experimental forced-choice test, children were asked only one question about each pair: either which of the choices was chrome or which of the choices was rattan. Children were questioned about one familiar item and one unfamiliar item, each of a different substance. The questioning procedure was the same as for the pretest on well-known objects. For the familiar rattan condition, children were shown the rattan hat and told, "See this? It's rattan." They were then shown a plastic hat and a piece of rattan and asked, "Which one is rattan, this stuff here (pointing to the piece of rattan) or this thing here (pointing to the hat)?" The unfamiliar rattan condition was the same except that the crescent-shaped container was substituted for the hat. For the familiar chrome condition, children were shown the metal cup and told, "See this? It's chrome." They were then shown a ceramic cup and a piece of metal and asked, "Which one is chrome, this stuff here (pointing to the piece of metal) or this thing here (pointing to the ceramic cup)?" The unfamiliar chrome condition was the same except that the tongs were substituted for the cup.

When these preschool children were asked about well-known objects and substances, they were quite able to answer the questions correctly. That is, when they were asked about cats and cars, they pointed overwhelmingly to cats and cars, pointing to the object rather than the substance 1.96 out of a possible 2 times. When asked about wood and sand, they pointed to wood and sand, pointing to the object only .48 out of 2 times. Since the object was in fact made of the relevant substance, pointing to the object when asked about the substance is not, strictly speaking, an error. A wooden cat, for example, is wood. Nevertheless, it was relatively rare for children to use that strategy, and for the most part they clearly differentiated between the two kinds of questions they were asked.

Since—as the pretest demonstrated and as expected from the work of Soja, Carey, and Spelke (1985)—3- to 5-year-olds have no trouble understanding this kind of question, we were now in a position to determine whether these children can use mutual exclusivity to reject a new term as an object label for a familiar object and interpret it as a substance term instead. We predicted that when children heard a novel term applied to a novel object (the odd-shaped container or the tongs), they would choose the object as the referent of the term, but that when they heard the term applied to a familiar object, they would choose the substance as the referent of the term. In other words, we predicted that children should select the substance in the familiar object condition more often than in the unfamiliar object condition. This prediction was supported. The mean number of object responses was .57 out of 1 for the unfamiliar object condition compared to only .13 out of 1 for the familiar object condition. Thus, in support of the mutual exclusivity hypothesis, when children heard a novel term applied to a familiar object, they rejected the term as a label for the object and interpreted it as a substance term instead.

In sum, these studies provide evidence that children do, in fact, assume that words tend to be mutually exclusive. Study 1, along with the studies reported by Golinkoff et al. (1985) and Hutchinson (1986), demonstrate that when children hear a novel object label, they assume that it refers to a novel object rather than to an object whose label they already know. This finding is not due to a general preference for novel objects, as it is seen only when a novel label is mentioned. To use mutual exclusivity in this situation, children can adopt a simple strategy of mapping the novel label onto the novel object. The remaining studies explored whether children adhere to the mutual exclusivity principle when this simple strategy can no longer be used.

If a novel label is applied to an object for which children already have a label, then they should, by mutual exclusivity, reject the new term as an object label. If that object is the only one present, however, then children cannot interpret the term as a label for a different object. Instead, they must analyze the same object for some property or attribute to label. Studies 2–6 provide evidence that 3- and 4-year-olds try to maintain mutual exclusivity of terms even in this more difficult situation. Studies 2 and 3 explored whether children can use mutual exclusivity to reject a term as a label for an object and interpret it as a label for a part of the object instead. In this case a new noun was attributed to an object and children had to decide whether the term referred to the object itself or a salient part of the object. Children interpreted a novel label as referring to the object itself when the object did not yet have a label. In contrast, as predicted, they interpreted the label as referring to the part when the label for the object was already known. Studies 4–6 examined whether children would use mutual exclusivity when taught a substance term, by attributing the substance term to an object. If the object was unfamiliar, then half or more of the children thought that the substance term was the label for the object. They agreed, in this case, that a similar object of a different material should have the same label. Even when the new term was an adjective or mass noun, then, children occasionally still interpreted it as a label for the object. In contrast, if the object was familiar, children rejected the new term as a category label. They denied, in this case, that a similar object of a different material should have the substance label and instead selected the substance as the referent of the term.

Parental Labeling

The studies and other evidence reviewed so far suggest that children first assume that a new label refers to an object category, and that category terms are mutually exclusive. It would simplify learning if adults' labeling practices conformed to children's expectations. Otherwise, children will misconstrue many terms. First, adults should tend to provide object labels in accord with the child's assumption that novel terms refer to categories of similar objects. Second, if an adult is providing something other than an object label and therefore violating the child's assumption, it would help if the adult clearly marked that this was an exception. That is, the adult should somehow convey to the child that the new term is something other than an object label. If the child assumes that category terms are mutually exclusive, a good way of indicating to the child that the new word is not a category term would be to introduce that new word in the presence of the already known category term. Hearing a known category term applied to the same object should then signal to the child, on the assumption of mutual exclusivity, that the new term is not a category term.

In fact, to the extent we can determine parents' labeling practices from the available evidence, their use of terms accords remarkably well with these assumptions. Ninio and Bruner (1978) studied 40 mothers looking at picture books with their infants. They found that 95% of ostensive definitions referred to the whole object depicted. Thus, the overwhelming majority of the labels mothers gave to infants would fit with the assumption that the first word heard will be the object's label. In the remaining cases mothers explicitly included the category term in the utterance that introduced a term for a part or property of the object. For example, in the 40 dyads, there were 52 naming utterances referring to parts of objects or parts of the body. In all but 2 of these, either the part was named immediately after the whole or the whole was explicitly mentioned along with its relation to the part. For example, mothers said, "Here is a train. Here are the wheels," "These are the girl's eyes," "Where are the girl's feet?", "Look what a lovely doll. Where is the doll's nose?" Ninio (1980) presents evidence that when a mother asks her young child, "What's this?", the child almost invariably answers with an object label, even when the mother makes clear from an adult's perspective (by touching or tapping a specific part) that she is asking about a part.

Studies on parents' labeling of categories reveal that parents label objects differently depending on whether they are providing basic level or superordinate level category terms (Callanan 1985; Shipley, Kuhn, and Madden 1983). These parental labeling strategies fit well, not just with mutual exclusivity, but also with another assumption that children make about word meanings, namely, that a novel term should refer to the object at roughly a basic level of categorization. Parents rarely use simple ostensive definition to provide a superordinate label for an object, yet this is an exceedingly common way of introducing a basic level label. Although adults would be very likely to point to a helicopter and say, "That's a helicopter," they would be very unlikely to point to a helicopter and say, "That's a vehicle." Adults thereby prevent children from erroneously treating novel superordinate category terms as basic level labels for objects.

Parents introduce superordinate category terms in two ways. The first is by labeling groups of objects rather than single objects (Callanan 1985; Shipley, Kuhn, and Madden 1983). Callanan found this tendency to be so striking in parents that they would explicitly define superordinate terms as referring to a group of things together—as though they were defining collections rather than classes. The parents in her study said, for example, "All of them together are vehicles," "A whole bunch of things together that you ride in are vehicles." (This, of course, is incorrect since even a single vehicle is a vehicle.) Moreover, she found that parents sometimes violated the singular-plural distinction in ways consistent with a collection interpretation. Parents occasionally said things like "What is all this called (pointing to several machines)? Is it a machine?" and "OK, is a car and a truck a machine?" As argued in chapter 8, collections are a simpler hierarchical structure for children because they do not violate mutual exclusivity. This erroneous labeling by parents may fit with children's way of first establishing hierarchical relations.

The second strategy parents use to teach superordinate category labels is to first provide a basic level label for the object and then provide the superordinate category term (Callanan 1985; Shipley, Kuhn, and Madden 1983). In fact, Callanan found that parents used basic level category terms just as much when teaching superordinate level category terms as when teaching basic level category terms themselves. Moreover, parents who were asked to teach their children new superordinate terms first used basic level terms even when the basic level categories were unfamiliar to the children, for example, calling something "a hassock" before calling it "a piece of furniture." When parents do provide the superordinate category term, they often explicitly mention the inclusion relation ("A car is a kind of vehicle"), which might also clarify the relation. As Callanan notes, this basic level anchoring with unfamiliar basic level terms increases the amount of new information children must learn. Such basic level anchoring should be very useful, however, given assumptions of mutual exclusivity and contrast. By first providing the basic level term, parents preemptively block the superordinate category term from being treated as a basic level term.

Multiple Representation

So far mutual exclusivity has been discussed as a constraint that children place on language per se. On the other hand, mutual exclusivity could derive from children's beliefs about objects, not just from their beliefs about object labels. That is, children may believe that an object has one and only one identity—that it can only be one kind of thing—and that an object's identity is revealed by object labels. Mutual exclusivity would then be an assumption that children make about objects, which leads to a parallel assumption about object labels. Flavell (in press) argues that young children assume that each thing in the world has only one nature—an assumption that adults may sometimes share. Unlike adults, however, children do not understand that each thing may, nevertheless, be mentally represented in more than one way. For example, children's poor performance on perspective-taking tasks is said to involve problems in dual coding. On this view, young children find it hard to understand that a given perceptual array can look quite different from two different perspectives because they treat two different appearances of the same object as though they implied two different identities for the same object. According to Flavell (in press), this limitation on multiple representation is revealed in a number of diverse tasks, including visual and conceptual perspective taking and understanding the appearance-reality distinction, as well as assuming mutual exclusivity.

The Generality of the Mutual Exclusivity Constraint

The question of whether the mutual exclusivity assumption in language derives from an assumption about objects raises a more general question: What is the best level at which to formulate this constraint? One possiblity is that it is narrowly specified as a constraint on word meanings. That is, it may be specifically a linguistic constraint. Another possibility, as just discussed, is that it could have its origin in children's beliefs about objects—that an object can have only one identity. Because labeling confers identity on objects, mutual exclusivity would be seen in language as well, but it would not be primarily a linguistic constraint. A final possibility is that mutual exclusivity, or perhaps some more general principle such as one-to-one mapping, might be a domain-general constraint, appearing in various manifestations across many diverse domains. Karmiloff-Smith (1979), Karmiloff-Smith and Inhelder (1975), and Carey (1978) have argued that children may begin acquiring knowledge in a domain by learning basic concepts in relative isolation but that after a while they are driven to try to organize and systematize their knowledge. Mutual exclusivity and a one-to-one mapping principle are simple, primitive forms of systematization. Basically, they work to keep relations between elements distinct and to maximize the predictability from one element to another. Some implications of a general one-to-one mapping bias are that it would lead children to expect perfect correlations between elements in a domain, to reject counterexamples and exceptions to general rules and to exaggerate regularities in their environment. Thus, mutual exclusivity might be either a language-specific constraint or a domain-general constraint, and at this point it is unclear which is the more appropriate level at which to characterize it. Whatever the generality of the constraint, however, it clearly applies to language.

The Principle of Taxonomic Organization

In some cases the assumptions of taxonomic organization and mutual exclusivity are in conflict, one leading the child toward object labels and the other leading away from object labels. The assumption of taxonomic organization directs children, upon seeing an object and hearing a novel term, to interpret the term as a label for the object—not as a label for one of its parts, not as a label for its substance, and so on. The obvious limitation of this assumption is that children must learn many kinds of terms, not just object labels. The assumption of mutual exclusivity, on the other hand, directs children to reject a novel term as a second label for an object and motivates them instead to interpret the term as a label for one of its parts, its substance, or some other property. The taxonomic assumption clearly has priority when the object being labeled has no previously known label, since mutual exclusivity does not apply in such a case. When one object has a known label and another has no known label, then both mutual exclusivity and the taxonomic assumption can be met. When only one object is present, for which the child already has a label, these two principles may to some extent compete. In these cases, when children find some other property of the object reasonably salient, they should adhere to mutual exclusivity and interpret the term as referring to this property. If, on the other hand, there is no obvious alternative interpretation for the meaning of a novel term, children may violate mutual exclusivity and follow the taxonomic principle, treating the term as a second object label.

Implications for Language Acquisition

Taken together, the present studies suggest how the assumption of mutual exclusivity can help children acquire not only cateogry terms but other kinds of terms as well. First, at a minimum, it enables children to reject one hypothesis or one class of hypotheses about a term's meaning; the new term should not be another object label. Second, the mutual exclusivity assumption has a motivational force. Having rejected one meaning for a term, children would be left with a word for which they have not yet figured out a meaning. This should then motivate them to find a potential meaning for the term, leading them to analyze the object for some other property to label. In this way, the mutual exclusivity assumption motivates children to learn terms for attributes, substances, and parts of objects. It also predicts that children should be much better able to learn color terms, shape terms, and so forth, on objects that have already been labeled.

As mentioned earlier, this function of mutual exclusivity helps overcome a major limitation of the taxonomic assumption that leads children to look for object labels. Although the taxonomic assumption provides a critical first hypothesis about word meanings, children must eventually be able to learn terms for properties of objects and not just terms for objects alone. These two principles complement each other, then, the taxonomic principle applying first, and the mutual exclusivity principle applying in cases where children already know a label for an object, motivating them to learn terms other than object labels. To envision how the mutual exclusivity principle can be used to successively constrain the meanings of terms, suppose a child who already knows "apple" and "red" hears someone refer to an apple as "round." By mutual exclusivity, the child can eliminate the object (apple) and its color (red) as the meaning of "round" and can try to analyze the object for some other property to label.

There are still many unanswered questions about how this analysis would proceed. There might be a hierarchy of hypotheses that children consider on hearing a new term, beginning with an object label and then moving in some predetermined order through part terms, substance terms, size, color, weight, temperature terms, and so on. Alternatively, the strategy might be to analyze each object for its most salient characteristic and to take that as the meaning of the novel term. That is, substance, for example, might be a likely candidate meaning for some objects but not for others. The potential hypotheses will very likely be affected by other cues, including grammatical form class and the linguistic and nonlinguistic context in which a new term is heard. The mutual exclusivity principle does not speak to these issues about how hypotheses are generated, but it does suggest that, as each successive word is learned, it further constrains the meanings of those yet to be learned, thereby helping children figure out their meanings.

Although in many cases the lexicons of natural languages are consistent with mutual exclusivity (as in many basic level category terms), there are inconsistencies as well. As mentioned earlier, one reason that children may have trouble dealing with hierarchically organized category terms is that they violate mutual exclusivity. At some point children obviously violate the assumption to allow multiple labels for the same object. It seems unlikely that the mutual exclusivity principle is abandoned at some age, never to be used again. Adults almost certainly would be likely to perform just as children did in study 1 of Markman and Wachtel 1988. When hearing a novel label in the presence of an object with a known label and an object without a known label, adults too would likely interpret the term as referring to the as yet unlabeled object. Although the assumption probably persists into adulthood, it might weaken with age or experience, as the speaker learns that many categories are organized into class-inclusion hierarchies and overlapping sets. Another possibility is that early in life children have the capacity to override mutual exclusivity, on a case-by-case basis, as long as there is enough evidence that it should be violated. It remains to be seen what constitutes "enough" evidence. Perhaps hearing a second label ("animal") applied repeatedly to an object with a known label ("dog") would eventually enable children to violate mutual exclusivity and accept the second label. This should be especially true, for slightly older children, if someone provides information about the relation between the two labels, for example, by stating that a dog is a *kind of* animal. Thus, the mutual exclusivity principle is resistant to multiple labeling but not impervious to it. The principle should be most useful and most evident, then, on children's initial exposure to a new term.

Chapter 10
Summary and Conclusions

To acquire the conventional classification system of their culture, children must learn both the categories that are deemed important or useful and the category terms that their language contains. Both of these inductive tasks pose many challenges to young children, who must categorize objects in ways that are culturally conventional, despite the enormous number of ways that are theoretically possible. Similarly, they must learn what labels refer to, despite the indefinite number of possible meanings category terms could have. How is it that children, with considerable limitations on their attention spans, memory, analytic skills, and other information-processing abilities, are able to solve these problems? To understand how children accomplish this, we need to reevaluate some of the assumptions and beliefs that have guided past work, including assumptions about the nature of categories and about the means by which categories are acquired. In this concluding chapter I will review some of the assumptions of the traditional view of concept acquisition that I think have led us astray. I will then highlight some of the arguments that I have made throughout this book that challenge these assumptions and that pose alternative solutions to the problem of how children acquire categories.

Traditional Theories of Concept Acquisition

Traditional theories of concept acquisition presupposed the classical view of concepts: that categories can be defined by a set of necessary and sufficient features that determine which objects are members of the category.

On the classical view, when learning a new concept, children first encounter a small sample of the extension of the category. From this sample, they must figure out what the intensional definition is. I have argued that this view presupposes that to acquire a concept a child needs (1) analytic abilities for decomposing the object into its properties, (2) a powerful hypothesis-testing system for generating, evaluating, and revising hypotheses, and (3) an ability to use the intensional criteria to evaluate subsequent objects to determine whether they are members of the category.

Although young children fail to solve many of the traditional classification and concept formation tasks (see chapter 7), they nevertheless are capable of acquiring a great many categories and category terms. If we focus on children's success in acquiring natural categories and not on their failure in solving experimental tasks, then we must account for their accomplishments. Either very young children have much more advanced information-processing abilities than we typically credit them with, or such abilities are not needed to account for children's initial success. Much of this book took the latter possibility seriously: that children solve the inductive problem involved in concept acquisition, in part by means that do not require the highly analytic, hypothetical-deductive reasoning assumed by the traditional theories.

Acquisition of Category Terms

The problem of induction in acquiring category labels can be seen most clearly in the case of ostensive definition, where someone points to an object and labels it (see chapter 2). In this situation a novel term could refer to an object category, but it could also refer to a part of the object, or to its substance, color, weight, and so on. The term could even refer to some external relation between the object in question and another object, such as a spatial relation, a causal relation, or a relation of possession. More generally, objects can be related through the variety of ways in which they participate in the same event or theme (cats eat mice; people read books; birds build nests). These assorted external relations between objects are referred to as thematic relations. The fact that two objects are connected by a powerful thematic relation does not, however, make them the same kind of thing. Although the association between spider and web is very strong and the relation is an important one for our understanding of spiders, we do not think of spider and web as being things of the same type. (Or, to the extent that we do think of spiders and webs as being the same, it is not by virtue of the fact that spiders weave webs.)

Although adult categories are not based solely on such thematic relations, traditional theories suggested that such thematic groupings form the basis of children's categorization. I argued that this strong claim is unlikely but that children do often find thematic relations particularly salient and interesting, as many studies of classification in children have revealed. Children often show a greater interest in thematic than in taxonomic relations between objects.

If this is the case, then why do children not interpret category labels as labels for the thematic relation they are attending to? The solution I have proposed is that young children place constraints on possible word meanings such that thematic relations are suppressed in favor of taxonomic relations, and, in particular, in favor of taxonomic relations between whole objects. That is, when children hear a novel label, they assume it refers to a whole object, not to its parts, its substance, its color, and so on (the whole object assumption) and that it refers to objects of this type, not to other objects it is thematically related to (the taxonomic assumption).

Experimental evidence shows that in the absence of a label, children often sort on the basis of thematic relations between objects, but that when an object is labeled, they interpret the label as referring to objects that are taxonomically rather than thematically related (Markman and Hutchinson 1984; Waxman and Gelman 1986). For example, in the absence of labels, children often selected a car and a tire as being the same kind of thing. When the car was called "a dax," however, and children were asked to find another dax, they more often selected a bicycle because car and bicycle are both in the same superordinate category, vehicles.

The whole object and taxonomic assumptions help children solve the induction problem by ruling out many potential meanings of a novel term. The enormous range of relational meanings would be eliminated from consideration by the constraint that nouns refer to object categories. By reducing the hypothesis space in this way, this constraint simplifies the problem of learning category terms.

The whole object and taxonomic constraints direct children to map a new label onto objects of the same type. But which of the very many possible object categories might children select? The next four chapters addressed this problem by considering what is known about different kinds of categories.

The Internal Structure of Categories

The discussion of conceptual diversity began, in chapter 3, by examining issues concerning the internal structure of categories. The classical view of concepts and the family resemblance view contrast in their predictions about the internal structure of categories.

The classical view of concepts has intuitive appeal in that most of us believe that we should be able to define the words that we know. It is a simple and elegant view of categories and provides a straightforward way of combining concepts. Further, it specifies in a natural way what it is that a child needs to learn to acquire categories. Finally, certain distinctions in philosophy and logic, such as analytic truth, depend on the classical view. Nevertheless, there is some evidence that concepts conform to a family resemblance structure instead. Concepts often appear to lack simple definitions. Instead of having necessary and sufficient features that define it, a category often exhibits a cluster of features, none of which is necessary or sufficient.

Evidence for the Family Resemblance View
There are two main sources of evidence in favor of concepts being defined by family resemblances. One comes from lists of properties that subjects generate when they are asked to list properties of category members. The sets of properties subjects list more often conform to a family resemblance structure than to a classically defined concept structure. This cannot be taken as strong support for the family resemblance view, however, because there may be implicit task demands that prevent subjects from listing properties they know to be true (Murphy and Medin 1985; Tversky and Hemenway 1984). Thus, subjects may fail to list necessary and sufficient properties, not because they do not know them, but because they judge them to be irrelevant to the task at hand.

Another major source of evidence supporting the family resemblance view is the existence of graded structure. Subjects are relatively consistent in their ability to judge whether or not an exemplar is a good or typical member of its category. Graded structure would be unexpected on a classical view of concepts because every exemplar would fulfill all of the necessary and sufficient features that define the category.

Perhaps the strongest evidence in favor of the family resemblance view is people's persistent failure to come up with classical definitions for many words that they nevertheless know well.

Problems with the Family Resemblance View
There are three problems with the family resemblance view. First, feature lists that experimental subjects generate do not provide strong evidence in favor of this view because they may be limited by the implicit demands of the situation. Second, there are problems with interpreting graded structure as evidence for a family resemblance view. Armstrong, Gleitman, and Gleitman (1983) have demonstrated that even classically defined concepts such as "odd number" have a graded structure. Thus, the existence of a graded structure cannot be used to argue against a classical definition. Third,

concepts defined by family resemblances should be linearly separable (Medin 1983), yet subjects do not generally find it easier to learn categories that are linearly separable than those that are not (Medin and Schwanenflugel 1981).

Developmental Implications of the Family Resemblance Structure
To the extent that categories are organized by family resemblances, we need to consider the developmental implications of such an organization (see chapter 3). Mervis and Pani (1980) demonstrated that instances that better exemplify a given category should be easier to learn than more peripheral instances, and that the category itself may be acquired more effectively if it is first taught with prototypical instances rather than peripheral ones. The traditional view of concept formation did not speak to the issue of which exemplars would promote better learning.

Family resemblance structure also has implications for the kinds of strategies children might use to learn a category (Kossan 1981; Kemler-Nelson 1984). Brooks (1978) argued that even adults' knowledge of categories is in some cases likely to be exemplar based rather than based on more abstract defining rules. For example, even adults are more successful at acquiring categories defined by particularly complex rules if they concentrate more on learning about individual exemplars than on trying to figure out the defining rule. Given young children's more limited information-processing abilities, an exemplar-based strategy may be most effective for them in trying to learn categories defined by family resemblances (Kossan 1981). This contrasts with traditional theories that assume that categories must be learned by hypothetical-deductive methods.

Reasons for the Existence of Family Resemblance Structure
The existence of family resemblances forces us to consider why categories should have a family resemblance structure. Three kinds of explanations were offered in chapter 3. It is possible that these explanations are all partially correct and that family resemblances may be multiply determined.

The first possibility is that family resemblances result when people stretch categories to allow for exceptions. On this view, even if people preferred classically defined concepts to those defined by family resemblances, many categories could end up being defined by family resemblances anyway. The assumption here is that it may often be most useful or natural to compromise and allow an object to be considered a member of a given category even if it does not fulfill all of the necessary and sufficient features of that category.

A second possibility is that family resemblances are the consequence of lay theories. If categorization is determined by lay theories
(Carey 1985; Murphy and Medin 1985), then family resemblances
will arise when they make sense in terms of a given explanatory
structure.

A third possibility is that categories organized by family resemblances result from nonanalytic or holistic processing (Kemler-
Nelson 1984). Using overall similarity to define a category may be
adaptive in that it may prevent children from prematurely deciding
on dimensions to define a category that could be wrong (Wattenmaker, Nakamura, and Medin 1988). Moreover, as Brooks (1978) and
Kossan (1981) point out, if children adopt an analytic strategy for
objects and categories that are too difficult for them to analyze, then
they will lose important information about the exemplars without
gaining information about the relevant rules that define the category.
In contrast, nonanalytic strategies help children retain needed information about exemplars.

Nonanalytic strategies may also help children solve the induction
problem of how to decide that an object label refers to the object as a
member of a taxonomic category, rather than to its size, shape, color,
position, and so on. By not analyzing an object into these features in
the first place, children avoid the problem of later having to rule them
out. Thus, limitations on children's analytic abilities can be seen as
an advantage in the sense that they limit the hypothesis space. Exemplar-based, holistic strategies focus the child on whole objects
rather than sets of features. Thus, the nonanalytic abilities that result
in categories having family resemblance structures fit well with the
taxonomic and whole object assumptions discussed in chapter 2.

Basic, Superordinate, and Subordinate Level Categories

In addition to varying in internal structure, categories vary in terms
of their level within a hierarchy. Although the taxonomic and whole
object constraints (perhaps reinforced by nonanalytic, exemplar-
based strategies for acquiring categories) lead children to interpret a
novel term as a label for an object category, they do not specify which
of the many possible object categories children consider. In particular, they do not specify whether a term refers to an object at a subordinate, basic, or superordinate level of categorization.

Basic Level Categories
Several critiera have been suggested to differentiate basic from superordinate level categorization (see chapter 4). Objects forming basic

level categories tend to have the same overall shape, many features in common, many parts in common, and many functions in common and tend to contrast well with other categories at the same level. Yet tests of these individual criteria have often failed to show that any of them is sufficient for determining the way in which people categorize. Perhaps instead, as I have suggested, the basic level may be the point in the hierarchy where these criteria tend to converge. Still, if there is one criterion that may have a special status in defining basic level categories, it is likely to be their correlated structure. Categories are not defined by arbitrary combinations of attributes. Instead, they capture correlations of attributes that exist in the world (Rosch and Mervis 1975); for example, creatures that have feathers, have beaks and claws rather than mouths and paws or hands. The basic level of a given hierarchy was hypothesized to be the most inclusive level that reflects the correlational structure of the environment. The correlational structure of categories has been shown to play an important role in categorization (Medin 1983).

Superordinate Categories as Ad Hoc Categories
One reason superordinate categories may be more difficult for children than basic level categories is that they function more like ad hoc categories (categories that have recently been created to achieve a goal (Barsalou 1983)). Although ad hoc categories possess an internal structure similar to that of common categories, there are important differences in the way the two kinds of categories are represented; and it is these differences that may parallel the developmental differences in the representation of categories. The main difference lies in how explicitly the category is represented. For adults, common superordinate categories are likely to be explicitly represented or associated with their exemplars. In contrast, Barsalou (1983) argues that most ad hoc categories are probably implicitly represented. The associations or categories are inferrable from information about the objects in question but are not likely to be thought of without some compelling reason. One may think of a chair as "something to hold open a door with" when one is faced with the problem of finding something with which to hold open a door, but not just on encountering chairs in any context. Given that ad hoc categories are only implicitly represented, they should be less accessible in memory than common categories.

On analogy with adults dealing with ad hoc categories, children may fail on tests of classification at the superordinate level not only because of structural differences between superordinate and basic level terms but also because they are usually forced to deal with categories that, for them, are as yet only implicitly represented (Horton 1982). For categories that are explicitly represented, children have been found to have less difficulty on sorting tasks. This argues against a view of conceptual development that claims that young children are unable to learn superordinate level categories or to understand principles of categorization. It suggests instead that development consists of categories becoming progressively freed from particular contexts and becoming more explicitly represented.

Violation of Mutual Exclusivity
Superordinate terms may also be more difficult to learn because they violate the mutual exclusivity principle. Given that children acquire basic level terms first, superordinate terms and subordinate terms will violate mutual exclusivity. A child who knows that a given object is a dog will be troubled or confused by claims that it is a poodle or is an animal.

In conclusion, the work on hierarchical levels bears on the issues raised in chapter 2 about how children determine which of the many possible object categories a new label could refer to. For several different reasons, children may be led to consider the term as applying to some intermediate level of categorization—something approximating the basic level. This is not because children formulate a number of possible hypotheses about hierarchical level and then somehow rule out all but the basic level. Instead, it is because the basic level will be the most simple, natural, or salient level for children. Something approximating the basic level is likely to be what first comes to mind when children see an object and hear a label, assuming they do not already have a label for the object. Many factors converge to make superordinate categories more difficult or less salient for children compared to basic level categories. Superordinate categories have few perceptual features in common and are often defined by common function instead; they may be only implicitly represented and may require a context to be retrieved or generated; and they violate the mutual exclusivity principle.

Natural Kinds

Natural kinds are objects that occur in nature (for instance, tigers, lemons, diamonds) that have a very rich correlated structure. In chapter 5 I argued that the correlational structure of natural kinds is important not only for the acquisition of categories but also for the implications and consequences of categorization.

The richness of the structure and the belief that unobservable properties are common to members of a natural kind predict that natural
kinds will often be used to support inductive inferences from one
category member to another. That is, if categories are structured so
as to capture indefinitely rich clusters of information, then new features learned about one category member will often be projected onto
other category members as well.

Gelman and Markman (1986, 1987) have provided evidence that
young children assume that objects that are members of the same
category will share many features. Children may assume that category members have unforeseen properties in common—properties
that are not apparent from their perceptual features. On each of a
series of problems children had to decide whether a given object possessed one or the other of two attributes. The perceptual appearance
and the natural kind category of the object shown to the children led
to divergent conclusions. For example, children saw a tropical fish
and were told that it was a "fish" and that it breathes underwater.
They saw a dolphin and were told it was a "dolphin" and that it pops
out of the water to breathe. They then had to decide how a shark—
an object that looks like a dolphin but is called a "fish"—breathes.
Children based their inductive inferences on the shared category
rather than on perceptual similarity.

These findings are surprising in light of the common belief that
children's cognition is strongly influenced by perceptual appearances. According to this view, young children should rely more on
perceptual characteristics than on category membership of objects for
drawing inductions. In contrast to what would be expected on this
view, by age 3, children expect natural kinds to have a richly correlated structure that goes beyond superficial appearances. They use
category membership to support inductions, even where perceptual
appearance and category label lead to different conclusions. In addition, children have made some progress in determining which properties are reasonable to project to other category members.

On the other hand, 3- and 4-year-olds have a great deal to learn
about which kinds of categories support which kinds of inductions
over which sets of properties. They need to determine which properties can be expected to be shared by members of different types of
natural kinds. In a study by Gelman and Markman (1986) children
based their inductions on common category membership even for
properties such as weight that adults know to be determined by superficial perceptual features.

In addition to differentiating between different kinds of properties, children must distinguish between different kinds of categories. Categories of artifacts, for example, do not pick out objects in nature that have indefinitely many properties in common. One possibility is that from an early age children expect categories named by language to be richly correlated and to therefore promote inductive inferences. Only after learning more about various domains would children come to restrict their inferences.

Children must also learn which properties are most relevant for determining category membership (Keil, in press). Being given category labels and then being asked to infer information from one member to another is simpler than having to form the category without knowing beforehand which properties are relevant. In forming a category "from scratch," children are likely to be more strongly influenced by perceptual appearances.

Language and Richly Structured versus Arbitrary Categories

Building on the argument about the structural richness of natural kinds, I proposed that there is a continuum defined mainly by the richness of the correlational structure of the categories, that ranges from natural kind categories at one extreme to highly arbitrary categories at the other (see chapter 6). This continuum spans roughly what people might consider to be natural, good categories of objects ("rabbit," "tree") to what they might more likely consider to be descriptions of objects ("yellow," "tall"). Descriptions that are turned into categories (say, "yellow things") appear quite arbitrary.

On the basis of this distinction, I proposed six differences that should obtain between richly structured and arbitrary categories:

1. Richly structured categories should promote inductive inferences more than arbitrary categories.

2. Richly structured categories should be viewed as capturing something fundamental about an object, whereas arbitrary categories should be viewed as providing less essential information.

3. Richly structured categories may be viewed as identifying what an object *is*, whereas arbitrary categories specify what it *is like*.

4. Membership in a richly structured category will be seen as relatively enduring and permanent, whereas membership in an arbitrary category may be seen as more transient.

5. Richly structured categories may be more likely than arbitrary categories to be organized into taxonomies of subordinate, superordinate, and coordinate classes.

6. People, including young children, may view richly structured

categories as being mutually exclusive. They should be less reluctant to view an object as being a member of multiple arbitrary categories.

I also argued that there is an imperfect but useful correlation between the richness of the category and grammatical form class: nouns tend to point to richly structured categories, and adjectives tend to point to more arbitrary categories. This correlation is very rough but may still be used in interpreting nouns and adjectives.

Experimental evidence supports both of these hypotheses. The distinction between richly structured and arbitrary categories has psychological reality for both adults and children. Further, to some extent, people interpret nouns as referring to richly structured categories and adjectives as referring to arbitrary categories or descriptions.

Systematization of Categories

In addition to figuring out how to form single object categories, children must figure out how categories relate to each other. Class inclusion and mutual exclusivity are two important ways in which categories are organized with respect to each other.

Hierarchical Organization

In chapter 7 I focused on determining whether children represent categories hierarchically. To consider this question, we need to have criteria for deciding whether someone has represented one category as being included in another (Markman and Callanan 1983). Categorizing a given object in two different levels of a hierarchy provides evidence for only a primitive, implicit hierarchical organization. This criterion is trivially satisfied by any concept. Requiring that one of the concepts be nonperceptually based, as many superordinate categories are, provides a more stringent criterion, but it is not failproof. Understanding that class inclusion is an asymmetric, transitive relation provides the clearest evidence for hierarchical organization.

The Piagetian class-inclusion problem is an overly conservative measure of whether children represent class-inclusion hierarchies. Children can understand the asymmetry and transitivity of class inclusion and still fail the class-inclusion problem.

In many studies of children's object sorting, sorting by categories can occur only at the superordinate level. This research is typically taken to bear on the principles by which children acquire categories. I argued instead that object sorting at the superordinate level should be interpreted as evidence for multiple categorization. In most such procedures children already know the basic level categories of the objects to be sorted. Thus, to sort correctly at the superordinate level, children must take into account two categories: the object's basic level category and its superordinate level category. Children often do not perform well on these sorting tasks until they are at least 6 years old. However, sorting tasks have many extraneous demands that make object sorting a conservative measure of children's knowledge of class inclusion. To successfully solve the classification problems, a child must find the categories to be salient, explicitly represented, and readily accessible. Knowledge that is less explicitly available may be obscured by the procedure. The requirement to form spatial arrangements, the large number of objects to be sorted, the wording of the instructions, and children's relative unfamiliarity with the categories all pose problems for them and may interfere with their categorical knowledge.

Studies of classification in infancy, using habituation procedures or simple selection tasks, have provided evidence that children as young as 1 year old have begun to represent some common superordinate categories (Ross 1980; Faulkender, Wright, and Waldron 1974). By greatly simplifying the demands placed on the infants, these procedures provide a more sensitive measure of children's knowledge. On the other hand, they have not as yet determined the precise basis for children's perception of similarity of objects that are part of the same superordinate category.

Very little evidence exists on children's understanding of the transitivity and asymmetry of class inclusion. One of the few studies to test this knowledge directly indicates that by age 4 children have the capacity to represent these relations and that by age 6 the representation of asymmetry and transitivity is quite robust (Smith 1979).

On the weaker criterion for class inclusion, then, there is evidence that the ability to represent class-inclusion hierarchies exists in 1-year-old babies. This primitive representational ability presumably becomes more explicit and more readily accessed as children grow older, such that by age 4 children have begun to understand the asymmetry and transitivity of class inclusion.

Collections versus Classes
Children may have another way of systematizing categories that conflicts with class inclusion: the assumption that categories are mutually exclusive (that is, that a given object belongs to only one category). Since class inclusion violates mutual exclusivity, children's expectation that categories should be mutually exclusive impedes

their ability to work out class-inclusion relations. The assumption of mutual exclusivity thus helps explain why young children have difficulty with class-inclusion relations. It may also help explain why children find the part-whole organization of collections easier to represent than class-inclusion hierarchies (see chapter 8). The collection structure does not violate mutual exclusivity by giving a particular object two labels of the same type. In a class-inclusion structure an oak "is an" oak and "is a" tree; in a collection structure it "is an" oak but "a part of" a forest.

One source of evidence in support of this analysis is that children sometimes erroneously impose a collection structure on class-inclusion hierarchies that they have been taught. This tendency to distort class-inclusion relations into collections has been found both for older children learning artificial categories (Markman, Horton, and McLanahan 1980) and for 2-year-olds learning natural language hierarchies (Callanan and Markman 1982). These very young children sometimes misinterpret superordinate category terms as though they referred to collections. For example, a child who agrees that a set of dolls and balls are "toys" will deny that a single doll is a toy and, when asked to "Show me a toy," will pick up all the dolls and balls rather than just one.

Because children are working out hierarchical relations find collections easier than class inclusion, one way of simplifying the problem of learning superordinate category terms would be to use collective nouns to represent superordinate categories. However, although it would be easier for children to refer to superordinate categories with collective nouns, collective nouns could not be used for this purpose; one of the main functions of class-inclusion hierarchies is to support transitive inferences, and collections do not readily allow such inferences to be made. However, mass nouns can provide an appropriate substitute for collective nouns. That is, languages can capitalize on the fact that, like collections, mass nouns have a kind of part-whole organization but that, unlike collections, they allow transitive inferences to be made. Many superordinate category terms in English are mass nouns, for instance, "furniture," "jewelry," "clothing," "food," "money." If the purpose of referring to superordinate categories with mass nouns is to help children learn them, then this should be true of languages other than English. In fact, in over 20 languages studied, there was some tendency for superordinate terms to be denoted by mass nouns (Markman 1985). Another prediction from this analysis is that teaching children new superordinate category terms as mass nouns should be more effective than teaching them as count nouns, a hypothesis that was indeed supported in two studies of young children learning new categories (Markman 1985).

Mutual Exclusivity
In chapter 9 I formulated the mutual exclusivity principle specifically with respect to category terms: namely, children assume that a given object will have one and only one label. Several kinds of evidence suggest that children expect terms to be mutually exclusive, including evidence from vocabulary acquisition, overgeneralization of terms, and language acquisition in bilinguals. Much of this evidence, however, is either anecdotal or restricted to production data. I argued that children's comprehension of terms would provide the strongest evidence about whether they adhere to the mutual exclusivity principle.

Experimental studies of children's comprehension support the hypothesis that children expect terms to be mutually exclusive. One line of research demonstrates that when children hear a novel label, they assume it refers to a novel object rather than to an object whose label is already known (Golinkoff et al. 1985; Hutchinson 1986; Markman and Wachtel 1988). They can maintain mutual exclusivity in this situation simply by mapping the novel label onto the novel object. Several other studies have addressed whether children can use mutual exclusivity to guide their hypotheses about word meaning when this simple novel label–novel object mapping strategy is not possible.

By mutual exclusivity, when a novel label is applied to an object for which children already know a label, they should reject the new term as a second object label. When no other object is present, however, they cannot treat the novel term as a label for a novel object. In order to adhere to mutual exclusivity in these cases, they must adopt some other strategy. They might, for example, reject the novel term as a second label and simply fail to come up with any possible meaning for the term. Or they might try to analyze the object to find some other property or attribute to label. Even in this more difficult situation young children continue to adhere to the mutual exclusivity principle. Three- and 4-year-olds can use mutual exclusivity to help them learn part and substance terms (Markman and Wachtel 1988).

Thus, the assumption of mutual exclusivity can help children acquire novel category terms, via the novel label–novel object mapping strategy. Moreover, it can help children acquire other kinds of terms as well. By disallowing multiple object labels, the mutual exclusivity assumption enables children to reject a whole class of hypotheses about a word's meaning. This negative aspect of mutual exclusivity— stating what a term cannot mean—is supplemented by the positive sense in which mutual exclusivity can motivate children to seek out alternative word meanings. If a most favored hypothesis has been rejected, then the child might recognize that he or she is faced with a novel term to which no meaning is yet attached. Knowing that the term as yet lacks a meaning will motivate children to look for something other than a whole object as a possible referent for the novel term. This will lead them to examine the object for possible parts, substances, colors, and so on, to label. Thus, by adhering to mutual exclusivity children will be motivated to learn not only category labels but terms referring to parts, substances, and other properties as well.

The taxonomic and whole object assumptions direct children to interpret a novel term as a label for the object and not for one of its parts, its substance, its color, and so on. This is an important way in which to limit hypotheses to begin the task of word learning. On the other hand, children must of course be capable of learning terms that refer to parts, substances, and other properties as well. By rejecting two object labels for the same object, the mutual exclusivity assumption helps overcome this limitation of the taxonomic and whole object assumptions. Given a novel label and a previously unlabeled, novel object, then the taxonomic and whole object assumptions apply. In this case both the whole object and mutual exclusivity assumptions can be fulfilled and the child will interpret the novel label as referring to the novel object. But when a novel term is applied to an object that already has a known label, the mutual exclusivity and whole object assumptions compete. At least when some property of the object is salient, children will in these cases override the whole object assumption and adhere to mutual exclusivity instead.

Another advantage of mutual exclusivity, if applied to other terms as well as object labels, is that it can successively constrain the meanings of terms. As each new term is added to the child's vocabulary, mutual exclusivity will limit the possible meanings that another novel term can take.

Mutual exclusivity has costs as well as benefits. The fact that class inclusion violates mutual exclusivity may be one reason that young children have trouble learning class-inclusion relations. Children must become capable of or willing to violate mutual exclusivity in order to successfully acquire hierarchically organized terms. As suggested in chapter 9, perhaps at any age children have the capacity to override mutual exclusivity as long as they are presented with enough information or evidence that a given object has multiple labels. If so, then mutual exclusivity would be most useful and most effective when children first encounter a new term. Its main function would be to guide children's initial hypotheses about the word's meaning.

Conclusions

I have tried throughout this book to frame the dual problems of how children acquire categories and how they acquire category terms from the perspective that these are problems of induction. The puzzle in both cases is how children so quickly organize objects into those categories that the culture deems useful or important, given the enormous number of possible ways to categorize and label objects. This problem arises both in terms of thinking about the acquisition of single categories and in terms of how categories are related to each other.

One main thrust of much of the work reviewed in this book has been that young children are biased learners and that this provides a partial solution to the problem of induction. Children approach the learning of categories and of category terms with biases, predispositions, and assumptions that restrict the range of possibilities and often lead them to fast learning. Moreover, even children's apparent limitations, such as their tendency to be nonanalytic, may be an advantage from this perspective, in that these limitations also help effectively narrow down the hypothesis space they need to consider.

This view also helps explain developmental differences in the acquisition of categories—that is, why some categories are more difficult for children than others. The learning of categories and category terms will be hard or easy for children depending on the expectations they have about the nature of categories and category terms. Categories that fit children's expectations will be easier to learn than categories that violate them. The other side of the coin is that looking at which categories children find hard or easy to acquire should offer clues about what biases and expectations children have.

Natural languages are flexible and do not fully conform to children's expectations. Thus, the biases and assumptions that often lead to success can mislead children as well and thereby explain the errors they make: for example, why children occasionally misinterpret adjectives as referring to objects, why they have difficulty with class inclusion, and why they tend to misinterpret superordinate category terms as collections.

Yet for the most part the expectations children bring to the task of concept learning are helpful. I have argued throughout this book that children must acquire categories in ways that circumvent the need for sophisticated hypothesis testing. The most powerful alternative is that young children may be equipped with certain assumptions about the nature of categories and about the nature of category terms. These assumptions guide children in their attempt to acquire categories.

References

Anglin, J. M. (1977). *Word, object, and conceptual development*. New York: W. W. Norton.

Armstrong, S. L., L. R. Gleitman, and H. G. Gleitman (1983). On what some concepts might not be. *Cognition* 13, 263–308.

Asher, S. R. (1978). Referential communication. In G. J. Whitehurst and B. J. Zimmerman, eds., *The functions of language and cognition*. New York: Academic Press.

Au, T. K. (1987). Children's use of information in word learning. Doctoral dissertation, Stanford University.

Au, T. K., and E. M. Markman (1987). Acquiring word meanings via linguistic contrast. *Cognitive Development* 2, 217–236.

Barsalou, L. W. (1983). Ad hoc categories. *Memory & Cognition* 11, 211–227.

Barsalou, L. W. (1985). Ideals, central tendency, and frequency of instantiation as determinants of graded structure in categories. *Journal of Experimental Psychology: Learning, Memory and Cognition* 11, 629–654.

Barsalou, L. W. (1987). The instability of graded structure: Implications for the nature of concepts. In U. Neisser, ed., *Concepts and conceptual development: Ecological and intellectual factors in categorization*. Emory Symposia in Cognition 1. Cambridge: Cambridge University Press.

Barsalou, L. W., and D. R. Sewell (1984). *Constructing representations of categories from different points of view*. Emory Cognition Project Report #2, Emory University, Atlanta, GA.

Bateman, W. G. (1916). The language status of three children at the same ages. *The Pedagogical Seminary* 23, 211–231.

Bloom, L. (1970). *Language development: Form and function in emerging grammars*. Cambridge, MA: MIT Press.

Bohn, W. E. (1914). First steps in verbal expression. *The Pedagogical Seminary* 21, 578–595.

Bolinger, D. (1967). Adjectives in English: Attribution and predication. *Lingua* 18, 1–34.

Bolinger, D. (1977). *Meaning and form*. London: Longman.

Bourne, L. E. (1966). *Human conceptual behavior*. Boston, MA: Allyn and Bacon.

Bourne, L. E., B. R. Ekstrand, and R. L. Dominowski (1971). *The psychology of thinking*. Englewood Cliffs, NJ: Prentice-Hall.

Bowerman, M. (1987). Commentary: Mechanisms of language acquisition. In B. MacWhinney, ed., *Mechanisms of language acquisition*. Hillsdale, NJ: Lawrence Erlbaum Associates.

Boyd, W. (1914). The development of a child's vocabulary. *The Pedagogical Seminary* 21, 95–124.

Brandenburg, G. C. (1915). The language of a three-year-old child. *The Pedagogical Seminary* 22, 89–120.

Brooks. L. (1978). Nonanalytic concept formation and memory for instances. In E. H.

Rosch and B. B. Lloyd, eds., *Cognition and categorization*. Hillsdale, NJ: Lawrence Erlbaum Associates.

Brown, R. (1956). *A study of thinking*. New York: Wiley.

Brown, R. (1957). Linguistic determinism and the part of speech. *The Journal of Abnormal and Social Psychology* 55, 1–5.

Brown, R. (1958). How shall a thing be called? *Psychological Review* 65, 14–21.

Brown, R. (1973). Language and categories. In *A first language: The early stages*. Cambridge, MA: Harvard University Press.

Brown, R., and C. Hanlon (1970). Derivational complexity and order of acquisition in child speech. In J. R. Hayes, ed., *Cognition and the development of language*. New York: Wiley.

Bruner, J. S., J. J. Goodnow, and G. A. Austin, eds. (1956). *A study of thinking*. New York: Wiley.

Bruner, J. S., R. R. Olver, and P. M. Greenfield, et al. (1966). *Studies in cognitive growth*. New York: Wiley.

Callanan, M. A. (1985). How parents label objects for young children: The role of input in the acquisition of category hierarchies. *Child Development* 56, 508–523.

Callanan, M. A., and E. M. Markman (1982). Principles of organization in young children's natural language hierarchies. *Child Development* 53, 1093–1101.

Callanan, M. A., and E. M. Markman (1985). Why collective nouns help children to solve the class inclusion problem: A test of the large number hypothesis. Ms., Stanford University.

Carey, S. (1978). The child as word learner. In M. Halle, J. Bresnan, and G. Miller, eds., *Linguistic theory and psychological reality*. Cambridge, MA: MIT Press.

Carey, S. (1982). Semantic development: State of the art. In L. R. Gleitman and E. Wanner, eds., *Language acquisition: The state of the art*. Cambridge: Cambridge University Press.

Carey, S. (1985). *Conceptual change in childhood*. Cambridge, MA: MIT Press.

Carey, S. (1988). Lexical development: The Rockefeller years. In W. Hirst, ed., *The making of cognitive science: Essays in honor of George A. Miller*. Cambridge: Cambridge University Press.

Carey, S., and E. Bartlett (1978). Acquiring a single new word. *Papers and Reports on Child Language Development* 15, 17–29.

Ceraso, J., and A. Provitera (1971). Source of errors in syllogistic reasoning. *Cognitive Psychology* 2, 400–410.

Chapman, I. J., and J. P. Chapman (1959). Atmosphere effect re-examined. *Journal of Experimental Psychology* 58, 220–226.

Churcher, J., and M. Scaife (1982). How infants see the point. In G. Butterworth and P. Light, eds., *Social cognition*. Chicago: University of Chicago Press.

Clark, E. V. (1973). What's in a word? On the child's acquisition of semantics in his first language. In T. E. Moore, ed., *Cognitive development and the acquisition of language*. New York: Academic Press.

Clark, E. V. (1983). Meanings and concepts. In J. H. Flavell and E. M. Markman, eds., *Handbook of child psychology*. Vol. 3: *Cognitive development*. New York: Wiley.

Clark, E. V. (1987). The principle of contrast: A constraint on language acquisition. In B. MacWhinney, ed., *The 20th Annual Carnegie Symposium on Cognition*. Hillsdale, NJ: Lawrence Erlbaum Associates.

Cohen, L. B., and B. A. Younger (1981). Perceptual categorization in the infant. Paper presented at the Eleventh Annual Jean Piaget Symposium, Philadelphia, PA, May.

Collins, A., and E. Loftus (1975). A spreading activation theory of semantic processing. *Psychological Review* 82, 407–428.

Conant, M. B. and T. Trabasso (1964). Conjunctive and disjunctive concept formation under equal-information conditions. *Journal of Experimental Psychology* 57, 250–255.

Curtis, K. A. (1973). A study of semantic development. M.A. thesis, Psychological Laboratory, University of St. Andrews.

Daehler, M. W., R. Lonardo, and D. Bukatko (1979). Matching and equivalence judgments in very young children. *Child Development* 50, 170–179.

Dean, A. L., S. Chabaud, and E. Bridges (1981). Classes, collections, and distinctive features: Alternative strategies for solving inclusion problems. *Cognitive Psychology* 13, 84–112.

Dockrell, J. (1981). The child's acquisition of unfamiliar words: An experimental study. Doctoral dissertation, University of Stirling.

Faulkender, P. J., J. C. Wright, and A. Waldron (1974). Generalized habituation of concept stimuli. *Child Development* 45, 1001–1010.

Flavell, J. H. (1963). *The developmental psychology of Jean Piaget*. Princeton, NJ: Van Nostrand.

Flavell, J. H. (1977). *Cognitive development*. Englewood Cliffs, NJ: Prentice-Hall.

Flavell, J. H. (in press). The development of children's knowledge about the mind: From cognitive connections to mental representations. In J. W. Astington, P. L. Harris, and D. R. Olson, eds., *Developing theories of mind*. Cambridge: Cambridge University Press.

Flavell, J. H., E. R. Flavell, and F. L. Green (1983). Development of the appearance-reality distinction. *Cognitive Psychology* 15, 95–120.

Fodor, J. (1972). Some reflections on L. S. Vygotsky's "Thought and Language." *Cognition* 1, 83–95.

Freedman, J. L., and E. F. Loftus (1971). Retrieval of words from long-term memory. *Journal of Verbal Learning and Verbal Behavior* 10, 107–115.

Gale, M. C., and H. Gale (1900). *The vocabularies of three children of one family to two and a half years of age*. Minneapolis, MN.

Gelman, R., and R. Baillargeon (1983). A review of some Piagetian concepts. In J. H. Flavell and E. M. Markman, eds., *Handbook of child psychology*. Vol. 3: *Cognitive development*. New York: Wiley.

Gelman, S. A. (1984). Children's inductive inferences from natural kinds and artifact categories. Doctoral dissertation, Stanford University.

Gelman, S. A., P. Collman, and E. E. Maccoby (1986). Inferring properties from categories versus inferring categories from properties: The case of gender. *Child Development* 57, 396–404.

Gelman, S. A., and E. M. Markman (1985). Implicit contrast in adjectives vs. nouns: Implications for word-learning in preschoolers. *Journal of Child Language* 12, 125–143.

Gelman, S. A., and E. M. Markman (1986). Categories and induction in young children. *Cognition* 23, 183–208.

Gelman, S. A., and E. M. Markman (1987). Young children's inductions from natural kinds: The role of categories and appearances. *Child Development* 58, 1532–1541.

Gelman, S. A., and M. Taylor (1984). How two-year-old children interpret proper and common names for unfamiliar objects. *Child Development* 55, 1535–1540.

Gentner, D. (1978). What looks like a jiggy but acts like a zimbo? A study of early word meaning using artificial objects. *Papers and Reports on Child Language Development* 15, 1–6.

Gentner, D. (1982). Why nouns are learned before verbs: Linguistic relativity vs. natural partioning. In S. A. Kuczaj II, ed., *Language development: Syntax and semantics*. Hillsdale, NJ: Lawrence Erlbaum Associates.

Gerard, A. B., and J. M. Mandler (1983). Sentence anomaly and ontological knowledge. *Journal of Verbal Learning and Verbal Behavior* 22, 105–120.

Gholson, B., M. Levine, and S. Phillips (1972). Hypotheses, strategies and stereotypes in discrimination learning. *Journal of Experimental Child Psychology* 13, 423–446.

Gibson, J. J. (1979). *The ecological approach to visual perception.* Boston: Houghton-Mifflin.

Gillham, B. (1979). *The first words language program.* London: George Allen & Unwin Ltd.

Gleitman, L. R. (1981). Maturational determinants of language growth. *Cognition* 10, 103–114.

Goldin-Meadow, S., M. E. P. Seligman, and R. Gelman (1976). Language in the two-year-old. *Cognition* 4, 189–202.

Golinkoff, R. M., K. Hirsh-Pasek, A. Lavallee, and C. Baduini (1985). What's in a word?: The young child's predisposition to use lexical contrast. Paper presented at the Boston University Conference on Child Language, Boston, MA.

Goodman, N. (1955). *Fact, fiction, and forecast.* Cambridge, MA: Harvard University Press.

Gordon, P. (1981). Syntactic acquisition of the count/mass distinction. Paper presented at the 1981 Stanford Child Language Research Forum, Stanford University.

Gordon, P. (1985). Evaluating the semantic categories hypothesis: The case of the count/mass distinction. *Cognition* 20, 209–242.

Greenberg, J. H. (1966). Some universals of grammar with particular reference to the order of meaningful elements. In J. H. Greenberg, ed., *Universals of language,* 2nd ed. Cambridge, MA: MIT Press.

Grice, H. P. (1975). Logic and conversation. In P. Cole and J. L. Morgan, eds., *Syntax and semantics.* Vol. 3: *Speech acts.* New York: Seminar Press.

Grieve, R. (1975). Problems in the study of early semantic development. In C. Drachman, ed., *Salzburger Beiträge zur Linguistik II.* Gunter Narr, Tübingen.

Grimshaw, J. (1981). Form, function, and the language acquisition device. In C. L. Baker and J. J. McCarthy, eds., *The logical problem of language acquisition.* Cambridge, MA: MIT Press.

Harris, P. (1975). Inferences and semantic development. *Journal of Child Language* 2, 143–152.

Haygood, R. C., and L. E. Bourne (1965). Attribute- and rule-learning aspects of conceptual behavior. *Psychological Review* 72, 175–195.

Herrnstein, R. J. (1982). Stimuli and the texture of experience. *Neuroscience and Biobehavioral Reviews* 6, 105–117.

Homa, D., and R. Vosburgh (1976). Category breadth and the abstraction of prototypical information. *Journal of Experimental Psychology: Human Learning and Memory* 2, 322–330.

Horton, M. S. (1982). Category familiarity and taxonomic organization in young children. Doctoral dissertation, Stanford University.

Horton, M. S., and E. M. Markman (1980). Developmental differences in the acquisition of basic and superordinate categories. *Child Development* 51, 708–719.

Hunt, E. B., and C. I. Hovland (1960). Order of consideration of different types of concepts. *Journal of Experimental Psychology* 59, 220–225.

Husaim, S., and L. Cohen (1981). Infant learning of ill-defined categories. *Merrill-Palmer Quarterly* 27, 443–456.

Hutchinson, J. E. (1984). Constraints on children's implicit hypotheses about word meanings. Doctoral dissertation, Stanford University.

Hutchinson, J. E. (1986). Children's sensitivity to the contrastive use of object category terms. Paper presented at 1986 Stanford Child Language Research Forum, Stanford University.

Huttenlocher, J. (1974). The origins of language comprehension. In R. L. Solso, ed., *Theories in cognitive psychology: The Loyola Symposium*. Potomac, MD: Lawrence Erlbaum Associates.

Huttenlocher, J., and F. Lui (1979). The semantic organization of some simple nouns and verbs. *Journal of Verbal Learning and Verbal Behavior* 18, 141–162.

Inhelder, B., and J. Piaget (1964). *The early growth of logic in the child*. New York: Norton.

Jennings, D., T. Amabile, and L. Ross (1980). Informal covariation assessment: Data-based vs. theory-based judgments. In A. Tversky, D. Kahneman, and P. Slovic, eds., *Judgment under uncertainty: Heuristics and biases*. New York: Cambridge University Press.

Karmiloff-Smith, A. (1979). Language as a formal problem-space for children. Paper presented at the MPG/NIAS Conference on "Beyond description in child language."

Karmiloff-Smith, A., and B. Inhelder (1975). If you want to get ahead, get a theory. *Cognition* 3, 195–211.

Katz, J. J. (1964). Semantic theory and the meaning of good. *Journal of Philosophy* 61, 739–766.

Katz, J. J. (1972). *Semantic theory*. New York: Harper & Row.

Katz, N., E. Baker, and J. Macnamara (1974). What's a name? On the child's acquisition of proper and common nouns. *Child Development* 45, 469–473.

Katzner, K. (1975). *Languages of the world*. New York: Funk & Wagnalls.

Keil, F. C. (1979). *Semantic and conceptual development: An ontological perspective*. Cambridge, MA: Harvard University Press.

Keil, F. C. (in press). The acquisition of natural kind and artifact terms. In W. Dempoulas and A. Marras, eds., *Language learning and concept acquisition*. Norwood, NJ: Ablex.

Kemler, D (1981). New issues in the study of infant categorization: A reply to Husaim and Cohen. *Merrill-Palmer Quarterly* 27, 457–463.

Kemler, D. (1983). Holistic and analytic modes in perceptual and cognitive development. In T. J. Tighe and B. E. Shepp, eds., *Perception, cognition, and development: Interactional analyses*. Hillsdale, NJ: Lawrence Erlbaum Associates.

Kemler-Nelson, D. (1984). The effect of intention on what concepts are acquired. *Journal of Verbal Learning and Verbal Behavior* 23, 734–759.

Kossan, N. E. (1981). Developmental differences in concept acquisition strategies. *Child Development* 52, 290–298.

Kripke, S. (1971). Identity and necessity. In M. K. Munitz, eds., *Identity and individuation*. New York: New York University Press.

Kripke, S. (1972). Naming and necessity. In D. Davidson and Harman, eds., *Semantics of natural language*. Dordrecht: D. Reidel.

Kucera, H., and W. Francis (1967). *Computational analysis of present-day English*. Providence, RI: Brown University Press.

Lambert, W. E., and A. Paivio (1956). The influence of noun-adjective order on learning. *Canadian Journal of Psychology* 10, 9–12.

Lockhart, R. S. (1969). Retrieval asymmetry in the recall of adjectives and nouns. *Journal of Experimental Psychology* 1, 12–17.

Lyons, J. (1966). Towards a 'notional' theory of the 'parts of speech.' *Journal of Linguistics* 2, 209–236.

Macnamara, J. (1972). Cognitive basis of language learning in infants. *Psychological Review* 79, 1–13.

Macnamara, J. (1982). *Names for things: A study of human learning.* Cambridge, MA: MIT Press.

Mandler, J. M. (1979) Categorical and schematic organization in memory. In C. R. Puff, ed., *Memory organization and structure.* New York: Academic Press.

Mandler, J. M. (1983). Representation. In J. H. Flavell and E. M. Markman, eds., *Handbook of child psychology.* Vol. 3: *Cognitive Development.* New York: Wiley.

Mandler, J. M., S. Scribner, M. Cole, and M. DeForest (1980). Cross-cultural invariance in story recall. *Child Development* 51, 19–26.

Mansfield, A. F. (1977). Semantic organization in the young child: Evidence for the development of semantic feature systems. *Journal of Experimental Child Psychology* 23, 57–77.

Maratsos, M. P. (1982). The child's construction of grammatical categories. In L. Gleitman and H. E. Wanner, eds., *Language acquisition: The state of the art.* Cambridge: Cambridge University Press.

Maratsos, M. P. (1983). Some current issues in the study of the acquisition of grammar. In J. H. Flavell and E. M. Markman, eds. *Handbook of child psychology.* Vol. 3: *Cognitive development.* New York: Wiley.

Markman, E. M. (1973). Facilitation of part-whole comparisons by use of the collective noun "family." *Child Development* 44, 837–840.

Markman, E. M. (1978). Empirical versus logical solutions to part-whole comparison problems concerning classes and collections. *Child Development* 49, 168–177.

Markman, E. M. (1981). Two different principles of conceptual organization. In M. E. Lamb and A. L. Brown, eds., *Advances in developmental psychology.* Hillsdale, NJ: Lawrence Erlbaum Associates.

Markman, E. M. (1984). The acquisition and hierarchical organization of categories by children. In C. Sophian, ed., *Origins of cognitive skills.* The Eighteenth Annual Carnegie Symposium on Cognition. Hillsdale, NJ: Lawrence Erlbaum Associates.

Markman, E. M. (1985). Why superordinate category terms can be mass nouns. *Cognition* 19, 311–353.

Markman, E. M., and M. A. Callanan (1983). An analysis of hierarchical classification. In R. Sternberg, ed., *Advances in the psychology of human intelligence,* vol. 2. Hillsdale, NJ: Lawrence Erlbaum Associates.

Markman, E. M., B. Cox, and S. Machida (1981). The standard object sorting task as a measure of conceptual organization. *Developmental Psychology* 17, 115–117.

Markman, E. M., M. S. Horton and A. G. McLanahan (1980). Classes and collections: Principles of organization in the learning of hierarchical relations. *Cognition* 8, 227–241.

Markman, E. M., and J. E. Hutchinson (1984). Children's sensitivity to constraints on word meaning: Taxonomic vs. thematic relations. *Cognitive Psychology* 16, 1–27.

Markman, E. M., and J. Seibert (1976). Classes and collections: Internal organization and resulting holistic properties. *Cognitive Psychology* 8, 561–577.

Markman, E. M., and G. F. Wachtel (1988). Children's use of mutual exclusivity to constrain the meanings of words. *Cognitive Psychology* 20, 121–157.

Medin, D. L. (1983). Structural principles in categorization. In T. J. Tighe and B. E. Shepp, eds., *Perception, cognition, and development: Interactional analyses.* Hillsdale, NJ: Lawrence Erlbaum Associates.

Medin, D. L., and P. L. Schwanenflugel (1981). Linear separability in classification learning. *Journal of Experimental Psychology: Human Learning and Memory* 7, 355–368.

Medin, D. L., W. D. Wattenmaker, and S. E. Hampson (1987). Family resemblance, conceptual cohesiveness, and category construction. *Cognitive Psychology* 19, 242–279.

Mervis, C. B. (1980). Category structure and the development of categorization. In R. Spiro, B. Bruce, and W. Brewer, eds., *Theoretical issues in reading comprehension*. Hillsdale, NJ: Lawrence Erlbaum Associates.

Mervis, C. B., and M. A. Crisafi (1982). Order of acquisition of subordinate, basic, and superordinate level categories *Child Development* 53, 258–266.

Mervis, C. B., and J. R. Pani (1980). Acquisition of basic object categories. *Cognitive Psychology* 12, 496–522.

Mervis, C., and E. Rosch (1981). Categorization of natural objects. In M. R. Rosenzweig and L. W. Porter, eds., *Annual review of psychology*, vol. 32. Palo Alto, CA: Annual Reviews, Inc.

Mill, J. S. (1843). *A system of logic, ratiocinative and inductive*. London: Longmans.

Miller, G. A., and P. N. Johnson-Laird (1976). *Language and perception*. Cambridge, MA: Harvard University Press.

Murphy, C. M., and P. Messer (1977). Mothers, infants and pointing: A study of a gesture. In H. Schaffer, ed., *Studies on mother-infant interaction*. London: Academic Press.

Murphy, G. L., and D. L. Medin (1985). The role of theories in conceptual coherence. *Psychological Review* 92, 289–316.

Murphy, G. L., and E. E. Smith (1982). Basic-level superiority in picture categorization. *Journal of Verbal Learning and Verbal Behavior* 21, 1–20.

Murphy, G. L., and E. J. Wisniewski (1985). Categorizing objects in isolation and scenes: What a superordinate is good for. Ms., Brown University.

Nelson, K. (1973). Structure and strategy in learning to talk. *Monographs of the Society for Research in Child Development*, 38149.

Nelson, K. (1974). Concept, word, and sentence: Interrelations in acquisition and development. *Psychological Review* 81, 267–285.

Nelson, K. (1976). Some attributes of adjectives used by young children. *Cognition* 4, 13–30.

Newport, E. L. (1984). Constraints on learning: Studies in the acquisition of American sign language. *Papers and Reports on Child Language Development* 23, 1–22.

Newport, E. L., and U. Bellugi (1978). Linguistic expression of category levels in a visual-gestural language: A flower is a flower is a flower. In E. Rosch and B. B. Lloyd, eds., *Cognition and categorization*. Hillsdale, NJ: Lawrence Erlbaum Associates.

Ninio, A. (1980). Ostensive definition in vocabulary teaching. *Journal of Child Language* 7, 565–573.

Ninio, A., and J. S. Bruner (1978). The achievement and antecedents of labeling. *Journal of Child Language* 5, 1–15.

Nisbett, R. E., D. H. Krantz, and Z. Kunda (1983). The use of statistical heuristics in everyday inductive reasoning. *Psychological Review* 90, 339–363.

Olver, R., and J. Hornsby (1966). On equivalence. In J. Bruner, R. Olver and P. Greenfield, et al., eds., *Studies in cognitive growth*. New York: Wiley.

Osherson, D. N. (1978). Three conditions on conceptual naturalness. *Cognition* 6, 263–289.

Osherson, D. N., and E. E. Smith (1981). On the adequacy of prototype theory as a theory of concepts. *Cognition* 9, 35–58.

Paivio, A. (1963). Learning of adjective-noun paired-associates as a function of adjective-noun word order and noun abstractness. *Canadian Journal of Psychology* 17, 370–379.

Pinker, S. (1984). *Language learnability and language development*. Cambridge, MA: Harvard University Press.

Pitcher, G., ed. (1966) *Wittgenstein: The philosophical investigations.* New York: Anchor Books.

Premack, D. (1976). *Intelligence in ape and man.* Hillsdale, NJ: Lawrence Erlbaum Associates.

Putnam, H. (1977). Is semantics possible? In S. P. Schwartz, ed., *Naming, necessity, and natural kinds.* Ithaca, NY: Cornell University Press.

Quine, W. V. O. (1960). *Word and object.* Cambridge, MA: MIT Press.

Revlis, R. (1975). Two models of syllogistic reasoning: Feature selection and conversion. *Journal of Verbal Learning and Verbal Behavior* 14, 180–195.

Ricciuti, H. (1965). Object grouping and selective ordering behavior in infants 12 to 24 months old. *Merrill-Palmer Quarterly* 11, 129–148.

Rips, L. J. (1975). Induction about natural categories. *Journal of Verbal Learning and Verbal Behavior* 14, 665–681.

Rips, L. J., E. J. Shoben, and E. E. Smith (1973). Semantic distance and the verification of semantic relations. *Journal of Verbal Learning and Verbal Behavior* 12, 1–20.

Rosch, E. (1975). Cognitive representations of semantic categories. *Journal of Experimental Psychology: General* 104, 192–233.

Rosch, E. (1973). On the internal structure of perceptual and semantic categories. In T. E. Moore, ed., *Cognitive development and the acquisition of language.* New York: Academic Press.

Rosch, E., and C. B. Mervis (1975). Family resemblances: Studies in the internal structure of categories. *Cognitive Psychology* 7, 573–605.

Rosch, E., C. B. Mervis, W. D. Gray, D. M. Johnson, and P. Boyes-Braem (1976). Basic objects in natural categories. *Cognitive Psychology* 8, 382–439.

Ross, G. (1980). Categorization in 1- to 2-year-olds. *Developmental Psychology* 16, 391–396.

Savage-Rumbaugh, E. S., D. M. Rumbaugh, S. T. Smith, and J. Lawson (1980). Reference: The linguistic essential. *Science* 210, 922–925.

Savin, H. B. (1973). Meanings and concepts: A review of Jerrold J. Katz's semantic theory. *Cognition* 2, 213–238.

Scaife, M., and J. Bruner (1975). The capacity for joint visual attention in the infant. *Nature* 253, 265–266.

Schwartz, S. P. (1977). Introduction. In S. P. Schwartz, ed., *Naming, necessity and natural kinds.* Ithaca, NY: Cornell University Press.

Shipley, E. F., I. F. Kuhn, and E. C. Madden (1983). Mothers' use of superordinate category terms. *Journal of Child Language* 10, 571–588.

Slobin, D. I. (1973). Cognitive prerequisites for the development of grammar. In C. A. Ferguson and D. I. Slobin, eds., *Studies of child language development.* New York: Springer.

Slobin, D. I. (1977). Language change in childhood and in history. In J. Macnamara, ed., *Language learning and thought.* New York: Academic Press.

Smiley, S. S., and A. L. Brown (1979). Conceptual preference for thematic or taxonomic relations: A nonmonotonic age trend from preschool to old age. *Journal of Experimental Child Psychology* 28, 249–257.

Smith, C. L. (1979). Children's understanding of natural language hierarchies. *Journal of Experimental Child Psychology* 27, 437–458.

Smith, E. E., and D. L. Medin (1981). In *Categories and concepts.* Cambridge, MA: Harvard University Press.

Smith, E. E., and D. N. Osherson (1984). Conceptual combination with prototype concepts. *Cognitive Science* 8, 357–361.

Smith, E. E., D. N. Osherson, L. J. Rips, and M. Keane (in press). Combining prototypes: A selective modification model. *Cognitive Science*.

Smith, L. B. (1979). Perceptual development and category generalization. *Child Development* 10, 705–715.

Soja, N. S., Carey, S., and E. Spelke (1985). Constraints on word learning. Paper presented at the 1985 Biennial Convention of the Society for Research in Child Development, Toronto, Canada.

Sommers, F. (1965). Predictability. In M. Black, ed., *Philosophy in America*. Ithaca, NY:
Cornell University Press.

Starkey, D. (1981). The origins of concept formation: Object sorting and object preference in early infancy. *Child Development* 52, 489–497.

Stegner, W. (1976). *The spectator bird*. Lincoln, NE: University of Nebraska Press.

Sternberg, R. J. (1982). Natural, unnatural, and supernatural concepts. *Cognitive Psychology* 14, 451–488.

Sugarman, S. (1982). Developmental change in early representational intelligence: Evidence from spatial classification strategies and related verbal expressions. *Cognitive
Psychology* 14, 410–449.

Thorndike, E. L., and I. Lorge (1944). *The teacher's word book of 30,000 words*. New York:
Bureau of Publications, Teacher's College, Columbia University.

Trabasso, T., A. I. Isen, P. Dolecki, A. G. McLanahan, C. A. Riley, and T. Tucker (1978).
How do children solve class-inclusion problems? In R. S. Siegler, ed., *Children's
thinking: What develops?* Hillsdale, NJ: Lawrence Erlbaum Associates.

Tversky, A. (1977). Features of similarity. *Psychological Review* 84, 327–352.

Tversky, B. (1983). Parts, partonomics, and taxonomics. Ms., Stanford University.

Tversky, B. (1985). The development of taxonomic organization of named and pictured
. categories. *Developmental Psychology* 21, 1111–1119.

Tversky, B., S. Havousha, and A. Poller (1979). Noun-modifier order in a semantic
verification task. *Bulletin of the Psychonomic Society* 13, 31–34.

Tversky, B., and K. Hemenway (1984). Objects, parts and categories. *Journal of Experimental Psychology: General* 113, 169–193.

Valentine, C. W. (1942). *The psychology of early childhood*. London: Methuen.

Voegelin, C. F., and F. M. Voegelin (1977). In *Classification and index of world's languages*.
New York: Elsevier.

Vygotsky, L. S. (1962). *Thought and language*. Cambridge, MA: MIT Press.

Wattenmaker, W. D., G. V. Nakamura, and D. L. Medin (1988). Relationships between
similarity-based and explanation-based categorization. In D. J. Hilton, ed., *Con-
temporary science and natural explanation: Commonsense conceptions of causality*. New
York: New York University Press.

Waxman, S., and R. Gelman (1986). Preschoolers' use of superordinate relations in
classification. *Cognitive Development* 1, 139–156.

Wexler, K., and P. Culicover (1980). *Formal principles of language acquisition*. Cambridge,
MA: MIT Press.

Whorf, B. L. (1956). *Language, thought and reality*. Cambridge, MA: MIT Press.

Winer, G. A. (1980). Class-inclusion reasoning in children: A review of the empirical
literature. *Child Development* 51, 309–328.

Wittgenstein, L. (1953). *Philosophical investigations*. New York: Macmillan.

Wittgenstein, L. (1958). *The blue and brown books*. New York: Harper and Brothers.

Index